About the Author

Peter Fieldman was born in North London in 1943. Having worked in international real estate and as a NUJ writer, he has travelled widely. His involvement in the world of politics, business and the media has enabled him to acquire a considerable knowledge of European and international affairs and an understanding of different cultures and languages. Growing up during the "Trente Glorieuses" he has experienced the good times as well as economic and political crisis.

After a grammar school education he took a gap year working in a factory in France's Dordogne region to improve his knowledge of French as well as appreciate the delights of French food and wine. He then spent nine months in the United States; an adventure, which began dramatically arriving the day after President Kennedy's assassination in November 1963. On his return to Europe an interest in bullfighting led to several visits to Spain during Franco's regime, following Hemingway's footsteps in Pamplona and Madrid.

He began a career in advertising, journalism and public relations in London but having fallen in love with France at an early age seized the opportunity to work in Paris and found himself on the left bank in May 1968 witnessing the student uprising and the last years of Charles de Gaulle's presidency, as well as meeting his future Italian wife.

Alternating between London and Paris as well as writing he discovered an interest in real estate which led to a change of career and he found himself at the forefront of the British expansion across Europe investing and developing offices and shopping centres for an international real estate company.

As a committed European he became involved in politics joining the Liberal party and standing as a candidate in Kensington council elections. He also took a backseat role in his wife's London restaurant looking after the wine list.

During this period he and his wife purchased a property in Sussex, from where they often took friends to Battle Abbey and made numerous trips across the Channel to the Somme and Normandy to research the two world wars and especially the Norman invasion of England.

In 1988 with his wife and two sons he finally said goodbye to England and returned to France acquiring a property in Paris and close to the Mediterranean coast near Aix en Provence. Although pursuing an interest in real estate, as a member of the NUJ he regularly contributed articles on European topics, and also began to write screenplays, a blog and take a serious interest in photography. In 2003 he and his wife spent a sabbatical year in Spain to study at the Universidad Complutense in Madrid joining one of their sons who had moved to the Spanish capital and started a family with his Spanish wife. Their other son spends his time between London and Beijing. After more than two years of research the historical novel, *1066 The Conquest*, was published in London. However despite two visits to the

Cannes Film Festival his screenplay based on the book has yet to be taken up by a production company.

Although Peter and his wife still retain the villa near Aix en Provence they travel overseas extensively and divide their time between Paris, Madrid and his wife's home city, Florence, enabling him to pursue a passionate interest in history, geo-politics, art, writing, the cinema, music and travel.

Dedication

While acknowledging the contribution of many other prominent political figures, who left an indelible print on society, I have to dedicate this book to the memory of Stephane Hessel in particular whose book Indignez-Vous persuaded me to follow his example and raise the issues confronting the world.

Peter Fieldman

THE WORLD AT A
CROSSROADS

AUSTIN MACAULEY
PUBLISHERS LTD.

A CIP catalogue record for this title is available from the British Library.

ISBN 9781784556846 (Paperback)
ISBN 9781784556853 (Hardback)

www.austinmacauley.com

First Published (2015)
Austin Macauley Publishers Ltd.
25 Canada Square
Canary Wharf
London
E14 5LQ

Printed and bound in Great Britain

The Pirates of Wall Street ® Peter Fieldman

Labour is the superior of capital and deserves much the higher consideration.

Abraham Lincoln, 3 December 1861

Contents

Preface

The object of this essay is to provide an overview of the major issues and events confronting the world today. I do not claim to be Thomas Piketty, Paul Krugman, Robert Reich or any other economist. I am not a well known personality from the world of politics, entertainment or sport whose comments and views are guaranteed publicity. I am a citizen like many others; one of the baby boomers, who has been fortunate to have lived through the good times and weathered the many crises around the world during the past half a century. I am also privileged to have had the opportunity to travel and live in many countries both within Europe and overseas. I have lived under conservative and left wing governments, monarchies and republican regimes and have seen leaders come and go. But until the last six years I have never witnessed so much inequality, disparity of wealth, greed, corruption and a loss of morality and ethics. After reading Stephane Hessel's book, "Indignez-vous" (Time to Revolt) I was determined to expound my own views and opinions on the state of the world as one of the silent majority whose voice deserves to be heard.

I have specifically avoided the use of graphs, figures, statistics and numbers, used by governments, economists and the media to bombard the public, which are often not understood. Please understand it if some comments are repeated in different chapters as it is hard to separate all the relevant issues I wish to raise as well as the reforms I believe are necessary for economic prosperity and peace. All are intrinsically linked in an increasingly interconnected world. And if, by the time you read this, some of the facts or information, are out of date, it is a reminder that we live in a time of rapid change.

The world has reached a crossroads. Robert Kennedy said, "Fear not the path of truth for the lack of people walking on it." His observation remains just as pertinent today. The path we need to tread is a moral one requiring a change of mentality to engage in a redistribution of wealth and a fairer and safer society.

Introduction

Imperial Rome is the centre of the empire, undisputed master of the world but with this power inevitably comes corruption. No man is sure of his life, the individual is at the mercy of the state, murder replaces justice, rulers of conquered nations surrender their helpless subjects to bondage, high and low alike become roman slaves, roman hostages, there is no escape from the whip and the sword.

That any force on earth can shake the foundations of this pyramid of power and corruption and human misery and slavery seems inconceivable.

Quo Vadis

More than six years have passed since the subprime crisis brought the world's economies to the brink of financial meltdown. Yet we are no nearer resolving the causes of the worst economic downturn since the Great Depression. The crisis has been like a receding tide, exposing what lies hidden beneath the surface. And much of what we have found is decaying or rotten. Abraham Lincoln and Martin Luther King believed all men are equal, but it is clear that some are more so than others. Since the outset of the crisis the wealth has gone to the richest one percent of the population, who bear a large responsibility for causing it. The wealthiest eighty-five people in the world possess more than the three billion poorest people on the planet. It is unsustainable. Growing inequality has become a major scourge in our societies and has reached unacceptable levels putting democracy, social cohesion and peace at risk.

Despite providing a unique opportunity for governments to engage in the fundamental changes and structural reforms urgently needed in our societies, little has been done and strict regulation of the banking sector has failed to materialize. The unregulated and uncontrolled speculation that caused incalculable damage to the world's economies has not been restrained but allowed to continue without adequate supervision. Markets fluctuate erratically at the slightest rumour and we continue to face the risk of another catastrophic meltdown of the financial sector.

The major mistake – unless it was a deliberate and organized transfer of the nation's wealth – was to bail out the banking sector with billions of taxpayer's money and allow it to keep the money without asking for anything in return. Instead of repaying their debt to society the bankers have continued to pay themselves obscene salaries, stock options and bonuses and hand out millions in dividends while the majority of the population has been facing drastic austerity measures leading to a loss of jobs and homes and a tough economic recession. America's promise of "No child left behind" has become "No banker left behind".

There have been massive fines imposed on banking and corporate entities for engaging in fraudulent activities, money laundering or fixing rates, but it has had no effect on the bankers themselves, or the auditors, regulators and bosses of rating agencies who have remained untouchable, resisting any form of control or intervention into their affairs. Their impunity has become one of the major injustices in our democratic law abiding societies.

In a speech to the French University of the Sorbonne in Paris in November 2012, Rafael Correa, President of Ecuador, spoke out about how the developing world had made the mistake of looking after the interests of the financial sector to the detriment of the economy and people, leading to economic and social problems throughout South America.

The money lent by the US was used to import goods rather than set up manufacturing plants and then interest charges, which hit 20% in some cases, meant the developing nations could not afford to cover their debts. He warned that Europe was guilty of making the same mistakes with its obsession in bailing out the banks resulting in massive national debts and draconian austerity measures. National debt has reached more than 100% of the GDP of many nations. This situation suggests poor management or negligence and incompetence on the part of governments and the teams of experts who advise them.

And all this comes at a time when we face major economic, technological, demographic, environmental, political and social changes. The world is being transformed by the internet. Power is escaping from Governments as the major internet companies by pass regulations and laws, able to communicate with billions of people around the world instantaneously. The technological revolution will ultimately lead to less need for unqualified low paid staff and a consequent rethink of importing immigrant workers.

Economic power is shifting to Asia while Russia and the Latin American nations are finally beginning to exert their influence over world affairs. The West has to become less arrogant in dealing with the rest of the world. We may think our liberal societies and way of life are superior but we should not forget that Chinese culture dates back more than five thousand years. The USA is engaged in an economic war to retain its dominant position and the fall in oil prices and rise of the dollar are part of a calculated strategy. Nevertheless the old colonial and economic powers in Europe and America are going to have to accept sharing economic and political power with a consequential loss of influence or face economic, political and social decline. The revelations over the NSA spying on top French political leaders has come as a major embarrassment for the US Government and has put WikiLeaks back in the spotlight. The initial tough reaction is unlikely to cause any long-term damage to the special relationship that exists since it is obvious that nations spy on each other for both political and economic purposes. It simply demonstrates that politics is an immoral game. But if you can't trust your friends, who can you trust?

Media coverage of the 2014 European elections eclipsed the elections in India, where the long standing ruling National Congress Party was ousted in favour of the Hindu Nationalist Bharatiya Janala party, the BJP, led by 64-year-old Narendra Modi. He presides over the second most populated nation on earth after more than a decade as Chief Minister of the Gujarat region. The reforms he has promised will perhaps have a more profound effect on world affairs than election results in Europe.

Despite its mighty military presence and unprecedented spy and surveillance operations, the United States has made it clear it no longer seeks to police the world. This decision comes at a time when there is growing competition out there. China has made no secret of its plans to extend its control over the South China Sea, ignoring opposition from Vietnam, Japan and Malaysia. Russia has demonstrated that it will not risk losing its strategic interest in the Crimea or the Ukraine and has established a Eurasian Economic Union with its ex-Soviet partners Belarus and Kazakhstan. Armenia, Kyrgyzstan, Tajikistan and Uzbekistan have all shown interest in joining this new club. Despite the war in Iraq, the country is still in chaos and coupled with the violence in Syria, the influence of radical Islamic groups is spreading across the whole Middle East as well as within Europe, bringing with it atrocities of a bygone age.

Increasingly, smaller states, as well as terrorist groups, are now able to acquire sophisticated weapons using the Internet and cyber networks to cause incalculable damage. Military dominance cannot defeat guerrillas or terrorists on their own ground. This was made clear during the Vietnam War more than fifty years ago.

Politically the world is no longer divided into the two opposing powers of the cold war. It is becoming more complex and precarious. The so-called Arab spring turned out to be a winter of discontent with Islamic groups seeking power and, as we are witnessing with Afghanistan, Egypt, Iraq, Syria, Somalia, Sudan and Yemen, conflicts are not simply about one side facing another, or good against evil, but involve varied political, religious and economic interests each fighting its own cause. The long drawn out Israel-Palestine crisis demonstrates the complexity of reaching a satisfactory peaceful agreement when there are so many conflicting issues at stake.

The changing scene makes it paramount for European states to forge a united front. If Europe expects to remain a global economic and political force, Europe's leaders must accept closer integration and some loss of power and sovereignty instead of pursuing national interests. The results of the Euro elections with the rise of populist groups caused an electroshock among the major parties, which clearly have not learnt any lessons. Matteo Renzi, whose Italian PD party won an overall majority, seems to have appreciated the problem and how to react. "To defeat the extremist or populist parties governments have to deal with the issues which the majority of the population want addressed." This is precisely what governments have failed to do.

Despite repeated elections in many countries or changes in leadership, politicians are still facing resistance on the part of vested interests clinging on to their privileges. At the same time the debt crisis and problems of the single currency in Europe have led to unprecedented austerity measures, increased taxes, privatizations, cut backs in social services and investment and government intervention on a massive scale to shore up the financial sector.

Germany is facing criticism for its ability in managing its books and maintaining a huge current account surplus. But surely it is for other countries to pull up their socks and emulate Germany rather than deride the success of its economic policies.

The debt and euro crisis and the disparity between north, south, and east Europe, will not be resolved until there is closer integration through some form of federal structure including political, financial and tax harmonization in order to bring confidence back to the economy. This is fundamental since without confidence and trust there can be no future.

The victory of Alexis Tsipras and his left wing Syriza party in Greece caused panic in Brussels and could lead to fundamental changes in the economic policies of the European Union. Naturally the Greek stock market collapsed but that was only to be expected given Tsipras's promise to stop privatizations, end the tax privileges of the elite and shipowners and end the austerity measures, which have caused so much economic and social damage to the Greek people. Yet despite the risk of a "Grexit" his campaign made it clear that he supports the European Union and wishes to remain in the Eurozone and Nato; hardly the words of a left wing revolutionary despite his criticism of the Troika – the EU, IMF and ECB. The risk is that any rescheduling of the country's huge debt could have a domino effect on other weak member states. Tsipras sent his finance minister, Yanis Varoufakis, to negotiate with the Troika. While his flamboyant presence made him an instant success with the media it antagonised European officials who did not agree with his debt-swap plans. The Greek tragedy is turning into a Wagnerian opera – interminable. There are meetings and more meetings but are we being told the truth about the Greek debt situation when it is obvious that the aim of the creditors is to force the country to privatize national assets for the benefit of financial and corporate interests?

Globalization, the absence of currency controls, the removal of the Glass-Steagall Act and lack of banking regulation have all contributed to an unprecedented transfer of wealth from nation states to the privileged elite, the financial sector and international corporations who take advantage of offshore companies and bank accounts in the world's tax havens. Capital can be shifted in and out of a country at the click of a mouse making fixing budgets and long-term planning virtually impossible.

The world has become a tax-free playground for those with the wealth and the right contacts. Wealth is being accumulated not through talent or work but through simply holding assets, whether real estate, stocks, art or cash, which ultimately ends up being handed down to future generations who have done little or nothing to earn their generous inheritance.

The power of the multinationals, able to relocate their manufacturing activities, destroy jobs and transfer their profits out of sight of government treasury departments, which lose vital tax revenues, is a major cause for concern. The natural and mineral resources in the developing nations of Africa, Asia and Latin America, are still being exploited by Western corporations and while the commodity markets can make fortunes for speculators, the profits too often fail to trickle down to the indigenous populations. The wealth generated ends up in the pockets of corporate bosses or corrupt political leaders in offshore bank accounts or luxury real estate, while the majority of the people are either forced to live in poverty or attempt to emigrate to the desired locations of North America, Western Europe and Australia, adding to the influx of illegal immigrants. Marc Rich, the founder of Glencore, who died in 2013, typified the global capitalist predator, amassing a colossal fortune at the expense of the impoverished mining workers in the developing nations. Fortunately the Internet has provided NGOs like Oxfam, Avaaz, Change and One, with the means to bring some of the worst cases of injustice to a worldwide audience. But little has changed since the Capitalist Pyramid poster was printed in Cleveland Ohio in 1911 to illustrate the exploitation of the people. (Appendix I)

Excessive remuneration packages have led to an unsustainable wealth gap exacerbated by the use of fancy financial engineering invented by the banking sector to enable the rich to avoid taxes. And astonishingly these schemes have met with government approval. It is twenty-five years since the Berlin Wall came down. But it is infinitely more difficult to break down the walls separating the privileged elite and establishment, which for so long have pulled the strings behind elected political leaders, from the majority of the population.

Main Street is still under the boot of Wall Street and politicians have done little to try and persuade the leaders of the financial and corporate sectors in Wall Street and the City of London that they can no longer help themselves to such a large slice of the national earnings cake, leaving crumbs for everyone else. Yet stock markets are back to where they were before 2008 and in some cases breaking new records.

Behind the scenes there is a power struggle as the elite lobby their friends in government to keep them in the lifestyle to which they have become accustomed. The top 1% of our societies is only concerned with influence, power and status, which it believes has been bestowed upon it by some divine right.

This became abundantly clear during the collapse of Bear Stearns and Lehman Brothers when these staunch exponents of free markets queued for bailouts desperate to cling on to their positions, their huge salaries, bonuses and pensions.

The accumulation of wealth has also increased bribery and corruption. In many countries it has become institutionalized and, like a cancer, eaten its way into the political, financial, business, and sporting, world as we now know with the FIFA scandal. Government institutions are supposed to be the trustees of the state. But these are no longer safe from unscrupulous and immoral politicians and their friends, who have no hesitation in stripping out the nation's wealth for themselves. This is not reserved for far off nations with dictators; Russia and the Ukraine are among the worst offenders and corruption permeates throughout the corridors of power in democratic Western societies too. Organizations like Transparency International and the Anti Corruption group in the European Commission have estimated that corruption in the European Union costs one hundred and twenty billion Euros each year. Corruption is not just immoral and criminal but can ruin nation states which lack sufficient funds for education, housing health, infrastructure and social programmes and are forced to increase taxes to compensate the loss of revenue. The impression is that rather than being stamped out, corruption is becoming worse, with politicians failing to take steps to deal with it.

Despite an increasing number of politico/financial scandals, since 2008 only a handful of politicians, bankers or business leaders have been indicted for corruption, professional negligence, mismanagement, speculative losses, money laundering or fraud. In Spain alone more than two thousand politicians around the country face charges relating to bribery or fraud but the courts seem reluctant to speed up the legal process implying that those at the top benefit from impunity. Astonishingly for a democratic society, there are more than seventeen thousand high level public officials (los aforados) who benefit from immunity from prosecution in the courts. To combat increasing public disaffection with the country's political class, Alberto Ruiz Gallardon announced plans to reduce the number to just twenty-two. However his resignation as minister of justice over the abortion issue meant that any decision to end this insidious practice was put on hold.

Bankers and corporate boardrooms are going to have to come to terms with a new world order. Tighter regulation and controls and a fairer and more equitable redistribution of earnings and taxation are needed to bring stability to world markets, whose economies are now so intrinsically linked. Governments, corporations and individuals, from the highest paid CEO to the lowest paid worker, must share a sense of responsibility, accountability and morality.

But there are also compelling economic and social reasons. Governments have to accept that the middle and poorer classes just cannot afford to continue subsidizing the rich. Increasing taxes and forcing austerity measures on the majority of the people cannot work over the long-term without creating serious economic and social problems. Without a prosperous middle class with adequate spending power no economy can survive, let alone, grow. But around the world whole populations, businesses and Nation States are in debt to global financial interests, intent on squeezing them dry when they should be increasing the flow of money into the economy.

In Greece, Portugal and Spain, perhaps the European countries worse affected, massive street demonstrations and strikes have sent a message to political leaders that the vast majority can no longer support the austerity measures and cut backs, the job losses, home repossessions, and uncontrolled immigration, which are destroying the fabric of society. The protests, often violent, have extended to countries like Brazil, Egypt and Venezuela with governments forced to react in their own way.

The growth in the world's population in the poorest countries of Africa and Asia has become one of the greatest challenges facing mankind. Lacking a proper education and a future as well as persecution from their own governments, hundreds of thousands of destitute men, women and children have chosen to migrate to the richer western nations, many losing their lives in the process. The west does not know how to deal with a chaotic situation in which genuine asylum seekers and refugees are hard to distinguish from economic migrants simply seeking a better life.

The increase in immigration, both legal and illegal, has been the catalyst for right wing parties in France, Austria, the Netherlands, and the UK to gain ground. Greece, worried about the rise of its ultra right wing party, Aurora Dorada, cracked down on its leaders but could not stop it campaigning and obtaining some success in the Euro elections and it took third place in the national elections.

The growing economic wealth of several African countries should have brought more equality, but corruption, exploitation and conflicts have failed to improve the lives of millions of sub-Saharan Africans. Incredibly Robert Mugabe still wields considerable influence.

The Arab Spring was supposed to bring democracy to North Africa. Instead it has resulted in ethnic and sectarian violence and chaos, not democracy, which was an illusion. The military coup in Egypt was aimed at dealing with the rise of the Muslim brotherhood, considered a radical Islamic group, while there is no end to the sectarian violence in Afghanistan, the Central African Republic, Iraq, Libya, Nigeria, Pakistan, Somalia, Sudan, Syria or Yemen. Christian communities, whose roots go back thousands of years, have been systematically targeted to the point of disappearing from the map, with little or no reaction from Western governments.

The creation of the European Union thankfully brought an end to military conflicts and territorial conquests among member states, which had endured for more two thousand years. But it has been less successful in dealing with economic and social conflicts and does not know how to deal with the Ukraine situation.

The brutal murder of the cartoonists at French weekly satirical newspaper, Charlie Hebdo, by Muslim extremists was a tragedy waiting to happen. Despite the public outrage and media coverage of French political leaders voicing their anger, as well as improving their popularity rating, France and Europe have been both incompetent and negligent in dealing with the problem of radical Islam. The war against the West has been progressing for more than two decades. France has the largest Muslim population in Europe with over five million people, mainly from North Africa and the controversial description of "apartheid" used by Prime Minister, Manual Valls was not exaggerated. But it is not state organized. Whether it is due to racism, social exclusion or a cultural divide, the reality is that most of the Muslim population chooses to live apart from the mainstream French society in segregated communities concentrated in the deprived sectors of towns and cities making them ideal targets for radicalization. Most Western European nations face the same problem with the immigrant population of Muslim origin unable to integrate.

We are at a crossroads: the pursuit of austerity measures with a subsequent increase in inequality is to follow a path to economic collapse, a breakdown of values and social disorder, with the risk of civil unrest on a large scale in both the rich and poor nations which could inflict permanent damage to our democracies. Or we can take the path to a world in which morality and ethics determine our future.

History tells us that empires and civilizations eventually fall and come to an end. The Persians, Greeks, Chinese, Romans, Mayas, Incas all disappeared. Historians have various explanations to explain the sudden collapse of the powerful Teotihuacan civilization, which existed in Mexico during the first eight hundred years of our age:

Internal revolts against the established ruling power, social difficulties caused by the excessive increase in population and the consequent ignoring of the plight of the people by the ruling elite.

Political leaders should bear this in mind.

Political Morality

Government is nothing more than the combined force of society, or the united power of the multitude, for the peace, order, safety, good and happiness of the people...there is no king or queen bee distinguished from all others, by size or figure or beauty of colours, in the human hive. No man has yet produced any revelation from heaven in his favour, any divine communication to govern his fellow men. Nature throws us all into the world equal and alike....

John Adams, 1772

Over 240 years after his death, John Adam's observation is more than relevant. The fact is we no longer live in true democracies and freedom is limited. If there is one single factor that defines democracy today it is the failure or refusal of governments to listen to the will of the people. Political parties have simply become commercial brands spending their time electing leaders to market and promote policies, which are carefully packaged to give the impression they are working in the interests of the people.

Party politics dominate our lives and the media. But the main political parties seek only to maintain their influence and power looking no further than the next election. Politicians are obsessed with popularity polls and secrecy at a time when transparency is called for. Election promises, which are rapturously applauded during campaign speeches, are rarely, if ever, translated into reality. Politicians love to talk and tweet, little else.

There has been a growing tendency since the end of the Second World War for governments, which possess an overall majority, to ignore other parties and take no account of their ideas or proposals. Bipartisanship leads to elitist political groups separated from the people they are supposed to represent. They seem incapable of making decisions or offering clear programmes. And any decisions and laws made by one party are overturned when the opposition comes to power. My simple question to all politicians in opposition, who criticize the policies of the incumbent government and propose their latest policies for bringing change is: "So why didn't you do it when you were in power?

The growing absence of consensus makes it difficult to engage in any radical or meaningful reforms for the benefit of the nation or the people. Politicians spend more time thinking about changing constituency borders to suit their own parties. The tradition of electing mayors, which is commonplace in Europe, does have the advantage of bringing democracy to the people by being able to deal with local problems at local level. The UK has finally begun to consider devolution by giving more power to cities to run their affairs under elected mayors. Nevertheless the results of the Euro elections illustrated too well that the majority feel they have been abandoned by the State; privatizations, lack of jobs, growing inequality, insecurity, failure of the justice system, increased taxation, uncontrolled immigration, loss of identity, absence of family values and a decline in moral standards. The institutions, which were the guardians of the state, are now puppets of the political system.

Adolfo Suarez, the Spanish Prime Minister who was instrumental in bringing democracy to Spain after forty years of dictatorship, who died in March 2014, understood the importance of dialogue. Despite the difficult task and complexity of having to deal with people with opposing views and total distrust of each other after the civil war, it was his ability and willingness to collaborate with opposing political parties and the military, together with the King, Juan Carlos, which enabled the government to bring stability and engage in the necessary reforms for the benefit of the country during the period known as "La Transicion".

The introduction of proportional representation in many countries has resulted in more coalition governments. But the fragmentation of votes often results in the inability to take decisions or pass laws, which are endorsed by all the parties and governments cannot function. Britain has been used to a two party system but in order to take power in 2010, the Conservative party had to negotiate a deal with the Liberal Democrats to govern, which was never a happy marriage. And it took Angela Merkel over two months to form a coalition government following the 2013 German elections due to protracted negotiations in order to reach agreement with other parties.

The UK can hardly be called democratic since it remains a Feudal society in which a minority of wealthy landowners possess most of the country and benefit from tax privileges, which go back centuries. Under the first past the post system, the smaller parties can be left without any representation at all in parliament despite obtaining a respectable percentage of the vote. This is precisely what happened in the May 2015 elections when the Conservatives obtained an overall majority with just 38% of the vote while hardly increasing their number of votes compared to 2010. Labour too increased slightly their total support but lost too many seats. How can parliament be representative when the Scottish National Party with one and a half million votes has fifty-six seats at Westminster while UKIP with almost four million votes has just one seat and the LibDems with over two million votes only have eight seats? The British public can look forward to another five years of Cameron unless he hands over to Boris Johnson at some point. Despite the polls and a lack of significant proposals for the future of the country, the result was a clear sweep for Cameron who managed to wipe out his principle adversaries, Miliband and Clegg in the process. Miliband stepped down and Clegg resigned. There must be many LibDem MPs regretting the loss of their seats; a far cry from 1962 when "Orpington Man" first entered Westminster.

Any change in the system to introduce more proportional representation now looks a long way off. On the other hand too many parties lead to countries becoming ungovernable. Italy is a perfect example of how political divisions led to a never ending round of elections over the years with coalition governments. Beppe Grillo's Cinque Stelle party started a revolt against the status quo with some success but despite Silvio Berlusconi's unceasing ability to put a spanner in the works, it is Matteo Renzi, Italy's Prime Minister, whose meteoric rise to power shocked the political establishment, who has promised to end the eternal political infighting and bring stability to the country. His success in obtaining parliamentary approval to reform the electoral process is a step in the right direction. Italicum, as it is known requires a party to obtain 40% of the vote in order to obtain a majority in parliament. If no party reaches 40% the two parties with the most votes go into a second round to determine who governs. Enabling one party to have a clear mandate to govern will reduce the influence of the losing parties and their leaders which has naturally upset Renzi's detractors. His reforms also reduce the power of the Senate.

The merry-go-round of European leaders means that political leaders are constantly meeting, getting to know and dealing with new faces, hoping they will be able to work together. However, as we see every day, differences in political and economic thinking can make European cooperation difficult to achieve.

Although vaunted as giving the European people the power to elect their representatives, the European and local and regional government elections cannot be considered truly democratic. Voters are asked to choose a party rather than a person and end up with the candidates chosen by the parties as their elected representatives. One of the consequences of the liberalization of financial markets in the global economy is that governments have less power and capacity to manoeuvre. Regardless of the political leaning of the party in government, motives for taking political decisions have little bearing on the economy or to improve the prosperity of the people or the country, but to bow to the demands of lobbies or political friends, to appease specific interest groups and especially, to maintain power.

Nowhere is this clearer than in the USA where political rivalry almost brought the nation to a complete stop. The loss of both the Congress and Senate to the Republicans in the mid-term elections has made it even more complicated for Barack Obama to bring the changes he promised during his remaining time in office. The US Government is becoming a puppet of the powerful privileged elite whose vast wealth can influence the results of elections in return for economic and fiscal advantages as well as "buying" senior diplomatic posts. It is a virtual coup d'état by the military industrial complex Dwight D Eisenhower once warned about.

In Italy Silvio Berlusconi fought to stay in power and benefit from parliamentary immunity by deferring the mounting number of court cases brought against him to avoid conviction. But like many powerful rulers before him he was eventually subdued, not by his enemies, but by defectors in his own party. However by clinging on to the leadership of Forza Italia he is still omnipresent.

In a country, which controls its banking industry, Jose Mujica, the ex-president of Uruguay, has been an outspoken critic of the growing power of the financial sector. "The distance of politicians from the people is creating resentment and worse is when the people no longer believe in its government. In the leading nations there are financial interests weighing down on governments with the power of the devil. The dog doesn't wag the tail, the tail wags the dog."

Not only have politicians grown isolated from the people, but there has been a loss of integrity. The debt crisis has raised the question of their ability to lead and take the correct decisions countries need. Politicians are so tied up with their party's interests or their own personal ambitions, they have forgotten that they are elected to manage the country and look after the well being of citizens. They should heed the advice given by John Maynard Keynes in 1926: *The political problem of mankind is to combine three things: economic efficiency, social justice and individual liberty.*

Looking back through history it is interesting to see how art was used to maintain an aura of power and influence of leaders, specifically aimed at misleading the people. Statues or paintings of powerful monarchs, emperors or military leaders posing majestically with robes or beautifully engraved armour and weapons were aimed at convincing the people of their status and importance.

Today the media has taken over this role allowing politicians to portray themselves as world leaders and demonstrate how indispensable they are to a wide audience. The UK perpetuates this aura of power by maintaining the outdated honours system. The Queen has the task of awarding titles, usually with reference to the British Empire – a distant memory – placing many undeserving people on a pedestal, which only exacerbates class divisions. It seems absurd that there is room for "Sirs" and "Lords" in the 21st century, who often obtain their titles by making financial contributions to political parties and, occasionally, end up discredited. People like Stephen "Lord" Green, ex-HSBC director and ex-Trade Minister who is at the centre of a major tax evasion scandal. These pillars of respectability are really Del Boys in pinstriped suits, only with less morals. I think Wikipedia's description of Great Britain is accurate: "An island in the North Atlantic off the north west coast of continental Europe."

Thanks to press and television, politicians have become celebrities concerned only about their image, their privileges and status. The international political meetings and conferences too often result in photo sessions of the leaders with big smiles for the camera and little else.

Political correctness has gone too far. Politicians are terrified of making a "faux pas" which is immediately pounced on by ethnic minority leaders or journalists who often take matters out of context. Nobody can call a spade, a spade any longer, only shovels. In the multicultural society, freedom of expression is being extinguished. Today if James Cagney said, "Come and get me you dirty rats" he would be censored and pursued by animal rights groups and police federations. Indian Chiefs who warned that, "White man speak with forked tongue" would be sued for making defamatory and racist remarks.

Many ex-presidents, political leaders and ministers seem more concerned about writing their memoirs, joining the speech making circuit, even receiving a Nobel peace prize and preserving or finding lucrative business contracts when they leave office. Some are grossly overpaid to travel and speak to paying audiences of corporate personalities who can network while listening to these ex-political figures giving them advice about how to run the economy or save the planet. I never understand why anybody would wish to pay so much to so few to hear them talk. The $250,000 a speech Clintons, who are supposed to have left office with serious financial problems, have grown rich through the publication of books and public speaking. Their charitable foundation has raised millions from wealthy individuals and corporations or foreign governments raising doubts over their special relationship with powerful interests. The success of memoirs or speech making tours are all the more surprising since the public learns either what they have already heard many times over or what they should have been told for free but were kept in the dark about, due to so-called state secrets, when the politicians were in power.

And while they are in power they are intent on being well paid. Euro MPs, members of parliament, senators and councillors across Europe have been helping themselves to ever increasing salaries, favourable tax breaks and guaranteed lifelong pensions when they leave office. They also have a habit of living above their means by spending public money.

This state of affairs is also prevalent within the Unions where contributions from members enable their leaders to lead extremely comfortable lifestyles. There are accusations of connivance between politicians, corporate bosses and union leaders to avoid strikes and social unrest so they can all maintain their own personal power and privileges.

In November 2013 the president of the Catalonia Region, Artur Mas, with fifty members of his parliament and their wives made an "official visit" to Israel where they were received with diplomatic honours usually reserved for a country's leader. Catalonia is not a nation state and this is an example of the abuse by politicians, mayors and councillors in many countries whose delegates spend public money on overseas junkets for themselves and their families. Another quirk of Senor Mas is his refusal to speak Spanish, only Catalan. TV and radio interviews have to be translated. It is the equivalent of Scottish, Welsh and Irish politicians refusing to speak English at Westminster and is hardly a way to forge a dialogue. Similar cases of luxury overseas travel by public officials have been exposed in England, while in France a minister once took a private jet to travel across the Atlantic for a short meeting at a cost of over one hundred thousand euros and, at the height of the financial crisis, Francois Hollande and Nicolas Sarkozy each took a private jet to fly to South Africa for the funeral of Nelson Mandela to avoid each other. Many of the directors of the now bankrupt Spanish savings banks have faced public outcry and been accused of using secret corporate credit cards for lavish spending involving hundreds of thousands of euros while their banks were sinking under massive debts. The scandal over the British MPs' expenses is tiny in comparison but just as relevant. It seems that luxury brands, first class travel and expensive hotels, cars and restaurants, thrive on people who love to spend other people's money rather than their own.

Regrettably corruption has become a plague in our societies and led to a general disaffection of politicians everywhere. Transparency International publishes its list of rogue states each year, which now include many Western nations. But the cultural differences between the Anglo Saxon and Latin countries means each reacts in a different way with regard to eradicating this scourge. Northern Europe tends to take a more serious view of bribery and corruption and affairs of the heart and if discovered, public figures are usually required to resign their posts. When the Profumo scandal erupted in London in the sixties it cost not only the career of a senior political figure but the suicide, if it was a suicide, of the main protagonist involved. Margaret Thatcher, publicly described as the Iron Lady, was a figurehead for the powerful financial elite and aristocracy who pulled the strings behind the scene and made sure they kept a major slice of the nation's wealth – especially from the North Sea oil bonanza.

In the Latin countries where decentralization has led to considerable political power being transferred to regional and local administrations, the relationship between politics and business becomes blurred. And when it comes to sex, unlike their northern counterparts, the Latin countries tend to ignore the private lives of their elected representatives. Local politics where mayors, town councillors and business people all know each other well and belong to the same golf or hunting clubs, leads to an incestuous relationship. Nepotism and cronyism is rife and exchanging favours is considered part of a way of life even if it leads to corruption and links with organized crime.

This is particularly relevant to Spain. The seventeen autonomous regions hold considerable power. They have their own culture, language, laws and taxes as well as a president and parliament, which have led to Spain becoming a mini European Union and just as ungovernable. The regions are run like medieval fiefdoms except whereas the leaders would have once been called Warlords, today they are known as Party Barons. The power of local governments has resulted in a huge number of major financial scandals. These involve the government, Regional parliaments, City councils, savings banks, real estate companies, secret payments in envelopes, Swiss or Andorran bank accounts, theft, tax evasion and waste of public funds, in an orgy of corruption involving hundreds of millions of euros by the political, banking and corporate elite. There are airports without passengers or aircraft, motorways leading nowhere and skeleton building sites. Even the Royal family has become entwined in the scandals and the abdication of King Carlos was considered by some to be a tactical move to end any further revelations, which might damage the monarchy.

Despite allegations of systemic corruption against some of the leading members of Spain's ruling PP party, they refuse to cooperate with investigating magistrates and are believed to have destroyed evidence. It is taking so many years to pursue the cases and engage in court proceedings there have been suggestions of interference or connivance at the highest levels of the judiciary system to protect those in power. Corruption is so endemic in political circles those involved simply do not believe they have done anything wrong.

Pandering to the various lobbies of banks and corporations, paid millions of dollars each year to obtain preferential treatment, suggests that our countries are actually run by and for the benefit of financial and corporate interests. If anybody needs evidence of the corrupt links between big business and politics just look at the boardrooms of the major international corporations or banks. Ex-ministers find highly paid positions in the boardrooms of the banks or quoted corporations where their influence can be crucial in gaining contracts or to obtain preferential treatment. This can only be seen as a reward for services rendered, not, as is usually argued, to bring their talents to benefit the company in question.

At the same time banks, multinationals and governments work hand in hand. The largest quoted corporations can no longer rely on business contacts. Corporate diplomacy is today a necessary evil in an ever more competitive world. Presidents and Prime Ministers are obliged to act as VIP representatives for their respective economies in order to obtain lucrative overseas contracts and ex-ministers often join the boards of companies with strategic economical interests in the financial, energy, utilities, defence, infrastructure and telecommunications sectors.

Santander's Emilio Botin, whose death in September 2014, left a void in Spain's business circles, was an influential figure in deals between the Spanish and Latin American governments, while Repsol's Antonio Brufau can often be seen in the presidential offices in Latin America representing Spanish oil interests. Tony Blair and Nicolas Sarkozy, freed from their political responsibilities, are well paid to jet around the world waving their national flags or representing private interests. The role of Spain's new King, Felipe VI, who is equally at home in the USA as in Latin America, is really that of CEO of Spain Inc. Current French president, Francois Hollande, has been busy selling military fighters to the Gulf States and during a visit to Cuba could not resist the opportunity of a meeting with ageing Fidel Castro, which may not have endured him to the country's American neighbours at a time when they have also begun to improve relations. Nation States are now subservient to banks and multinational corporations. When General Electric wanted to take over a strategic French company, Jeffrey Immelt, the CEO, was welcomed at the Elysee Palace by the French president. Many Western politicians, including Spain's Mariano Rajoy, have been seen flirting with Nazarbayev, the dictator of oil rich Kazakhstan. Goldman Sachs exerts considerable influence in the US Treasury and Federal Reserve with its 'people' – Henry Paulson, Robert Rubin, Rahm Emanuel and Tim Geithner, to name but a handful – who have been appointed Treasury Secretary.

The bank also has powerful connections throughout Europe with ex-directors, Mario Monti, Mario Draghi, Peter Sutherland, Karel Van Miert, Lucas Papademos influential in their respective countries and in the ECB. The Bank of England has become a haven for ex-Goldman Sachs people with Canadian, Mark Carney, the new Governor and several of his close associates infiltrating Threadneedle Street. Although there is no direct evidence, without these connections would it have been possible for Goldman Sachs to arrange preferential tax treatment with HMRC? And to rub it in, as part of a government reshuffle, France appointed an ex-Rothschild's banker as Minister of Finance.

The IMF and World Bank are controlled by establishment figures, who despite their reputation, have failed to reduce or eradicate poverty. The USA has always run the World Bank while Europe heads the IMF. This is a comfortable arrangement, which has allowed the Western powers to dominate world affairs. Think tanks like the Bilderberg Club, Berggruen Institute, exclusive investment groups such as Carlyle, the Freemasons and events such as Davos, cater for a privileged political and corporate elite, whose objective is to ensure that power and wealth remain in their hands. Instead of being treated as another London borough, the City of London Corporation is a virtual independent state just like the Vatican in Rome; a square mile run by and for powerful financial interests. It is an urban ghetto dating from the middle ages which has been preserved for wealthy bankers and lawyers. The European Union is no exemption with an estimated seven thousand five hundred lobbies in Brussels looking after the interests of corporate and financial interests.

All these cosy arrangements may well be coming to an end following the creation of the Asian Infrastructure Investment Bank, signed in Beijing in October 2014 by twenty-one nations designed to provide funding for major projects in the developing countries. However, the main threat to the power of the elite comes from the wide use of Internet and social networks, which have no frontiers and have led to controls and censorship in many countries and a witch hunt against "mavericks" like Julian Assange who was forced to seek protection in the Equator Embassy in London. To users, social networks are seen as a great advance for freedom; to the elite they are a serious encroachment on its power. The crackdown on the networks in Turkey and China shows how seriously governments take the threat.

Politics and business have always maintained an unhealthy partnership, especially in the arms industry. Since colonial times there have been close links between dictatorship regimes in the developing nations and Western governments. In exchange for arms or mining contracts, millions found their way into the pockets of corrupt politicians, dictators, arms dealers and middlemen. These funds were, and still are, often diverted to London, Paris or Geneva, to be invested in luxury real estate or secret bank accounts by the leaders of despotic regimes, leaving the people in squalor. There is no better way to keep power than to maintain a strong police and military force and a poor and illiterate population.

However the developing nations have started to flex their economic muscles and none more so than the South American nations, which have traditionally seen their natural and mineral resources exploited. A wind of change is blowing across the continent. Twenty-seven-year-old, Camilla Vallejo, is one of the new young, fresh faces in the Chilean Government. Despite the promises of previous premier, Sebastian Pinera, to reduce inequality, the country faced a series of demonstrations from students and workers. One of the principal student movement protesters, she was elected to parliament in the 2013 elections, which saw the return of Michele Bachelot as president. The new government in Santiago has engaged in a programme to reduce poverty by social reforms and extracting a greater share of profits from multinationals in the country. In Bolivia, President Evo Morales, has been at the forefront of giving the indigenous population a greater share of the earnings from the country's natural resources while engaging in major social advances. Dilma Roussef's election victory in Brazil is expected to lead to economic and social reforms as well as reduce corruption. The Petrobras financial scandal, which led to the removal and arrest of several top executives and political figures is an example of how seriously corruption is being treated. However Dilma Roussef's opponents have accused her of being aware of the massive financial fraud where eight billion euros is believed to have been siphoned away by directors and politicians to some of the world's more exotic tax havens. Enrique Pena Nieto of Mexico, Rafael Correa of Ecuador and Ollante Humilla in Peru have engaged in reforms aimed at retaining a greater share of their countries' natural and mineral resources. The Pacific Alliance has been created to increase trade links between Chile, Colombia, Mexico and Peru while Mercosur includes most other South American nations. China has sensed the changes and become a major partner for Latin America providing billions of dollars in loans for infrastructure projects in exchange for petrol without America being able to intervene.

The case of Argentina expropriating Spanish company Repsol's ownership of its YPF petrol company, demonstrates the gradual recuperation of national strategic assets by countries whose economic wealth has been concentrated in the hands of US or European interests acting for the benefit of their directors and shareholders.

At a conference in Madrid in 2014, Mexico's president Enrique Pena Nieto announced an ambitious programme to lift his country into the top ten world economies. He plans to end state monopolies, the power of vested interests and the corruption, which have stifled growth and led to huge inequality, by opening up the economy and attracting foreign investment. Six hundred billion dollars has been earmarked to develop the country's infrastructure, tourism, telecommunications and energy sectors. The aim is to increase production of the country's substantial oil and gas reserves although under the constitution all natural resources will remain the property of the state. Foreign investors will be invited to enter into partnership agreements with the state, which will thus be able to maintain control over the distribution of profits. Nevertheless, despite his optimism, the violence and corruption, which affect many areas of the country, have not abated. Powerful narcotics gangs continue to murder anybody who stands in their way giving the impression that the country is ruled by the drug barons. It is hard to understand their purpose. Making money illegally from drugs is one thing, but why assassinate so many innocent people in the process?

While most countries of Latin America strive to improve their economies, Venezuela seems to be the exception. Despite the loss of Hugo Chavez, his policies being pursued by Nicolas Maduro are leading to social divisions and unrest. Greed and corruption have meant that the people of the country, despite all the wealth from its oil fields, remain poor.

Opponents of the regime are imprisoned without charges. Lilian Tintori is the wife of Leopoldo Lopez, leader of the Voluntad Popular (Popular Will Party), He has been in prison for over a year and despite the threats to her life she has become the leading protestor against Maduro's repressive regime. The recent revelations that one of the country's most senior politicians has been involved in the international narcotics trade hardly helps to improve the country's standing.

Cuba, which has relied on Venezuela for economic aid, is also a nation waiting for change as the Castro regime reaches the end of its era. After half a century the US embargo failed to remove Cuba's leaders and President Obama has extended a hand of friendship with the aim of ending "El Bloqueo". The result of US policy has simply caused suffering to the majority of Cubans although they benefit from free education and health and now have the chance to own their own homes. After eighteen months of secret talks involving the Pope, it is high time to end the isolation of this beautiful island and friendly people who pose no military threat to America. A country, whose national hero, Jose Marti, was a poet deserves a better future and given its beaches, countryside, colonial past, gastronomy and love of music, tourism is likely to be the sector to provide it. I have travelled the country from east to west and believe the real concern is that when change comes, and it will, the sudden wall of money which will cascade into the country from Cuban Americans and big business, will lead to a return of the situation which existed prior to the revolution with gambling, prostitution and corruption instead of investment in infrastructure, building projects and economic reforms to benefit the people. I am concerned that the Museo de la Revolucion in Havana will fall victim to US pressure. It houses a vast array of press cuttings, videos, photos and items relating to the fall of Batista and rise to power of Fidel Castro and Che Guevara and naturally includes the Cuban victory at the Bay of Pigs. It provides a remarkable historical legacy which the Americans may not wish to be reminded of. And unless they relocate their embassy in Havana what are they going to do about the huge sign facing the entrance which reads "Venceremos." (We shall triumph)

After the fall of the Berlin Wall, Russia and many of the ex-communist states transformed themselves into fervent capitalist societies. Who would have believed that the notorious Checkpoint Charlie would metamorphose into a major tourist site? Yet the same privileged elite of ex-communist tsars and associates somehow managed to change hats and retain control over their countries' affairs. The hypocrisy of communist regimes was exposed. There has been unprecedented, systematic pillage of national assets – energy, mining, utilities and telecommunications – allowing the elite in or close to those in power, to become immensely rich within the space of a few years, while the vast majority of the population remains poor. Ukraine is an example of how the greed and selfish interests of political leaders can ruin a country. Changes in a regime do not always result in more freedom or equality for the people.

Freedom of expression is still limited and opposition to the oligarchs in power often results in imprisonment and sometimes, death by Mafia controlled groups bent on preserving their power. Russian and East European wealth finds its way into luxury real estate, cars, art and jewellery, pushing prices ever higher to the delight of estate agents, dealers and stores. Unfortunately, regardless of how they made their wealth, no questions are asked when the oligarchs invest in the West buying real estate and soccer clubs or opening accounts in offshore banks – an indictment of Western morality.

The fast expansion of economic power and opening up of China has seen a consequent rise in financial corruption, which has benefitted the political and corporate elite. Nevertheless the new regime has vowed to crack down on the abuse of power in cities across the country. The media disclosure of how political and military leaders and their families as well as businessmen were implicated in the transfer of billions of dollars to tax havens with the aid of Western accounting firms and banks highlighted the problems which the country faces as well as the apparent connivance of the global financial industry.

Organized crime is so entrenched in Italian society that many believe large sections of the economy are now under the control of Mafia groups. This includes bars with slot machines, restaurants, road construction and especially public services such as refuse collection, whose contracts are issued by town councils. The Naples region has been rocked by the discovery of toxic waste being dumped into fields polluting the earth and creating a health hazard for the nearby local communities demonstrating scant concern for the environment. A major scandal came to light in Milan where a multimillion euro fraud was exposed relating to the vast construction project to prepare for the Milan Expo Fair bringing work to a halt and concern that the expo would not open on time. In Venice investigators discovered a huge financial fraud linked to a major public works programme to build seventy-eight flood barriers in the lagoon against rising tides, which threaten the existence of the city. Those involved used the well-tried and trusted method of inflating the bid price for public works and distributing fake commissions. Tens of millions of euros of public funds have disappeared into the pockets of local politicians and contractors including, it has been alleged, Mafia interests. The mayor, together with several local politicians and prominent business people have been arrested in connection with the fraud which has shaken Venice to its fragile foundations. Anyone who thought the "Tangentopoli" scandals of the '90s had been eradicated were wrong. Several of those implicated belong to Prime Minister,

Matteo Renzi's party which has only reinforced his plan to insist on total transparency of how public money is spent. It is the only way to substantially reduce fraud and corruption.

France too has its share of political corruption, the latest concerning the UMP, political party of ex-president, Nicolas Sarkozy, which has been accused of illegal political funding. Sarkozy is also being investigated for a series of alleged illegal or unethical activities, which took place while he was in power. These include the multimillion euro pay off from bankrupt state controlled bank Credit Lyonnais to flamboyant ex-politician and businessman, Bernard Tapie, a case which has implicated IMF boss, Christine Lagarde, who was finance minister at the time, secret deals with the Gaddafi regime and payments to political parties from lucrative arms contracts overseas. These are linked especially to France's old African colonies, where the close relationship allowed dictators to invest in luxury Parisian properties and lead extravagant lifestyles. Outrage over the accumulation of wealth by dictators, accused of human rights violations, has actually led to a backlash with some of their Parisian assets being confiscated. Clearstream was a secret Luxembourg based fund, whose existence came to light following investigations by French journalists who believed it was used to channel funds to political parties. Local political leaders in the decentralized regions and larger cities such as Lyon or Marseille have also been accused of corruption and nepotism awarding lucrative public service contracts to companies owned by relatives or friends.

A high profile case involving Jean Noel Guerini, ex-president of the Bouches du Rhone Department, whose headquarters is in Marseille, demonstrates the lack of morality in political circles. Despite the charges against him he has not resigned and retains his privileged seat in the Senate with the immunity against prosecution it provides. Nobody seems to learn the lessons.

Soon after the death of Nelson Mandela, South Africa's President Zuma was accused of spending over twenty million dollars of public money to extend his private residence while millions of people are impoverished. And there is no better example of the hypocrisy of Europe with its double standards than the invitation extended to Teodoro Obiang, President of Equatorial Guinea, accused of torture and other human rights violations, to a conference in Brussels, allowing Zimbabwe's president, Robert Mugabe, to attend international events or erecting a tent in the Elysee Palace grounds for Libya's Gaddafi. Despite the corruption, whenever these leaders need medical attention they are welcomed in private hospitals in Europe's capitals and taken care of by the most renowned doctors and surgeons. Even the Nobel peace prize has lost its aura when personalities such as Henry Kissinger, a major player in US military and political affairs during the Vietnam War, are awarded this prestigious award.

The rot even extends to the Church. The so-called "Vatileaks" scandal exposed political intrigue, shady financial dealings using Swiss bank accounts in a fight for power and money in the confines of the Vatican City. This was first exposed in the 1980s when banker, Michaele Sindona, was running the Ambrosiano bank and Roberto Calvi ended up hanging from Blackfriars Bridge. Some say the bridge was deliberately chosen for this macabre execution because of its name. The death of Pope Jean Paul I in 1973 after just thirty-three days remains a mystery with suggestions that he was poisoned to prevent any investigation into the Vatican finances.

Before Pope Benedict XVI resigned, his butler, Paolo Gabriele, was sacked for handing papers to the press and then his banker, Ettore Gotti Tedeschi, was removed. Nuncio Scarano, known as "Mr Five Hundred Euros" for his alleged transporting of bags of cash, was indicted for money laundering and Tarcisio Bertone, the powerful Vatican secretary of state, chose to resign to avoid charges of corruption. Worse have been the revelations of paedophilia and sexual abuse by bishops. Was it a coincidence that these events led to the resignation of the first Pope since Pope Celestino V in 1294? Since being elected, Pope Francis has embarked on a journey to heal the wounds and restore the dignity of the Catholic Church.

Due to the Vatican scandals the world learnt of the highly secretive religious foundations; Opus Dei, Regnum Christi, Camino Neocatecumenal and Comunione e Liberazione, with millions of followers, some of whom hold political posts, and whose power and influence extend around the globe to ensure that the doctrine of the Catholic religion is upheld.

There are signs of a change in mentality among the new economic giants in Asia, which have to deal with huge populations. Despite ongoing corruption, the new leaders of the world's economic giant, China, and to some extent India, have realized the need to improve the standard of living of the majority of the people and crack down on inequality through the introduction of new economic and social measures.

This is something President Obama, in his second term of office, has been trying to do in his own country. Even before the midterm election disaster, he faced an uphill battle to change the views of the Republicans in Congress and the Senate. They have blocked every move to kick-start the economy through government spending on infrastructure projects, increased taxes on the top earners and approving the passage of the Obamacare health plan, which he ultimately achieved. His promise of change – "Yes we can", turned into "No we can't." The standoff resulted in the first government shut down in seventeen years resulting in eight hundred thousand state employees staying at home.

With encouraging signs of a reduction in unemployment figures, the US cannot allow its already unsustainable wealth gap to widen even further, creating more inequality and pushing millions into poverty and debt. How can the richest country in the world allow forty-five million of its citizens to live below the poverty line? The conflict between the president and the Republican controlled House of Representatives and Senate, coupled with the spying revelations has reduced the prestige of the USA across the world.

The European Union finds itself at a crossroads. While some member states seek closer political, financial and fiscal unity, others refuse to hand over sovereignty to Brussels and many regions are seeking more autonomy or even independence. These include Catalonia and the Basque regions of Spain, Scotland and Wales in the UK, and Corsica in France, which does not auger well for the future of the twenty-eight member states.

The financial crisis has put the future of the European Union on the line as member states cope with rising unemployment, cut backs in services, huge debts, bank losses, tax evasion, corruption and massive illegal immigration. The tragedies in Calais, Lampedusa, Ceuta and Melilla, and the rise in illegal immigration from north and sub-Saharan Africa, the Middle East and Asia, using Turkey and Greece to cross into Western Europe and making a mockery of the Schengen agreement, has highlighted the absence of clear immigration policies and led to the rise of both right and left wing populist parties. Europe's immigration policies are now being run by people traffickers in North Africa and Turkey who decide who should be transported to Europe and for how much. And when they arrive they are allowed to stay, which only encourages more desperate people to risk their lives.

In any family, when money is tight it naturally leads to arguments, squabbling and the risk of a break up. The European Union is no exception. The aim of a Europe with political, monetary and fiscal unity, far from becoming a reality, is growing more distant as member states are increasingly at odds with each other as well as with Brussels. No national political leader is prepared to give up sovereignty to Brussels. There is a European president and foreign secretary who wield little power or influence and whose existence is virtually ignored by foreign diplomats. The previous president, Juan Manuel Barroso admitted, "The Commission can only plan, propose and implement policies, but the decisions are made by national governments."

Could these irreconcilable differences lead to divorce and ultimately the break-up of the union? Great Britain has promised to review its current position and after Cameron's re-election a referendum is on the cards with a large percentage of the UK population prepared to consider an amicable separation. A new word "Brexit" has entered the euro language to describe the risk of the UK leaving the European Union. However despite the warnings of economic disaster, should Great Britain ever withdraw, as one of the largest European economies, the likelihood is that it would benefit from the same political and trade agreements which already exist with Norway and Switzerland. This could antagonise other major member states who may not appreciate an associate club member who can bend the rules and does not pay the full membership fees. However the main problem is not Great Britain but the way the European Union has evolved.

With six countries, the Common Market, as it was known, was an exclusive club, twelve members made it stronger and when it became fifteen, all from Western Europe, it was still manageable. But lacking a proper set of rules for the club, the adherence of ten Eastern European nations closely followed by Romania and Bulgaria, countries with economies and people still suffering from decades of communist rule, came too fast and too soon.

It has led to a two-tier union with a great deal of inequality and an influx of East Europeans to the wealthier Western countries creating social problems. The free movement of people is a noble concept. But in reality it is one-way traffic from east to west. This is not surprising when the average wage in many Eastern countries is less than 300 Euros a month with scarce job or social protection. Was it incompetence or simple lack of foresight by Europe's political leaders to have underestimated the number of Eastern Europeans who would head west looking for gold? Nobody envisaged that hundreds of thousands of Eastern European immigrants would place such a burden on the Western European jobs market, housing and health care systems, adding to the long list of aspiring immigrants from other continents.

After the Cyprus banking crisis, the Greek situation highlights the difficulty of managing twenty-eight nations each with its own particularities and points to mismanagement on a major scale. Greece is a tragedy in three acts.

Act I: Membership of the European Economic Community. After the removal of the colonels in Greece and dictatorships in Portugal and Spain, it was deemed vital to bring the "Club Med" nations under the protective umbrella of the then Common Market to ensure their democratic future. In addition, with Turkey and the Balkans on its border, Greece was seen as a vital link for Europe's defence. Enlarging the European Union would also boost economic development within the member states and France and Germany lost no time in providing Greece with military aircraft and submarines increasing its defence spending to the point of possessing one of the world's highest defence budgets.

Act II: Why did Europe's leaders allow the country to join the Euro when it lacked the necessary criteria? Europe's political leaders and finance ministers as well as the presidents of the IMF, Rodrigo Rato, Dominique Strauss Kahn and Christine Lagarde and the banking sector must have been aware of Greece's precarious economic situation. Yet all seemingly turned a blind eye or suffered from collective amnesia with regard to the absence of an efficient State administration. Even after Goldman Sachs had been accused of fiddling the books, nobody bothered to check the country's true financial position. The banking sector recklessly pumped money into Greece knowing the country would be unable to repay and then our Governments bailed out the banks leaving the debt to be born by the taxpayer. While most of the responsibility lies with decisions taken in Brussels, the Greek government has to be criticized for its administrative failures coupled with endemic nepotism, tax evasion and corruption throughout the country. Nevertheless with an economy representing just 2% of the Eurozone and a debt, which is insignificant compared to the major European nations, does Greece justify all the attention it is receiving? (See Appendix VI). After all Warren Buffet and a few cronies from hedge funds could have a whip round and pay the debt from their pocket money.

Act III. Geopolitical factors are back on the negotiating table. With the Middle East in turmoil and Turkey, the Balkans and North Africa posing a greater threat to Europe's security than forty years ago, neither the US nor the European Union can allow Greece to come under the influence of foreign powers such as Russia or China. Even if resolving the debt problem is paramount several Eurozone countries resent the idea of writing off Greece's debts. Why should countries, which pride themselves on good management, such as Slovakia, where incomes and pensions are actually lower than in Greece, pay for the colossal mismanagement and corruption of their Hellenic neighbours? The referendum returned a resounding "Oxi" reinforcing Tsipras, who sacrificed Varoufakis on the European altar. The whole of Europe is living above its means and reducing national debt is fundamental to every country's survival. A compromise solution will have to be found with Greece to avoid a disastrous domino effect across the continent, which without a fairer distribution of incomes and wealth, could signal the end of the European dream.

One of the consequences of the disparity of incomes came to light in Ibiza, known for sun, sea and sex and now slavery. The owner of seventy-two hotels in this holiday island was convicted for fraud, and the exploitation of more than one thousand staff, mainly from East Europe working for low pay, without time off and housed in primitive conditions. They put up with the harsh working conditions because they were paid three times more than at home. This disparity is one of the main reasons why Switzerland voted to close its doors to uncontrolled immigration believing it posed a threat to its social and economic cohesion.

Britain is adamant that European Union citizens who remain unemployed in another member state are excluded from receiving social benefits and can be sent back to their country of origin. It should be pointed out that there are already European laws designed to avoid people from one country becoming a charge on another state. Called the ninety day ruling, if anyone remains without a job or resources in another member state they can be required to leave. Even if it only concerns a minority, there are cases of East Europeans abusing their rights by not seeking work and living off benefits in the West. This applies in particular to the Roma community. If they have been singled out it is because they have been allowed to flout the laws of every country where they have settled. They live in illegal camps or squats, engage in crime and delinquency – some violent – and begging, which has exasperated the majority of the people. Yet despite the laws, which require them to return to their own countries, little has been done to implement them. Plans for the expansion of the European Union must be shelved for the foreseeable future if not forever; certainly until the rules of membership are written in stone and abided by every member state and the economies of the present Eastern European members begin to match those of Western Europe, a situation, which is not going to happen tomorrow. Even Jean Claude Junckers agrees. "No more members for at least five years," he declared during the Euro election campaign.

The remaining Balkan countries of Montenegro, Macedonia, Serbia and Bosnia-Herzegovina must therefore put their applications on hold as any new member states would undoubtedly make the Union more unmanageable than it is now, pushing the frontiers further east and, with their porous borders, increase the risk of corruption as well as illegal immigration and infiltration of potential terrorists from Asia and North Africa. The conflict in East Ukraine with its pro Russian population has not helped the case of Ukraine, Europe's largest nation in terms of size excluding Russia. Surely it would it be more logical for Ukraine, which shares a similar culture and economic interests with Russia, together with Moldavia, Georgia, Azerbaijan and Belorussia to become a federal state as part of the new Eurasian union with the ex-USSR countries. Or is there a risk of the region turning the clock back and resurrecting the USSR, as some political analysts fear?

Turkey's application must be refused not just on the grounds that the country is not geographically part of the European continent except for a small area around Istanbul, but also because it is predominantly a Muslim country with borders fronting most of the volatile Muslim states of the Middle East as well as the southern Caucasus. It would exacerbate the social problems faced in many Western countries with growing Muslim populations, as well as lead to a growing risk of terrorism. In plain language it would signal the end of Europe. Albania and Kosovo, although within Europe, should also be excluded on economic and religious grounds.

In an ideal world, it would appear to make more sense to create an economic and political block between the countries of the Middle East and North Africa to include Turkey, Syria, Jordan, Lebanon, Iraq, Palestine and Israel, extending to Egypt, Tunisia and Libya. Of course this is unrealistic at the present time while religious and ethnic conflicts continue to engulf the region.

Approximately one hundred years ago the Sykes-Picot agreement changed the face of the Middle East. Today, the Western powers cannot be expected to resolve the difficulties of the Arabs to attain peace. So far Saudi Arabia, with a new monarch, and the Gulf states do not seem to want to become embroiled in the ethnic conflicts on their doorstep or help alleviate the refugee problem. But events have demonstrated that they cannot keep their heads buried in the sand (or oil wells) and it is time they took responsibility for their own future as well as contribute towards bringing peace to the region.

While Europe's nations attempt to mend their differences and reach a compromise, they face rebellion at home. The concept of the nation state is being eroded by decentralization and demands for more regional autonomy as well as outright independence in some cases. The abdication of Spanish King, Juan Carlos I, in favour of his son, Felipe VI, has opened up discussions across the continent with regard to the delicate subject of the future of the monarchies: Monarchy or Republic? In those countries with constitutional monarchies the king or queen represents tradition and history dating back centuries. The older generation brought up with a sense of loyalty to the Royal families, are more inclined to accept the present system than the young population. This is especially relevant in multicultural societies with children from immigrant families, who do not possess the same attachment, interest in or knowledge of the country's past.

I was educated in the United Kingdom at a time when almost half of the world was part of the British Empire or Commonwealth. As my geography teacher kept pointing out on a globe, "The red bits are all ours." It gave the British a sense of superiority summed up by actor Peter Ustinov in the movie Topkapi. Drinking with a Turk in Istanbul he was asked if he was a foreigner. He replied instantly. "Oh, no, I'm English." I grew up with the queen on the throne and she is still there. European history was made up of kings and queens and their conquests and battles across the continent or, during the civil war, at home. The monarchy began to go wrong when the royal family transformed itself into a soap opera with the publicized romances, break up of marriages and scandals. William and Kate have tried to redress the loss of prestige but the UK population has gone through too much of a transformation for them to have any real long-term influence.

As an avid student of history from a young age, I became enamoured with France. It too had a history of monarchs and the chateaux and palaces around the country testify to the nation's glorious past. In England I was always on the side of the Cavaliers rather than the Roundheads, and in France, not surprisingly, I favoured d'Artagnan and the Three Musketeers rather than the Cardinal's troops. However when the people chose to rid the country of its aristocrats to form a republic they went a little too far, causing panic among the elite on this side of the channel, who feared a similar fate.

1968 was an eventful year with the Prague spring, the Tet offensive in Vietnam and the assassination of Martin Luther King and Robert Kennedy. I found myself in Paris in in the midst of the student revolution and learnt how a republic functioned. Except President Charles de Gaulle ruled the country exactly like a monarch. Respected by most, vilified by a few, who never ceased to try and assassinate him, he almost single handedly took the country from the 19th to the 21st century while he was in power. 1968, was the start for me, of a lifelong love of the country, its institutions, history, culture and enviable way of life. I lived on the left bank and participated in some of the student meetings and witnessed the upturned cars, barricades and fires. But the most emotional moment was at the end of May standing under the Arc de Triomphe watching hundreds of thousands of Gaullist supporters thronging the Champs Elysees in support of the president. By chance May 1968 coincided with the main holidays of the 1st and 8th of the month falling mid-week. With strikes and demonstrations disrupting the city, most companies took the opportunity to shut down for a long weekend – the "pont" (bridge). Miraculously Paris emptied as families took off for the country, somehow finding enough petrol to do so, returning to the fray on the Monday. Whatever the hardship, there was no way the strikes, lack of petrol, the mounting garbage in the streets and the violence was going to disrupt the French from their normal routine.

The following year a referendum went against de Gaulle, so he simply told the people, if you do not want me I shall go and he went. When he died there was no massive coach-drawn funeral procession through the streets of Paris or a place in the Pantheon, reserved for France's most illustrious citizens. According to his wishes, he was laid to rest in the village cemetery of Colombey les Deux Eglises, in the centre of France, close to his home. A remarkable man and leader, who put his country first.

This is something I have always felt wanting in the UK. Throughout my life I have never seen any British Government make decisions which actually benefit the people. My impression is that laws and policies are made for the financial benefit of a privileged corporate and wealthy elite. Little or nothing seems to be done to improve the quality of life of the majority of the population. In contrast the French do consider the well being of the people even if sometimes it results in demonstrations. For example many years ago, government officials came to the conclusion that the two week winter and spring half term holidays led to thousands heading for the mountains, creating massive traffic holds ups, accidents and overcrowded ski resorts. It was decided to divide the country into three academic regions spreading the holidays over a period of six weeks. The result was less road accidents while the ski resorts were still busy but more enjoyable for all.

Monarchies and republics are not really that different, it is the leaders who count. Despite 28 years in prison, when Nelson Mandela became president he took no revenge, but instead had the wisdom to understand that the country would collapse without the cooperation of the experienced white South African officials in government. Would Britain have surmounted the formidable challenge it faced in 1940 without the charisma, inspiration and determination of Winston Churchill? But monarchs and presidents can only survive in sovereign nation states without which they serve no purpose. And it is the very future of the nation state, which is under threat.

The Lander in Germany encouraged Welsh and Scottish nationalists to press for more freedom over their affairs, Corsica and Brittany continue to be a thorn in the French government's side, Catalonia never ceases in its aim to secede from Spain, while the violence in the Basque country, Corsica and Northern Ireland is a reminder of the passion aroused by nationalist groups, often with their own language. Has the Spanish government considered the consequences of an independent Catalonia or Pais Vasco? It would isolate the Iberian Peninsula from France and Europe.

Is Padania in northern Italy, merely a nationalist's dream or could it divide a nation in which the regions, for historical reasons, exercise considerable local power? Lately it is the turn of Venice to call for more autonomy. People forget that it was once a powerful maritime republic, which lasted for over one thousand years until 1797. Their arguments are based on what they see simplistically as a north-south divide with the wealth- creating north having to subsidize the underground economy and a tax-evading, Mafia controlled south.

The European Union can take heart over Scotland's referendum result. The "No" vote possibly prevented a domino effect occurring across the continent and led to Spain's government calling the Catalonian referendum unconstitutional. This did not prevent the Catalonian Regional Government organizing a consensus in November 2014 in which 80% of the two million people, out of a population of seven million, who voted were in favour of independence. Artur Mas continues to defy the Spanish Government with new parliamentary elections planned in September. If the British government keeps to its promises of more devolution, Scotland's decision may well turn out to be a success for its independent movement. The Scottish National Party's success in the UK elections might in fact provide it with more power than being independent as it now wields considerable influence in Westminster with David Cameron forced to devolve control over Scottish affairs. Unfortunately, referendums, promoted as the panacea of democratic participation, are often just the opposite; as was the case with the "No" vote to adopt the European Constitution. Since the political leaders didn't like the result, they simply organized another referendum.

The removal of frontiers has also led to a revival of cross border links; the Spanish and French Catalonian and Basque regions, Alsace with Baden Wurttemberg; the Franco-Italian Mediterranean region and further north the channel tunnel has been the catalyst for renewed links which the Kent and Calais regions possessed over six hundred years ago.

We should not forget that many European nations are relatively young having been created through wars, revolutions and treaties during the past three hundred years. This year is the two hundredth anniversary of the Battle of Waterloo, which to a large extent determined the borders of the present European nation states. But do these demands for more autonomy or independence point to a genuine desire to achieve more democracy and improve the well being of the people or simply a means to hand more power and privileges to regional or local politicians who see themselves as leaders on a world stage?

These regional conflicts and nationalist fervour have arisen at the same time as major changes have been taking place in the world's economies. We are now witnessing the result of these profound changes. Only nineteen countries use the euro while nine retain their own currencies making economic and financial unity virtually impossible to achieve and threatening Europe's role as an economic force in the world. Western Europe is affected by massive job losses as corporations delocalize, scale back activities or take advantage of the lack of fiscal harmonization to switch their operations to any country which offers the most favourable tax regime or lower production costs. Governments face a loss of tax revenue from tax evasion and corruption, which leads to cut backs in public services and investment as debt drags the economies ever further downwards.

The privatization of utilities, energy, health, transport, telecommunications and roads has handed over strategic national assets to the private sector which queues up to get their hands on these vital services which people cannot do without. The only beneficiaries have been corporate bosses and shareholders to the detriment of the majority of the people and increasingly to our democracies.

Powerful investors with colossal sums at their disposal – hedge funds, pension funds and Sovereign State funds – have begun to take an interest in other nations' strategic assets and commercial real estate. Billions of dollars are being invested in the USA, Europe and the Asia-Pacific region by sovereign funds, giving them considerable influence in other nations' economies. This is a relatively new form of interference and control in a country's affairs by foreign governments and could have serious short-term economic and political repercussions. There seems little difference between a state owned company and one owned by a sovereign investment fund; both are under the control of governments, except the latter happens to represent a foreign state.

Meanwhile Europe's sovereign states and politicians continue to live above their means, maintaining a lifestyle unsustainable in a changing world. Everyone agrees governments need trimming but no politician in power will accept a loss of influence and perks, dare to drastically reduce the number of civil servants, or reduce the number of levels of government. Yet this is fundamental if Europe is to retain its sphere of influence in world affairs.

If five hundred and thirty-five elected members can govern three hundred million Americans does Europe, with around five hundred million people, need almost five thousand members of parliament, two thousand five hundred senators as well as seven hundred and fifty-one European MPs? And if there is a case to reform the unelected House of Lords, it is that the eight hundred or so lords in Westminster represent nearly thirty percent of all Europe's senators. Clearly there is considerable room for a reduction in the number of our so-called "representatives of the people".

The crisis has brought to light the excesses and waste in government. Germany's federal system has sixteen Lander while France has more than thirty-six thousand local authorities, more than the rest of Europe combined together with one hundred and one departments (five overseas) and twenty-six regions (four overseas). The public service sector, which employs over five million people, has been blamed for stifling economic progress. Francois Hollande's government to its credit has managed to reduce the number of regions to thirteen although not without considerable local opposition.

The departments are resisting change. The origin of the departments goes back to the Napoleonic era when in order to govern it was decided to divide France in a way so that every corner of the department could be reached by horseback in a single day. In a world where every corner of the world can be reached in a day their relevance becomes questionable.

The iFRAP (Fondation pour la recherche sur les administrations et politiques publiques) is a think tank, which provides data on France's public sector. Its director, Agnes Verdier-Molinie has written a book called *On Va Droit dans le Mur,* which can be translated as *We are heading for disaster.* She explains that despite government cutbacks in personnel and services, the number of state employees has risen in the regions. With more than twenty percent of the country's workforce in the public sector, she believes that the number of local authorities needs to be reduced from its current number to just five hundred, that poor management, and duplication of functions and services lead to too much waste and that there are taxes which cost more to collect than raise revenue.

Spain, as previously mentioned, is virtually a mini European Union on its own divided into seventeen autonomous regions and two special overseas territories in North Africa coupled with thirty-eight provincial councils, which exercise considerable political and financial power. However this administrative decentralization is one of the reasons for the country's economic problems with seventeen Regional Presidents, over two thousand members of parliaments and sixty-eight thousand town councillors, who have brought the country to the verge of bankruptcy through profligate spending and corruption. In contrast, Matteo Renzi has promised to reduce Italy's numerous levels of government, which comprise twenty regions and ninety-five provinces, which spend while Rome fiddles. Transforming government will be tough but is inevitable. See Appendix II.

At the State of the Union conference in May which took place in Florence at the European University Institute, Italian ex-prime minister, Giuliano Amato, former French Minister for European Affairs, Elizabeth Guigou and Vaira Vike-Freiburga, ex-president of Latvia, called for a New Schuman Declaration for Europe to create a new eurovision. And it has nothing to do with singing and dancing.

Too many representatives of the people have turned into plunderers of the people while swathes of national, regional and local government as well as excessive bureaucracy have become synonymous with waste, unaccountability and corruption. Europe hands out money like confetti that often disappears into a black hole with too many of the projects benefitting from Europe's funds never materializing. The gravy train must be put on a new track and the new commissioners in Brussels have already been facing opposition over the EU budget with several member states refusing to contribute.

The Common Agricultural Policy is just one area needing a total overhaul. Rather than help poor struggling farmers, the CAP benefits the wealthiest landowners, who inexplicably receive massive subsidies they do not need or merit. The recipients are often investors like Britain's Duke of Westminster, rather than farmers, keen to place their money in land and benefit from the generous subsidies and favourable tax arrangements which the government bestows on them, such as exemption from inheritance tax. The purchase of vast tracts of cheap agricultural land in Romania by private funds has recently exposed the injustices of the present system. While poor Romanian farmers receive little or no help for their smallholdings, the new landowners rake in subsidies. It has led to a backlash and small farmers have joined forces to stop the destruction of their livelihood.

Too much money is unaccounted for as it disappears into dubious or illegal activities such as paying for non-existent sheep or infrastructure projects and building works never undertaken. There are too many examples of new motorways leading nowhere, unused airports or public edifices standing empty. During years of plenty, reckless and profligate overspending is immoral, during lean years it becomes both immoral and unacceptable. It is strange that with all the surveillance technology cameras and spying, which the public has been hearing about, governments seem very slow when it comes to locating the proceeds of all this corruption, organized crime, drug traffickers, fraudsters or tax evaders and identifying the criminals.

Not surprisingly confidence has evaporated and the people have become disillusioned with their political leaders and institutions as well as the European Union. The rise of Alexis Tsipras and the Syriza party, The Los Indignados in Spain, reborn as the Podemos party under Pablo Iglesias, the Ciudadanos (citizens) party from Catalonia led by Albert Rivera, Occupy Wall Street, Beppe Grillo's MoVimento Cinque Stelle in Italy and Turkish and Brazilian protest groups have raised the issues people want dealt with, but which successive governments have failed to address. There is a need for transparency and an end to the graft and endemic corruption that permeates through the corridors of power, local and national, contaminating everyone in its path. These new parties, call them populist if you will, are changing the face of politics and pose a threat to all the major parties. They use social networks and the internet to spread their message cheaply and fast to a generation of young voters who want a different political, economic and social model and an end to the corruption and power of the entrenched elite. Today's youth is better educated, well travelled, open to new ideas and of course embrace new technology and change without hesitation. The question is whether they can ultimately end the bipartizan political system to which we have become accustomed.

France's local elections at the end of March 2014 resulted in a catastrophic loss of towns and cities, which had traditionally been bastions of the socialist party – although it did hold on to the capital Paris – and a significant rise in the vote for the right wing party, the National Front. Local elections tend to deal with local issues and favour a popular mayor and the local authority rather than a political party. In November 2014 Nicolas Sarkozy returned to power as leader of the right wing UMP party. The idea to rename it as "Les Republicains" has met with considerable opposition but it did not prevent Sarkozy from a resounding victory in the 2015 regional elections gaining sixty-six departments while leaving the socialists with twenty-nine. The National Front increased its share of the overall vote but failed to achieve its aim of gaining control of a department. It is the second time in twelve months that the French voted their disaffection with President Francois Hollande and his government. Despite the UMP or Les Republicains' success, the result sent a clear message to every European government that people are uncoupling from the leading political parties and are either looking to the extremist parties or tearing up their voting cards. Politicians of all parties cannot continue to ignore the people's legitimate concerns regarding austerity measures, inequality, insecurity, justice, immigration and a fairer society.

Italy underwent a transformation. First the MoVimento Cinque Stelle's success in the 2012 elections breached the walls of the Palazzo Chigi in Rome and sent shockwaves through Italy's corridors of power. Then the Senate finally plucked up the courage to remove the, up until now, untouchable Silvio Berlusconi, while the PD party chose a young and charismatic leader with firm ideas to transform Italian politics.

Matteo Renzi, the ex-mayor of Florence, achieved his aim to become the country's leader and his programme calls for major reforms to both the parliament and senate. He has vowed to reduce bureaucracy and remove much of the old guard from power. His first government includes a new breed of younger politicians, half of which are extremely competent and articulate women – Renzi's Angels. For the past five years, each October, Matteo Renzi has presided over a three day jamboree in Florence organized by the PD party. Known as "Leopolda" after its location in the now defunct Leopolda railway station transformed into a conference centre, it comprises round tables and discussion platforms. It has met with huge success, but Renzi's opponents criticize it as a huge media event to promote his personality. Despite Renzi's promises of immediate reforms, which include the removal of chauffeur driven limos from many politicians and preventing any convicted politician from standing for office, it will be some time before we are likely to see any meaningful affect to reduce the power of the country's well-entrenched elite. And this is precisely the difficulty affecting every democratic nation.

The result of Spain's regional and municipal elections in May turned out to be a second "Transicion." After almost forty years of domination since the country became a democracy, the two major parties – the right wing PP and socialist PSOE – were shaken to their foundations by the rise of two new parties and the fragmentation of the vote.

The Podemos (We Can) and Ciudadanos (Citizens) parties did not exist four years ago yet their programmes have appealed to millions of Spanish voters tired of the austerity measures and rampant corruption in the corridors of power. Although the two major parties managed to obtain 52% of the total number of votes, down from 65% in 2011, the sudden incursion into the political arena of new arrivals could signal the end of bipartisan politics. Unlike four years ago when a tide of blue swept across the peninsular, the PP party of incumbent president, Mariano Rajoy, failed to win an overall majority in any constituency either conceding defeat or requiring pacts with opposition parties to maintain control while, the PSOE, hoping for a revival of its fortunes, saw its support dwindle to second or third place behind the emerging minority parties.

The greatest blow to the PP was the loss of the country's major cities where the Indignados effect was instrumental.

Madrid, Barcelona, Valencia and Sevilla will all come under socialist controlled assemblies. In the case of Madrid change comes after 24 years of a right wing dominated assembly. The Ahora Madrid, party, backed by Podemos, was beaten into second place by the PP, but with the support of the PSOE, the left have an overall majority. Ahora Madrid leader, Manuela Carmena is the new Mayor of the capital. At 71 years old the retired Supreme Court judge, ex communist and human rights activist faces a new challenge.

Barcelona also chose a woman as mayor for the first time. Ada Colau, 41, is a philosophy graduate and political activist. Her Barcelona en Comu (citizens party), backed by Podemos, managed to defeat the incumbent Mayor, Xavier Trias and pro independence party, CiU, by one seat. However she will have to form a coalition with other minority groups. As leader of the Plataforma de Afectados la Hipoteca (Platform for people affected by mortgages) she has been instrumental in helping thousands of families avoid eviction from their homes due to the property crisis. Her surprise victory has severely dented the plans for independence of the Catalonian Region's controversial President, Artur Mas.

Another prominent casualty was Rita Barbera, right wing Mayor of Valencia since 1991. The city has been rocked by political and financial scandals for almost a decade resulting in massive public debts, the resignation and arrest of prominent figures and several high profile court cases. Although never indicted herself, she has recently been accused of profligate spending of public money for personal use. The people finally said enough.

Pablo Iglesias and Albert Rivera, respectively leaders of Podemos and Ciudadanos, are both in their mid thirties and represent the new breed of young Spanish politicians, formed at university with academic backgrounds. While Podemos is unashamedly left wing, Ciudadanos, which was founded in Catalonia, considers itself centre left and more liberal.

Nevertheless both leaders seek to change Spanish politics and have won considerable support in their aim to combat austerity measures and create a fairer society as well as put an end to the elitist status quo with its cronyism and corruption between elected officials and the financial and corporate sector.

However while proportional representation might be more democratic, it does not lead to stable governments. Forming coalitions and negotiating pacts is a difficult process as the LibDems found out to its cost in the UK and Spain's new political map may well make the country difficult to govern. Perhaps it is time to reform the Constitution and introduce the two ballot system prevalent in France, and now in Italy, so that when one party fails to obtain a majority the two leading candidates face a second round to determine the victor.

Traditionally local elections are fought over local factors and do not reflect the way voters think when it comes to electing a Prime Minister and Parliament. Voters often return to the main parties whom they trust. Without a long established entrenched party machine or experienced politicians in the national assembly, will Podemos or Ciudadanos have time to convince the electorate that they have the ability to govern the country?

In this crisis, political leaders have been so concerned about protecting the wealthiest sector of society they have neglected the country's youth. With so many of Europe's young generation being left on the sidelines, governments are mortgaging their own future. By reducing the opportunities available through Erasmus and forcing the most educated generation in history to accept low paid jobs or emigrate in search of employment while encouraging or allowing mass immigration from the poor nations to provide cheap labour, the nations of Western Europe risk ending up like Third World countries.

The European elections are now all but forgotten. However, the various political campaigns clearly demonstrate that the continent is at a crossroads with many of the previously described issues at the top of the agenda. Although people could choose their European representatives under the proportional representation system, it is not certain that the electors really knew what they were voting for or for whom they were voting. There was no harmonization and each country's elections took place on different days. It seems clear that the results had far more to do with national politics than Europe and they caused a massive tremor felt from Scandinavia to Crete. The major parties were stunned by the rise of extremist and populist parties and the casualty list has been growing. Paradoxically while many member states were perceived to be voting against Europe, the Ukraine was voting in favour of closer European ties.

Great Britain's complacent major parties were shaken by the success of the UKIP party, a tsunami they failed to foresee. In France the success of Marine Le Pen and the Front National relegated the current ruling socialist party to an unheard of third place with President Francois Hollande winning the unwanted prize of being the most unpopular leader in living memory. Since he came to power, France has seen a change of Prime Minister, ministerial resignations, the loss of the Senate and two governments, which may or may not be capable of reversing the catastrophic situation in a country trying to cope with a debt of two thousand billion euros. The appointment of an ex-investment banker from Rothschild, Emmanuel Macron as Minister of the Economy, is a complete turnaround for Francois Hollande whose election campaign was based on a strong anti-banking message. Is it a case of Macron economics? Prime Minister, Manual Valls, was obliged to visit France's principal political and economic partners, Germany, Italy and England, to convey the message that "France liked business". But the move to a more liberal approach has enraged staunch socialist, Martine Aubrey, who ruined the country with her thirty-five hour week, blamed by the right for France's economical ills. Macron has announced a series of measures aimed at transforming the French business sector.

But the right wing party can hardly gloat. Dogged by years of infighting among its leaders, it is virtually bankrupt and convulsed by the corruption scandal involving illegal political funding during the last presidential elections. It led to the resignation of one of the party's leaders, Francois Cope, and following elections, the return to power of Nicolas Sarkozy. How can the UMP or "Les Republicains" or any new right wing party claim any right to run the country if it can't manage its own affairs? But like Berlusconi, Sarkozy never gives up.

The Charlie Hebdo tragedy turned out to be a short lived silver lining for both Francois Hollande and Manuel Valls, whose strong leadership in dealing with the terrorist attacks, gave the socialist party a boost until the regional elections brought them down to earth. Hollande has refused a French "Patriot Act" but nevertheless was forced to implement tough new security laws. No visitor to Paris can ignore the heavily armed soldiers patrolling the streets and protecting schools and religious centres or the increased police presence. The major parties are now too preoccupied with the presidential elections in 2017 than helping the country's economic recovery.

Another significant casualty of the Euro Elections was Spanish PSOE leader, Alfredo Rubalcaba, who resigned after the collapse of his party's share of the vote. But despite his party's expected victory, current prime minister, Mariano Rajoy was left to ponder over the meteoric success of the Podemos party (We can), which, with very little funding, won over one million votes and obtained five seats in the European Parliament.

In Greece, the radical left party of Alexis Tsipras swept to victory with the extreme right wing party Aurora Dorada, also gaining enough votes to obtain a seat. Extremist parties in

Denmark, Hungary, Austria and Sweden all increased their share of the vote even if they did not win. Only Geert Wilders' party in Holland failed to improve its position. There were no surprises in Germany where Angela Merkel comfortably rode out the storm and for the moment, the ultra right Pegida party is too small to have any influence.

As was expected, turnout was below 50%, averaging 43%, except in Italy where the ruling government party of Matteo Renzi actually increased its share, achieving an overall majority and reducing the influence of the parties of Beppe Grillo and Berlusconi – can this really be his last waltz? But Renzi's success was due to his current popularity and plans for reforming Italy, rather than Europe. It was Italy's turn to preside over European affairs for six months from July to December 2014 as part of the Union's rotating system, but without the new Commission in place, Renzi was unable to exert any influence.

French socialist Jean Christophe Cambadelis called the Euro Election results "A dark day for Europe". I would call it a wakeup call to which the major parties must take heed if they are to remain in power. The anti-European vote was not necessarily a desire to split from the Union but to reform Europe. Brussels and Strasbourg have become elitist bastions, with bureaucrats and technocrats too remote from the everyday lives of the people and with twenty-eight member states, unmanageable.

The principle handicap facing Europe is communication. While candidates jostle for a place on the gravy train there should be a simple rule that requires every candidate for a European post to possess a good knowledge of a language other than his or her own native tongue. English may be the most commonly used language but every member insists on documents being printed in their own language requiring hundreds if not thousands of translators.

The choice of the new leader of the European Commission was fraught with controversy. For the first time in the European Union's short history, the leader was chosen by popular vote and not by political bargaining behind closed doors. The candidates crisscrossed the continent to present their case at meetings on the understanding that the leader of the group with the most votes would be elected. After a great deal of negotiating the right wing candidate from Luxembourg, Jean Claude Junckers, was finally elected as president. He received tacit approval from Angela Merkel, but David Cameron made known his opposition. A difficult choice, but in the present economic and political climate can it be right to have an ex-Prime Minister of the largest tax haven in Europe as its new leader? Herman Van Rompuy and Catherine Ashton were replaced respectively by ex-Polish Prime Minister, Donald Tusk, and ex-Italian foreign minister, Federica Mogherini. Whether they will have a greater impact in their new roles than their predecessors, who remained largely irrelevant, remains to be seen. But the appointment of Mogherini, was seen as a coup for Matteo Renzi, Italy's Prime Minister.

The power of the extremist, populist parties to block the machine is limited, although they can put a spanner in the works. The solace for the leading parties is that they range from extreme left to extreme right, are by no means united in their aims, and ran campaigns based on issues which were more national than European. The contradictions were apparent: some parties seek to leave Europe while others want closer integration, some want to return to their own currencies while others embrace the euro, some are anti-Semitic while others are anti-Muslim, some are fervent anti-capitalist while others anti-socialist and so on. Nevertheless they are bound together with a desire for change.

People are beginning to demand reforms to restrict the worst excesses of capitalism and liberalization of the economy, which are leading to growing inequality and, of course, an end to the austerity measures. European Union bureaucrats are constantly talking about seeing the "green shoots" of economic recovery appearing. But instead all we get are Brussel sprouts. Political as well as corporate leaders must become more responsible and act in the long-term interest of their nations. There is still time to heed ex-British Prime Minister, John Major's famous dictum, "It is time to return to core values, time to get back to basics", which has been completely ignored. Those in public office must be accountable and where corruption, fraud or mismanagement is proven nobody should be able to benefit from impunity, which those in power seem to believe is their right. Instead, justice must prevail and those found guilty must be severely punished and lose their rights to stand for public office. The one lesson which every political leader should learn is that while they are among the most protected citizens in the world they are also the most expendable, replaced immediately on departure or death. Forbes list of the most powerful men and women on the planet should mention this simple fact. Nations and governments continue to function long after they have gone.

Uruguayan writer, Eduardo Galeano, accurately summed up the situation in which politicians invariably find themselves. *The most well intentioned of politicians end up prisoners of the system which devours them.*

Economic Morality

We will never find a purpose for our nation nor for our personal satisfaction in the mere search for economic well-being, in endlessly amassing terrestrial goods. We cannot measure the national spirit on the basis of the Dow Jones, nor can we measure the achievements of our country on the basis of the gross domestic product.

Robert Kennedy, 18 March 1968

The crisis gave governments the opportunity to end the insidious practice of private gains and public losses, which the financial sector adopted as the norm. While governments have been handing over billions to the banks to cover their massive losses or debts, too many downtown city areas are being transformed into derelict zones with boarded up shops, houses and apartments. Streets are plastered with "For Sale" or "To Let" boards. Small stores and traders are squeezed dry by higher rents, rates and taxes and customers with less spending power and families are evicted as banks repossess their homes. Queues line up outside job centres, poverty is increasing, suicides are on the increase and austerity measures and lack of credit are crippling both businesses and workers.

World leaders cannot ignore the growing inequality in the world, so visible in the streets of our cities. There is no need for statistics to provide data. To know what the weather is like people do not check the temperature or isobars, they look out of the window. In the same way inequality can be observed just by looking around us at the increasing number of beggars and homeless. It is astonishing to reflect that at a banking conference in Madrid in 2003, leading US economist, Paul Krugman, warned, "The world has stepped back to the inequality of the nineteen twenties."

A decade and one major crisis later, bankers and corporate bosses have continued to collect huge earnings and bonuses as if nothing happened. Every day brings more revelations of massive salaries, bonuses and severance packages being awarded despite huge financial losses. Reward for failure or even fraud, has become the norm. Boardroom chief executives too do not seem to appreciate that they are expendable and are replaced the moment they leave.

The issue of boardroom remuneration is high on the agenda for reform. It is generating, not jealousy, but animosity at the way those primarily responsible for the economic crisis – the CEOs and senior boardroom executives and traders of financial institutions as well as bosses of quoted corporations – have been allowed to award themselves massive salaries, bonuses and severance pay. The gap has widened to unrealistic and unjustified levels. And it is not only limited to the corporate world. Top civil servants and academic staff in universities have also been awarding themselves huge unjustified increases in pay while the majority of public employees and teachers have seen their earnings fall. Another issue which the crisis has exposed and is causing resentment in several European states, is the granting of substantial guaranteed pensions for life to MPs and Senators for serving a few years in office before they reach the age of fifty. As the political, banking and corporate elite collect fortunes, spare a thought for the thousands of workers who are vital to our lives; the fishermen who risk their own lives in all seasons and weather to bring food to our shores, garbage collectors, hospital staff, firefighters, law enforcement officers, cleaners, factory workers, public transport workers etc. They all play their part in society and deserve recognition.

The crisis has demonstrated the need for a review of top pay. We cannot continue to offer a carrot without a stick. If we go back twenty or thirty years, earnings of top executives were not only far lower than today in real terms, but the tax bar was placed at a much higher level. But with the global economy, opening up of borders, the absence of monetary controls and ease of transferring huge sums to tax havens, governments have pandered to the wealthy. They have stood by as boardroom executives awarded themselves unreal and often unmerited salaries and bonuses, golden hellos and goodbyes, free stock options, huge pensions and lavish tax breaks.

If CEOs were paid 10 or 20 times the average company salary twenty years ago why are they now being paid 100 or even 300 times the lowest salary? Are today's boardroom executives better managers and more talented? The evidence suggests not; companies functioned well, our economies prospered and those in boardrooms did their job with enthusiasm and efficiency without the huge earnings gap.

The privileged establishment in government, Wall Street and the City of London call for more competition and the need for the free movement of people. What they mean is more immigration to keep wages low, the ability to operate cartels or monopolies, the absence of personal financial risk, and freedom to hide their wealth in tax havens and protect their lifestyle and interests in ivory towers surrounded by high walls.

The crisis merely gave corporations the opportunity to justify the shedding of staff and reduce wages and salaries while increasing the earnings in boardrooms. They adhere to globalization when it comes to profits and their earnings, but want to keep taxes localized in offshore tax havens. We have seen where it has led; low pay, job insecurity, part time work, widening income gap, unemployment and poverty. Despite public outcry little has been done to curb the secrecy and greed of the bosses; in the USA ninety-five percent of the gains since the crisis began have gone to the top one percent. One in four Spanish citizens face poverty and exclusion, thirteen million have trouble making ends meet.

Surprisingly it was only tiny, rich Switzerland, whose reputation as a tax haven is often derided, which held a referendum on top pay. The organizers may have been disappointed with the result – a majority in favour against capping top earnings – but it remains on the government's agenda and there will no doubt be further efforts to clamp down on the outrageous earnings and severance packages for top executives in the country's banks and major companies, many of whom presided over losses and corrupt practices.

The European Union has followed Switzerland's example by calling for a curb on bonuses, especially in a time of crisis. This is a step in the right direction, which every country in Western Europe and the US would be wise to follow, including Great Britain whose powerful financial lobbies resist any change. But any curbs on either earnings or salaries requires multilateral cooperation to put an end to the spurious arguments of the corporate elite that lower salaries and less bonuses will lead to an exodus of talent.

The decision to abolish the Glass-Steagall Act was instrumental in causing the crisis and severe damage to the world's economies, and it was a democrat, Bill Clinton, who presided over its removal. The separation of retail and investment banking ensured that people's savings were looked after and banks acted more cautiously when considering where to invest client's funds.

Removing this firewall simply gave Wall Street bankers access to our money, which they have squandered in an orgy of speculation and greed. New creative investment vehicles were introduced which had nothing to do with the real economy but were used for gambling with other people's money. It was a boon for the financial sector. When they made fortunes the less they paid in taxes and when they lost money the government bailed them out with taxpayer's money. A huge financial industry called Wealth Management – code word for tax evasion – has developed into a major business with government approval.

The lack of supervision, either by government regulatory bodies or auditors, allowed the world's most respected and largest financial establishments to become engaged in rate fixing, mis-selling, exchange rate rigging, money laundering and fraud on a gigantic scale. Can the ratings agencies be trusted? Standard & Poor, Fitch and Moody's, have been criticized over their conflict of interest as paid advisors to Wall Street banks, while the regulators, who also came from Wall Street, turned a blind eye to the bad practices which led to the crisis.

There have been accusations that the bail out of US insurance giant AIG by the government in 2008 was nothing more than a conspiracy to defraud the American taxpayer and protect some of the country's leading banks. The government's injection of billions of dollars saved not only AIG but also Goldman Sachs, J.P. Morgan and other US and European banks, whose exposure to derivatives might have otherwise led to their defaulting and suffering the same fate as Lehman Brothers.

The wall of money handed out not only allowed the Wall Street banks to escape possible liquidation but ensured that the bankers and traders could continue to pay themselves astronomic earnings at a time when the majority of the population faced higher taxes, the loss of their jobs and homes and lower incomes.

In Italy the Antonveneta bank, Santander, J.P. Morgan, Abbey and ABN have been implicated in dubious dealings and offshore transfers involving seventeen billion euros, which nearly brought down the once venerated Monti dei Paschi de Siena bank. But so far little seems to have been done to investigate what is believed to be a massive financial fraud or the whereabouts of the missing funds.

However change is on the horizon. It may have taken six years, a major recession, millions out of work, massive national debts and loss of tax revenues but governments have finally begun to bring the worst offenders to court.

In the USA, J.P. Morgan, Goldman Sachs and Bank of America have been forced to pay billions of dollars in fines for their involvement in the mortgage scandal. HSBC was fined a substantial sum for money laundering and City Bank, Credit Suisse, Barclays and other leading Wall Street and City banks have been negotiating settlements for running a cartel to fix the Libor rates or rigging exchange rates. Europe's leading banking institution, BNP Paribas, has been accused of dealing with Iran and Cuba in breach of the US embargo and hit with a multibillion-dollar fine.

These illegal activities make the Brink's-Mat gold heist and great train robbery in England look like pocket money, except for one fundamental difference; while the robbers involved were pursued relentlessly around the world, the bank bosses have, so far, been allowed to escape judgment.

When losses are discovered there is either an admission of human error in an attempt to escape responsibility or collective amnesia by the bankers, CEOs, boardroom directors, audit companies and regulators. It suggests there have been conspiracies to hide losses or bad assets purely to protect the high salaries, bonuses and pensions.

Instead of punishing the bankers implicated in any illegal activities, governments have only imposed fines on the banks, which penalize clients, savers and shareholders leaving the untouchable bankers to continue receiving their bonuses. It is like sanctioning a car for dangerous driving and not the driver.

In Spain the government was quick to indict the driver and rail executives for imprudence and negligence after the crash in Santiago de Compostela, but bankers seem to be untouchable. Michel Barnier, special adviser on European defence, has said the bankers should face penal sanctions.

"The taxpayer should not pay for their mistakes." This does not seem to apply to Spain where the government has casually written off eleven billion euros through the sale of the bankrupt Catalonia savings bank to major bank BBVA, while the directors walked away with millions in indemnities and pensions. The ABN Amro bank takeover by the Royal Bank of Scotland was described as the worst merger in corporate history. Yet while the bank had to be rescued by the British Government the board directors walked away with their wealth intact. And where were the highly paid non-executive directors whose role is to look after the interests of shareholders?

The Volcker Rule in the USA, which finally obtained Congress and Senate approval in December 2013, seeks to limit and regulate financial speculation, which was the principal cause of the crisis, despite opposition from Wall Street. The Troika – BCE, European Union and IMF – have called for the banks to increase their reserves, which the banks seem reluctant to do. Interestingly while banks cannot find money to loan to small companies, causing problems for our economies, they seem to be able to pay these colossal fines out of petty cash. Just where do they suddenly find these billions? Does it come out of their profits? Is it our money from the bailouts they have been hiding or from subsidiaries in tax havens? One thing is clear, the fines have had no effect whatsoever on bankers' or traders' salaries and bonuses.

Nothing illustrates more the unacceptable face of capitalism than the traders of Lehman Brothers insisting on receiving their bonuses after the bank went under and RBS, and Lloyds, owned by the British Government, awarding bonuses and huge pensions for departing bosses, while being investigated for illegal rate fixing and posting huge losses. Matt Ridley, or as he likes to be known, The Right Honourable 5th Viscount Ridley, was chairman of Northern Rock from 2004-7 and presided over the financial ruin of the British bank. In July 2014 he received the Free Enterprise

Award by the Institute of Economic Affairs. Are City boardroom executives so cynical and out of touch with reality?

Given that the banks use our money to function – either to lend or for speculation – there is a strong case for a radical change of mentality in the financial sector as well as the transformation in the way banks treat clients. Since it is our money which is used by the banks, it would not be unreasonable for them to be required to distribute a share of the profits with clients, savers and deposit holders and not just to shareholders or the bankers themselves. Following the Cyprus bank crisis, governments began to limit the guarantees on people's bank accounts to around one hundred thousand euros. Why? The banks are supposed to be the guardians of people's savings. If clients do not wish to engage in risk taking investments, the guarantees should be one hundred percent of each person's savings. How can any confidence be restored in the banking sector when ordinary bank clients risk losing their savings because of risk taking by the bankers and traders over whom they have no control?

Perhaps the most unacceptable aspect of the present crisis is that the richest segment of society has not participated at all in the austerity measures imposed on the majority, continuing to increase their earnings and assets as if nothing has changed, despite many in the financial sector being responsible for the crash and economic crisis. This wall of money paid to the privileged elite needs to find a home and it has bloated real estate, art, yacht, cars and luxury brand prices to absurd levels. Auction houses break records as purchasers with seemingly bottomless pockets and oversized egos outbid each other to get their hands on works of art. What makes many of the mega deals suspicious is the practice of wealthy investors hiding their transfers, acquisitions or sales behind opaque offshore companies or trusts or using middlemen. The lack of transparency should be brought to an end. The very fact that the real beneficiaries do not want to be known can only lead to the conclusion that it is either illicit funds or to avoid tax. Even today's well known art buyers and generous philanthropists, who donate works to museums, can thank equally generous politicians who have made them wealthy by privatizing public assets and handing them over to a few privileged friends.

One of the consequences of the wealth gap is that real estate prices in top locations in the world's leading cities continue to escalate creating a widening disparity in the property market, putting homes out of reach of more and more people, who can neither buy them nor pay exorbitant rents. Values of some prime real estate have increased out of all logic compared to the price of land or construction costs. Vital public services are under threat when the police, council employees, firefighters, teachers, transport and hospital staff are unable to find accommodation close to their jobs.

New York, Paris and London, or their prime central areas, are singled out as among the worst examples in the Western countries. Property prices have reached unsustainable levels as developers have changed the skyline with modern loft-style apartments, described as safe deposit boxes for overseas buyers. Wealthy foreign investors, seduced by the glossy brochures of estate agents, who regularly organize property fairs overseas, have been piling into the market, afraid of being left out. While the most deprived locations turn into ghettos for the poor, these prime locations become walled castles for the mega rich, who inexplicably, have been free to purchase properties using offshore corporations or middlemen to hide the real owners. In London these acquisitions have been able to avoid council tax for years. The 2014 British budget rectified this abuse through increasing stamp duty on corporate purchases and, from 2015, introducing capital gains tax for previously exempt non-resident owners. Nevertheless these ultra expensive properties tend to remain empty, changing hands regularly as they are purely speculative purchases with doubts expressed as to the origin of the real owners or their funds. London's image as a tax haven where foreign dictators, criminals or tax evaders can hide their wealth has led to calls to end opaque transfers of real estate which have created a false market. There is something in the adage that those who want to hide the truth, have something to hide.

The money that cascaded into banks from investment and pension funds, coupled with the removal of regulations and globalization has led to a new breed of businessmen whose sole aim is to fill their own pockets. They invented complex financial instruments which they themselves failed to understand or control, like a Frankenstein monster let loose. What made it easier was that it was not even their money but money belonging to clients, investors or shareholders, who had entrusted them, directly or indirectly, to look after their savings. Mis-selling became endemic and regardless of whether the projected growth or returns were anywhere close to that promised in the glossy brochures, banks and fund managers extracted initial charges and annual fees, which too often diluted any long-term benefits.

The unacceptable face of capitalism became standard practice as banks, legal firms, the big four audit firms and accountants, hedge funds and private equity funds realized that the fees they could earn from mergers and takeovers, hostile or friendly, or from pure speculation with derivatives, credit default swaps (CDS) etc., far exceeded the earnings from traditional corporate or banking activities. Warren Buffet, the American financial guru from Omaha, Nebraska called them "financial weapons of mass destruction".

Derivatives, which began as contracts using the value of assets as security, were transformed into pure gambling ventures, speculating for short-term financial gain. Nobody seems to know for sure the extent of CDSs, toxic assets or how many billions are still at risk in company balance sheets or in the outstanding loans to towns and cities. In Spain alone it is estimated that the major banks hold over fifty billion

Euros in mortgaged real estate, much of which is overvalued at a time when seven hundred thousand homes do not have a single family member employed and cannot repay their loans.

Nobody has investigated or disclosed just how much of the money being invested comes from organized crime, corrupt political regimes, or from funds in tax havens, all of which pose a threat to the world's economies. The financial crisis gave governments the opportunity to bring more transparency to financial transactions by insisting that banks disclose the origins of the wealth of account holders to weed out corruption, the proceeds of crime and tax evasion. They also had the chance to return to the system, which operated under the Glass-Steagall Act; a separation of the investment activities from the retail banking function of the financial sector. But they have been facing tough opposition from the financial lobbies who resist any return to the older, traditional and safer method of protecting clients or lifting the veil of secrecy, which prevails.

Corporations have been traded and passed around regardless of the fate of the employees so that directors and traders could make fortunes from the increase in share price. Remember Mitt Romney's 2012 election campaign, which exposed his own company, Bain Capital, as a perfect example of how the private venture corporations function.

Too often, leveraged buyouts pile debt on to the companies and jobs are destroyed to extract short-term profits in order to increase the share price, which enables the company to be sold off at a profit. Private venture capital companies, often called vulture funds, have been accused of seeking short-term gains rather than acting in the long-term interest of the companies in which they invest. Many mergers have actually led to a loss in shareholder value, which results in demergers where, naturally the bankers and lawyers, who advise the companies, make even more fees.

Governments seem more concerned about what investors and the markets think than carrying out policies for the benefit of the country or people. Hedge funds and sovereign funds have billions at their disposal. Warren Buffet through his successful Hathaway Fund can virtually acquire any company (or for that matter, any nation state) he likes.

The growth in asset management and hedge funds, often operating from tax havens, with a total lack of transparency, have made the stock markets vulnerable since the huge amount of money under their control can manipulate stock market prices and movements as well as exert unwarranted influence in a company's affairs. The ten largest funds, which include names like BlackRock, Fidelity, Vanguard and the Norwegian Sovereign Fund handle billions of dollars. Hedge fund managers have been able to earn untold wealth through taking a percentage of the sums under their management and somehow have avoided paying their fair share of taxes, benefitting from exceptionally favourable tax regimes. Their wealth has given them enormous power in the financial markets.

After several years of inactivity the vulture funds are back and the number of mergers and acquisitions is on the increase as some economies begin to emerge from the crisis. While there might be some short-term advantages for the companies which come under the control of investment funds, it signals the gradual transfer of the industrial and manufacturing sector from industrialists to financiers, who do not always have the long-term interests of the company or their employees at heart.

The acquisition of soccer clubs too has demonstrated how owners attempt to cash in, sometimes to the detriment of the financial position of clubs, by loading too much debt. Scottish club Rangers is a prime example together with the allegations of money laundering by the Chinese boss of Birmingham city. Too many clubs in Europe have substantial debts and tax liabilities and would be out of business if the tax departments forced all of them to pay what they owe.

Organizations like the Qatar Foundation which are pumping millions into sport may have long term commitments but by limiting their investment to a handful of clubs are simply creating a wealth gap between the top teams and the rest of the soccer clubs. Is the Sky deal with the Premier League justified when it will suck talent to the UK from other countries' clubs? This disparity of wealth cannot be healthy for the future of the sport.

The Gulf state's money, whether through corruption or not, influenced FIFA into granting them the rights to hold the World Cup in 2022, criticized by many as being impracticable due to the excessive heat even if it does take place during the winter months. The treatment of Asian workers has added to the doubt and controversy about holding the competition in the Gulf state. The ownership of soccer clubs by oligarchs, corporations or sovereign states coupled with the growth in sponsorship and television rights, has raised the earnings of players, managers and agents to unprecedented and unrealistic levels. At least FIFA has bowed to pressure from Michel Platini to stop players being owned by investors. Surely soccer players must be salaried employees of their clubs, not slaves tied to corporate entities, whose only interest is the return on their investment? It would lead to even more transfers than at present purely for financial gain, making a mockery of the sport.

Part of the problem of the greed culture and insatiable appetite for short-term gains and shareholder value, lies in the way public corporations are run. Corporate directors of the leading quoted corporations and financial institutions have become the robber barons of the 21st century.

Boardrooms are filled with chairmen, CEOs, board directors, non-executive directors, remuneration committee members, advisers and recruitment consultants. Read the annual statements of quoted companies and the same names crop up. It is a Facebook for the elite, whose members award each other oversized remuneration packages on the basis of mutual back scratching in a conspiracy behind the closed doors of their lodges or private clubs, continually raising the earnings bar.

They have created an exclusive market, which cannot be undercut and argue that bonuses have to be paid to retain the best talent. Of course this is all spurious nonsense. It is time that they were told the game is up and that they must adapt to the real world.

When the American pilot, Chesley Sullenberger, was forced to ditch his aircraft in New York's Hudson River, with, miraculously, no loss of life, he said, "I was doing my job." One of the most remarkable unsung heroes has to be Tony Mendez, the CIA agent, who risked his own life by concocting an elaborate plan to rescue six Americans who had escaped being taken hostage after the American Embassy siege in Tehran in 1979. It was an extraordinary feat and he did his job in total secrecy.

These people didn't ask for, or expect, a bonus. Examples such as these should have set the standard for everyone. Unfortunately there is scant likelihood of a voluntary change of mentality and governments have demonstrated whose side they are on by doing so little to regulate the banks and force the bankers and corporate bosses to relinquish some of their earnings or bonuses during the present crisis.

It needs emphasizing that boardroom executives in quoted corporations are not risk taking entrepreneurs. They are employed by their companies and are paid generously to manage them on behalf of shareholders. It has become far too easy to become rich by sitting in a boardroom of a public company with a huge salary, bonus, stock options and generous pension and/or severance payout rather than take any business risk.

The stock options and bonus culture, which should be used as an incentive scheme for all employees, to give them an opportunity to profit from the fruits of their labor, has simply became standard practice in boardrooms. Receiving a high salary is only for getting up in the morning and turning up at the office. Bonuses, free stock options and pensions are written in stone and have nothing whatsoever to do with performance, or even the survival of their company. How can it be right that Lloyds Bank boss Antonio Horta Osoris, collects a multimillion pound bonus while announcing the loss of 9000 jobs? Watertight contracts and huge pensions are also distributed to this privileged elite on the basis of the need to retain talent. In reality they are insurance policies to guarantee fortunes for CEOs and executives in case they are ejected from their posts or are headhunted for another well paid position.

There is no economic or moral justification for such massive remuneration packages and huge pension pots for executives who take no personal financial risk. Far from acting as an incentive to perform, granting massive unearned bonuses and free stock options lead to arrogance and complacency.

There is no longer any incentive to succeed or for entrepreneurs to take personal financial risks when it is so much easier to be a boardroom director and earn a fortune within the space of one or two years regardless of performance. Ordinary managers whose role is the day to day running of the company, can be granted golden hellos, massive salaries, bonuses, free stock options and put millions aside into a pension scheme thus assuring a life of luxury before they even start work. Far too often failure has been rewarded as much as success. It would make more sense to encourage boardroom directors and employees to buy shares in their companies. This would give them a genuine vested interest to work harder for the long-term interest of the company. Nothing should be free.

There needs to be more democracy in the corporate world. Earnings need to be based on long-term performance and there is a strong argument for maximum wages in the same way that governments impose a minimum wage. If the bosses want to raise their salaries it should apply to everyone in the company. When staff is laid off there should be no increase in boardroom pay.

There should be an end to the practice of executives walking away with huge sums in compensation after only a few months in a job. This type of pay off is an insult to hard working employees with years of loyal service and must be discouraged.

An unhealthy relationship has arisen between big banks and big business at the expense of the thousands of small private companies. Governments have been so busy pandering to their friends in City or Wall Street boardrooms they have ignored the plight of the hundreds of thousands of small private companies, which form the backbone of our economies. While the bankers have handed out billions in loans to the multinationals, small private firms have been starved of credit. The ratio of debt to assets in many multinationals has been allowed to grow to the point where corporate liabilities exceed the value of their assets. The debt of many of the world's leading companies is more than the GDP of nation states. But regardless of the financial situation of banks or quoted corporations, boardroom pay increases while employees have their earnings capped or reduced or are sacked.

This kind of situation would bankrupt smaller companies and if applied to ordinary people, they would be on a credit black list or face ruin. This is why smaller companies, owned by families, are often more successful. They have a greater interest in looking after their company's future taking a long-term view to preserve their ownership for future generations. The major quoted multinationals are more intent on short-term projections to satisfy shareholders.

In a recession when so many workers are being asked to accept lower pay or lose their jobs, and in the light of the rate rigging and mis-selling scandals, it is simply unacceptable that those at the top continue to receive increases in pay and bonuses. Governments should impose a 100% tax on all bank bonuses in excess of 10% of their salaries and use the money for badly needed public services.

There are always those who strongly believe they are entitled to receive their over-generous salaries. Well, anyone who believes he or she is worth more than they are paid can become an entrepreneur and invest his or her own money. That is how it used to be.

Whether the huge earnings of pop groups and singers, cinema and sports stars are justified is more difficult to judge. They are paid massive sums because the public is willing to pay to see them. Pop groups and singers collect huge earnings because they actually sell albums or get bums on seats at concerts, and tennis, athletic or golf stars actually have to beat the competition to pocket the top prize money.

But in some cases the amounts earned have lost all sense of reality. Many cinema stars are paid millions regardless of the success of their movies. Football and basketball stars are paid fortunes regardless of the success of their clubs thanks to the wall of money cascading from television and sponsorship deals and to satisfy the egos of wealthy club owners. They do not understand what incentive schemes are all about.

Soccer clubs are now corporations and multinational businesses. More often than not the wealthiest clubs purchase the top players to prevent rivals from buying them, not because they fit in to their plans. Players have become mercenaries with no loyalty to a club and no real incentives to actually win competitions since their salaries are written in stone. And of course there is a conflict of interest with agents who make money from the constant trading of players. Where it starts to become unethical is when the more the stars earn the less they pay in taxes which is described in another chapter.

The downside is that many soccer clubs in the lower echelons of leagues in Europe, Africa and Asia have no money to pay their players. In Spain, players from Santander, a club which fell from grace, and had been unpaid for months, in an unprecedented move, actually refused to play forcing the referee to abandon a match. The pathetic Brazilian World Cup demonstrated how big business has taken over sport.

We require a total change of mentality to return to a fairer and more just society with a redistribution of the nation's wealth and an end to the power of banks, multinationals, corrupt governments and organized crime. Failure to act will inevitably lead to economic decline and social unrest on an unprecedented scale around the world.

The unacceptable level of unemployment in Europe is a major obstacle to economic recovery. The crisis has given businesses, large and small, the opportunity to shed staff and reduce salaries and wages while new labour laws have allowed them to offer part-time, precarious jobs or short-term contracts. Meanwhile the public sector receives preferential treatment with jobs for life, early retirement and other advantages. It is time to bring the public sector employees into line with the rest of the working population. Competition for work has also come from the opening up of Western Europe to poorer workers from Eastern Europe and immigrants from overseas. Permanent employment with respectable salaries may be a thing of the past and the question in the technological and internet age is will there be enough jobs for everyone in the world who wants to work?

If new jobs become available it is not the banks or multinationals which will provide them. They will come from the hundreds of thousands of small companies, which will lead the recovery when demand picks up. But the bosses of private companies either cannot obtain loans to expand or are often required to guarantee loans, risking their families and homes. In addition they face too many administrative burdens and pay too much tax. No wonder so many executives prefer the comfort of sitting in boardrooms than running their own businesses. Governments need to concentrate their attention on the private sector through increasing financial incentives and simplifying procedures and tax and spend less time pandering to the lobbies of the multinational corporations quoted on the stock markets. Given that the small private companies actually create more jobs than the quoted corporations, there is a strong case to persuade pension and major investment funds to invest a proportion of their funds in them rather than in the stock markets.

Unions have played an important role in protecting the interests of workers and are needed more than ever. But globalization and the crisis have reduced their influence and in this new international environment there is a need to rethink their position. Corporations have tended to push unions to the sidelines and reduce their involvement whenever they can, sometimes with the approval of governments – remember Margaret Thatcher's Britain. However, failure to take account of technological change and a lack of dialogue due to entrenched political views, too often leads to unnecessary conflicts and strikes causing disruption and inconvenience to the very people the unions are supposed to be protecting as well as violent confrontations with the police. Until the recent rail strikes, the German union model was upheld as a model of cooperation between workers and employers. So where do we go now?

While the World Trade Organization has been successful in negotiating free trade agreements to boost global economic growth and reduce poverty, there have been other negotiations, far less transparent, taking place to create what is known as the Trans Pacific Partnership. Approximately a dozen countries are believed to be preparing to endorse an agreement, which is seen as a charter to provide multinationals and banks unprecedented power over the world's economies.

According to its detractors, the agreement would undermine the laws of nation states by granting freedom to ignore consumer, labour and environmental laws. It would block copyright and patents, liberalize financial markets, restrict the use of generic medicines and determine the use of land, energy, telecommunications, natural and mineral resources, energy, healthcare etc. Corporations could sue nation states whenever they disagreed with their laws. In short, it is a charter to weaken governments to the point of becoming irrelevant and incapable of ensuring the well being of the people. The battle is not yet over.

In 2005 Nelson Mandela visited England and made a famous speech in Trafalgar Square thronged with thousands of admirers. He called for an end to poverty, more trade justice, the elimination of Third World debt and more financial aid. The crisis has shown that we do not seem to have grasped the importance of his message.

Financial Morality

Finally in our progress towards a resumption of work we require two safeguards against a return of the evils of the old order: there must be a strict supervision of all banking and credits and investments: there must be an end to speculation with other people's money, and there must be provision for an adequate but sound currency.

Franklin D Roosevelt, 4 March 1933

"We live in Financial Times" says the publicity for a well-known newspaper and it accurately sums up our world. Or it might be more appropriate to say that we live in fraudulent times. The abolition of monetary and currency controls coupled with the growth of tax havens has created a mountain of cash, usually tax free, which moves around the world looking for the highest returns and can be shifted at a moment's notice causing massive damage to the economies of nation states. The holders of this "hot money" can be compared to sharks constantly thrashing about in the water searching for food and devouring everything in their path.

Wall Street and the City of London are the hunting grounds for the most powerful predators and have done an incredible job in promoting themselves almost into cult status by engaging in systematic brainwashing. Not a day, not a minute, goes by without the media informing the public about stock market or currency movements as money and shares circulate.

The so-called financial experts and economists, who, with a few exceptions, failed to appreciate the banking crisis – members of the Dead Economists Society – bombard the public with daily statistics and economic graphs mesmerizing everyone and leaving the vast majority understanding little if anything at all. Professionals study the markets on a permanent basis and do not need hourly media reports, while the rest of the population, advised to invest over the long-term, has little interest in daily price fluctuations or economic data and more often than not, cannot understand them. The public is more interested in knowing that petrol has gone up or down by a few pence than learning that the price of Brent crude is fifty or one hundred dollars. And what is the point of excited financial journalists announcing that a stock index has opened or closed with a gain or loss of 0.3%? *Spread* is a current favourite we hear several times a day. But I doubt whether the average man or woman in the street could explain what it means. And I wonder if many people really understand the meaning of *quantitative easing*.

Despite specialist TV programmes and the financial press providing a constant barrage of financial data with prices moving up and down or across screens, and economists giving their economic data and advice, nobody forecast the crisis. So what is the purpose of this information? Does all this hyper activity have anything to do with the real economy?

Can anybody take stock markets seriously when the slightest rumour can send indices racing up or collapsing overnight adding to or wiping billions of dollars off the value of stocks for no apparent reason? When an unconfirmed message sent via Twitter can cause a 5% drop in share prices something must be wrong with the markets and their use of information. Interestingly when stock prices rise nobody seems concerned, but when they fall it creates panic. Perhaps it is time for the media to reduce its financial coverage and concentrate on matters which really affect people's daily lives. After all when the markets are closed for holidays, the world somehow copes.

We live in a world of intangibles dominated by the Internet. This ephemeral age has spawned a new form of corporate entity, which makes nothing, sells nothing, charges nothing to use, but is worth hundreds of billions of dollars. In my personal view Facebook, Twitter, LinkedIn, Snapchat and other social networks not only serve no useful purpose but are becoming dangerous to use. A purported nineteen billion dollars was paid by Facebook for WhatsApp, a company with less than one hundred employees and whose very existence depends on telecom companies. Many of these start-ups have one aim – the stock market. Glowing documents are produced by the banks appointed to arrange the flotation to entice investors, and with so much money looking for a home, billions are raised with astronomic values placed on these new quoted corporate entities. The capitalized value of these new firms is more than long established multinational conglomerates with global manufacturing plants employing hundreds of thousands of workers. Both directors and senior employees find themselves millionaires, if not billionaires overnight, and the bankers also cash in. The controversial private taxi operator, Uber, is an Internet company financed by venture capitalist firms including Goldman Sachs. With a handful of employees, it is capitalized at more than forty million dollars. The huge success of Alibaba's flotation was another example of how investors are enticed into investing in new Internet stocks to avoid being left behind. Whether there is room for all these companies in a competitive global marketplace or if they will succeed or justify their share price, is of secondary importance. The one certainty is that the venture capitalists will abandon ship with their gains at the slightest hint of a downturn.

Nevertheless many of these global, multibillion corporations are changing the way we live. Google, Facebook, Amazon, Apple and Microsoft may have made their founders mega rich but they are also reaching out to where no man has gone before. They have the ability to be in touch with billions of users or consumers and store data which governments can only dream about. They are the new masters of the universe.

Neither governments nor the banking sector have come to terms with their power to reach the people. All the laws in the world can be by-passed at the click of a mouse. New activities will provide thousands of jobs either full or part-time, which Governments will be unable to control. Instead of salaried staff, workers will be independent and self employed paying little or no charges or taxes. A headache for every Government used to rules and regulations.

The travel and leisure industries have been totally transformed by the Internet. Booking and reservation sites have altered the lives of millions of consumers who can check, compare and book flights, hotels, apartments, car rental, restaurants and theatres from their homes. These sites also provide client comments to add to the information available but the personal views cannot be substantiated and are unreliable.

The advent of new forms of currency and transfers via the net, are going to have a profound effect on the future of spending, saving, investing and transferring money. Within the space of a few years new companies have been created using the Internet for trading. There is no visible presence in the high street and little way of judging the reliability of using them. Crowdfunding is becoming an alternative and cheaper means to raise money by small companies often refused access to bank loans. The use of the virtual money, the bitcoin, which appeared from nowhere and whose value fluctuates without any logical or tangible reason, is growing and being used around the world. So far its presence as an alternative currency does not seem to concern governments despite recent events, which have seen the disappearance or loss of substantial sums as well as the operators themselves. PayPal is another alternative method of Internet payment which could have a profound effect on the banking system as we move towards a cashless society, and there are several Internet companies which specialize in currency transactions. What these new forms of payment offer is faster and cheaper transactions and tough competition for the high street banks which will have to adjust their own fees and charges to survive. The Internet has increased the speed at which transactions can be made and clients will no longer have to accept waiting for several days to clear cheques or make transfers while the banks sit on the money and charge for accessing one's bank account. The banking sector does not seem to be aware of the tsunami on the horizon.

The velocity of Internet transfers is also being exploited by traders using high frequency trading (HFT), which, although legal, is believed to manipulate prices in order to make millions through cheating investors. In the time it takes to receive an order to buy or sell, the traders are able to alter the price and make an extra profit without either the buyer or seller being aware of the difference. The rise of stock markets since the beginning of the crisis and the financial speculation, which continues unabated, can only add to the concern that we are facing another bubble.

Until the onset of the crisis the public traditionally trusted Wall Street and the City of London to look after its money and pensions, but is there any trust or confidence left? The growth in the number of financial advisers, whose role is to look after people's savings, has been matched by the increase in the number of cases of mis-selling or fraud. The response to the Cyprus bank crisis sent shockwaves around the world. Not only have banks speculated and lost people's savings but it now seems they can simply confiscate the money held on deposit. This is a whole new ball game, which could lead to a total collapse of the financial system.

Years ago most people never thought twice about depositing substantial sums of money or making transfers. The banks, with bank managers, were trusted implicitly to look after a client's savings. Today with Internet banking coupled with an increase in hacking and cyber crime, many people are concerned about the security of their savings. I believe that as the money used by banks belongs to its customers, every penny, euro or dollar of ordinary deposits, regardless of the amount, should be protected. For those who are prepared to take risks and speculate it is another matter.

But the uncertainty over how banks are managed suggests we need to return to a separation of retail banking and investment banking as it was before the abolition of the Glass-Steagall Act. To avoid the huge fluctuations in base rates we have witnessed in the past we need to fix fair but low interest rates for borrowers while providing an adequate return on investments for savers.

The HSBC revelations have opened up a Pandora's Box into the links between politicians, bankers and corporate bosses and how they collaborate to ensure the privileged elite avoid tax. Questions still need answering as to how and why the troika of Europe, the BCE and FMI allowed Cyprus and Greece to join the euro five years ago and did little or nothing to regulate or supervise operations.

With regard to Cyprus they all knew about the country's reputation as a tax haven and money launderer of Russian funds and how its banking sector was far too large for such a tiny state. Yet there has been no admission of responsibility for the mess and no heads have rolled. While the ordinary saver was faced with restrictions on withdrawals and transfers, there are rumours that the mega rich, with political friends, or Russian oligarchs, appear to have been informed in advance and were able to shift their funds across the Atlantic or elsewhere before the crash.

The Troika should also reflect on why it allowed Greece to accumulate so much debt without any supervisory action being taken years ago.

Currency trading was once a means for corporations to buy foreign currency when exporting or importing goods to ensure they would obtain the best rate. Today it has become a means to an end speculating on the rise or fall of different currencies to make quick gains. Statistics point to trillions of dollars being traded each day causing unjustified movements in currency prices, which cause considerable damage to the stability of the real economy and even nation states. And there is so much money traded it has led to fraud in the currency exchange markets.

The wall of money held by opaque hedge funds operating offshore, whose rampant speculation can lead to the manipulation of prices, coupled with an increase in derivatives and insider trading scandals, suggest that the financial, commodity and currency markets are high stake casinos and are no longer safe for either businesses or small investors looking for long-term security and growth. The warning signs have been flashing ever since George Sorus broke the Bank of England, or to be more accurate, forced the pound to leave the European Exchange Rate Mechanism. On 16 September 1992, on what became known as Black Wednesday, he speculated that the pound would fall. He made a gain of one billion pounds while the cost to the British Treasury was estimated at more than three billion pounds.

There is growing concern that the Asian Mafia organizations – Yakusa in Japan and Triads in China – which are so entrenched in their societies and control gambling rackets in Asia – have turned their attention to speculate in and manipulate the world's financial markets. And reports suggest that the Italian Ndrangheta has billions of euros at its disposal, much of which is generated by the cocaine industry.

And when the rating agencies are under investigation themselves for conflict of interest and deceit through falsely inflating ratings, and banks have been fined for mis-selling and blatant fraud, Wall Street and the City of London have lost all credibility to act as accurate barometers of the economic situation.

Nobody can ignore the euro crisis caused by the lack of agreement by member states to accept some loss of sovereignty in exchange for a kind of federal monetary union with a powerful central bank and harmonization of taxes and laws. But a return to individual currencies seems inconceivable in today's changing global economy. It would reduce Europe to a group of tiny countries competing with each other with no economic or financial clout to match the US or rising Asian powers. Devaluation is a double-edged sword. On the one hand it makes a country's exports more competitive while on the other it increase the costs of imports cancelling out any advantage.

If the European Union had followed the example of Iceland, perhaps the recession would have been less damaging. Iceland refused to pay the debts of private banks, let them go to the wall and indicted the bankers for their negligence. With the help of the IMF and thanks to the introduction of capital controls, it is on track to economic recovery.

In Richmond, California, the council of this small town took on Wall Street by blocking foreclosures on property. It used compulsory purchase orders to take over properties in debt and granted loans to the owners or allowed them to rent. Despite the threat of legal action by Wall Street lawyers, the mayor justifies this approach. "Better to leave people in their homes and let them pay what they can afford than have families on the streets. Better to bail out the people than the banks." In Barcelona, Spain, the PAH (Plataforma de Afectados por la Hipoteca) has become a powerful voice calling for local authorities and banks to renegotiate terms to prevent people being evicted from their homes.

This has raised the question of whether any bank should be allowed to sell off its mortgage portfolios to investment funds without the knowledge and agreement of the borrowers. This "packaging" of poor or toxic debts is what caused the financial crisis in the first place. It is becoming a legal and moral issue with any form of debt. A borrower enters into a contract with a chosen lender so why should the loan be traded to another unknown party, with whom the borrower has no legal engagement and who may not take into consideration the borrower's personal situation? This pass the parcel game applies to nation states and Argentina recently put a spanner in the works by refusing to repay billions of dollars to the American vulture funds, which somehow purchased the country's debt from the original lenders.

But the one single element needed to create a more equitable society as well as stimulate growth in the global economy, is the need for global reform of the present tax regimes. It is becoming increasingly apparent that individual states can no longer fix taxes unilaterally since it leads to tax competition, delocalization of companies and change of residence for wealthy individuals.

French actor Gerard Depardieu, who abandoned France for Russia, was the tip of the iceberg in this respect, with business bosses, celebrities of stage, screen, and especially sport, transferring their place of residence to tax havens just like soccer players changing clubs. It has to be said that the rich deserve some sympathy since governments constantly change the rules and move the goal posts making it virtually impossible to plan ahead either for individuals, families or companies. The crisis has led to a myriad of new laws and taxes creating a minefield. Instead of simplifying taxes and making them more equitable they have become complex, extremely unfair and hard to understand. The only beneficiaries are accountants and tax consultants.

The wealthy enjoy the freedom of movement of capital which the global economy has provided using it as a means to transfer money and avoid taxes. So tax regimes should also go global or at least be harmonized within the European Union and perhaps the USA. We need a new approach to ensure the financial sector serves the economy and there is a level tax playing field.

There are compelling moral and economic reasons to act now.

Moral reasons:

1. The banking sector caused the current crisis through an excess of greed, speculation and, as is becoming apparent, corrupt practices, insider trading and outright fraud.

2. The system of pay and bonuses operating in Wall Street and the City of London has simply widened the gap between

the wealthy privileged elite and the middle and poorer classes to unsustainable levels.

3. It is inconceivable that bankers and corporate bosses are allowed to award themselves massive salaries and bonuses when thousands face the loss of jobs and homes due to their irresponsibility.

4. Quoted corporations and the financial sector have been granted too much power and freedom due to globalization, the removal of currency controls, the abolition of the Glass-Steagall Act and deregulation.

5. The financial services industry has turned into an insatiable monster controlling people's destiny through excessive costs and fees charged for handling people's savings or investments regardless of the performance of the funds.

6. The unsatisfactory opaque practices in boardrooms allowed bosses like RBS's Fred Goodwin to ride off into the sunset in his fifties with his saddle bags filled with loot as a reward for having almost bankrupted his bank.

Economic reasons:

1. The financial markets dominate the economy to the detriment of the real economy in which hundreds of thousands of small private companies actually create the new jobs and economic growth.

2. Tax avoidance – or legal tax evasion – has become a major sector of the financial services industry. Inexplicably it comes with government approval, which allows City professionals to conjure up sophisticated schemes to enable powerful corporations and wealthy individuals to avoid paying tax. Thanks to creative accounting and computer technology they can simply shift profits and assets offshore into the myriad of tax havens, which governments, again inexplicably, tolerate.

3. The use of offshore banks and companies has led to the expansion of unregulated and opaque hedge funds which

operate from the tax havens using undisclosed "hot money" funds to create havoc in the stock markets through short-term, high risk, speculative activities which serve no economic purpose. Total transparency is required.

4. With the wealthy able to avoid taxes the burden falls on the middle and poorer classes. Coupled with the unfair distribution of earnings towards the mega wealthy, who cannot spend what they pay themselves, it is clearly damaging for the economy and social cohesion.

5. The crisis has led to a double whammy; governments face increased social benefits to pay the unemployed and poor while tax avoidance or evasion and unemployment means less tax revenue and an increase in the national debt.

6. In order to stimulate the economy there should be a cap on the earnings of those at the top (or raise taxes) and higher wages and less tax to increase the spending power of the vast majority of the population.

7. Investment banking must be separated from the retail banks, which should return to their role as protectors of people's savings and suppliers of credit to businesses and home owners, rather than act purely in the interests of their boardroom directors and shareholders.

8. There is no moral or economic logic in governments creating a tax system which maintains high tax rates for income, capital gains and death duties, when those at whom the tax is aimed simply avoid paying thanks to avoidance schemes which the same governments permit the financial sector to implement in order for it to generate substantial fees and charges from their clients.

9. European and American governments must take action to control the power of the multinational corporate and banking sectors and ensure they pay their fair share of taxes.

10. The financial sector draws too many young people lured by the potential of earning high salaries from other important sectors of the economy. This is damaging for the future of engineering, medicine, research, architecture, science

and other professions requiring long years of study and training.

Great Britain is one of Europe's leading world economies yet refuses to join the single European currency. Despite having retained its own currency, the country has not avoided the economic recession. The obsession to keep sterling, which is becoming irrelevant in international trading, is purely to satisfy the short-term and selfish interests of the City of London bankers who do not wish to relinquish their power and cannot accept sharing the financial stage with rivals Frankfurt and Paris and thus ensure Europe remains a major player in the world.

The fact is that the euro, despite its problems, improved the standard of living of most Europeans until the onset of the current economic crisis. The single currency has probably saved the continent from a potentially worse economic situation and a series of competitive devaluations which would have had disastrous consequences. It has also been a boon to business and private travellers eliminating currency fluctuations and bank charges across a large part of the continent. The obvious analogy is to imagine the United States with a different currency and central bank in each state.

David Cameron said, "We are all in it together." He is right. If Britain wants to be taken seriously and remain a leading European power it has little choice but to eventually join the euro. Unfortunately, both for businesses and the thousands of British pensioners who retired to Europe's sunshine belt, who have seen a decline in their living standards, the decision wasn't taken ten years ago. The crisis has made people wary of the single currency and Eurosceptics never stop blaming it for our current economic problems. But the future of the European Union with over five hundred million people representing 7% of the world's population depends on it becoming a major economic and political world player with a single currency.

We should not forget that despite economists and so-called experts advising governments, hardly anyone saw the crisis coming or if they did, they were ignored. Political leaders should not rely on them again. Governments have a duty to create a new global financial system through more stringent regulation and transparency to reduce the speculation that caused the crisis and, far more important, to end the corruption and fraud in order to restore confidence and trust in the financial and corporate sector. But the most important long-term objective has to be to oversee a major redistribution of the world's economic wealth without which peace and stability cannot be guaranteed.

Corporate Morality

The health of a democratic society may be measured by the quality of functions performed by private citizens.

Alexis de Tocqueville

My first job after leaving school was with a major London advertising agency. One of my roles was delivering reports to the directors. I had to take the elevator to the top floor where the carpeted corridor, wood paneled boardroom and luxuriously furnished offices were reserved for the directors, all men. It was another world with smoke filled, overheated offices. Years later, having risen to managerial level, I had to attend a meeting at the London offices of a multinational corporation. This time the directors not only had their own floor reserved for the company's elite, but a private lift and dining room. Lower down at the executive level there was another larger, less lavish, dining room and in the basement, the majority of the staff had to contend with a vast canteen. This corporate segregation at executive levels gradually receded as the move to open plan offices became popular and heralded a more democratic working environment, taking a cue from the Japanese. The earnings gap was not an issue despite the pyramid structure within companies, which existed between the boardrooms and office floor. Today, behind the shiny glass facades of the latest, architect award winning, innovative and sophisticated high rise office blocks, the CEOs and boardroom directors still run their organizations from a distant planet far removed from the open spaces below filled with thousands of employees. They are still private domains where decisions affecting the lives of the people are made, but instead of the wealth created by their employees being shared, it is reserved for themselves.

This is the corporate world today. Our economies have in fact been hijacked by the financial sector and multinationals and as the world's economies have become global with new emerging markets, economic expansion has also led to an increase in corruption, greed and immoral practices.

Helmut Schmidt was quoted as saying, "The profits of today generate the investments of tomorrow and the jobs of the future." This idealistic and long-term view of how the corporate world should function has been forgotten or ignored. Immediate profits and personal gain have become the corporate charter.

One of the most grotesque examples of corporate immorality was the sale of Rover, one of Britain's industrial jewels, to the Phoenix 4. The company was in grave financial difficulty but the decision by Stephen Byers, then Labour secretary of state for trade and industry, to allow Peter Beale, John Edwards, Nick Stevenson, and John Towers to become its new owner for £10 was a disaster for the company and employees.

But not for the directors who are believed to have somehow made off with an estimated £42 million through the use of sophisticated financial engineering leaving thousands of employees on the scrap heap. What is even more astounding is that despite allegations of corruption, intent to defraud and corporate negligence of the directors and Deloitte, the auditors involved throughout, the Senior Fraud Office did nothing.

The selloff of Britain's Royal Mail generated a considerable amount of controversy with accusations levelled against ministers for giving it away too cheaply. This does seem the case as the share price rocketed so soon after the public offering. The investment banks and advisors, which handled the sale have come under criticism for raking in fortunes in fees and then dealing in the shares for clients, which included hedge funds, all of whom made considerable profits, once again, to the detriment of the taxpayer. Was this down to incompetence or negligence in government or straight-forward connivance with the financial sector to rip off the public? This situation happens regularly whenever there is a major corporate flotation.

The demise of Phones 4 U also highlighted the dubious role of private equity funds whose clever financial engineering allowed them to make a profit while the company was left with a massive debt, forced to sell off its stores and lay off thousands of employees.

Wherever major arms deals have been negotiated payments to intermediaries and plain bribery have always been used to win contracts. Lately the use of offshore banks and companies in tax havens have allowed multinational corporations to engage in systematic tax evasion, much of it legal, thanks to governments rubber stamping complex avoidance schemes.

The horsemeat scandal in Europe has shown how regulations mean nothing. Deals are made and products transferred from one country to another, using intermediaries, often based in those countries offering the most favourable tax arrangements. These methods are used to cover the tracks and hide the origin of many products, as well as unnecessarily increasing the price. Despite legal requirements on packaging we no longer know what we consume. And when a well-known major brewery is accused of watering down beer to increase profits, it demonstrates how low the business world has sunk.

The electronic age has brought with it scams on an unprecedented scale finding naïve consumers or investors who are caught in the traps. The Nigerian scam ranks in the top ten. In order to be able to obtain a huge inheritance or investment from overseas, punters were seduced into handing over cash up front to these fraudsters in order to release the funds, which would be shared. Some, like this, are so obvious, it makes one wonder how they get away with it. And even if they are caught they still get away with it, the money, I mean, which has by that time disappeared into some secret offshore account.

It is rather late and hypocritical of the British Government, which endorses most of the avoidance schemes and runs many of the world's tax havens, to call for an end to the transfer schemes, which have allowed major corporations to cheat the system for so long. If politicians want to recover lost tax revenue they just have to abolish all the avoidance schemes and end the use of tax havens. And they could start by ending the private deals between major banking and corporate entities with HMRC to reduce their tax bills.

The economic crisis has been the catalyst for opening up a Pandora's Box of institutionalized corruption and fraud, which is now endemic. And it is not just limited to African dictatorships but permeates the corridors of power in democracies everywhere.

Not a day passes without another scandal over corporate payments to politicians, bribery, real estate land deals, bank fraud, rate fixing, mis-selling, pension rip offs, insider trading, bribery, kick backs, price manipulation in stock and currency markets, price fixing by cartels, excessive banking and corporate salaries and bonuses and just plain greed to rip off the consumers.

Even the major auction houses have been tainted with scandal. Works of art and antiques are sold at exorbitant prices to secretive buyers without knowledge of the origin of the money. Works found to be copied, forged or even stolen are sold to unsuspecting collectors. The result is a loss of trust and confidence in the markets.

Nowhere is the lack of corporate morality more apparent than in the financial sector as already mentioned. Banks have operated with impunity for years collecting fees, overcharging, rate rigging, mis-selling, speculating with our money on a massive scale and as the crisis demonstrated, engaging in fraud and money laundering while building up colossal losses and debts. Several years after the pensions and endowment policy scandals rocked the British financial establishment, the government has finally given some freedom back to the people by abolishing the requirement to take out annuities and allowing everybody with a pension to take responsibility for their own savings. This decision is a blow for the insurance industry used to making substantial fees from managing people's pensions. There have been calls for more transparency and laws to end the practice of individuals and corporations using shell companies, trusts or figureheads in tax havens to hide the names of the true owners of bank accounts, companies or real estate. This is paramount if governments are serious about reducing or eliminating tax evasion.

People tend to forget when hearing about unethical dealings, fraud and crime that the banks are deeply involved. Deregulation and the global economy have transformed bankers into accomplices. Without the cooperation of banks, there would be no money laundering, no tax evasion, no illicit transfers, no offshore accounts and no corruption. They have a great deal to answer for. But we must also accept that governments have given them too much freedom to handle our money.

One of the worst excesses has been the packaging up of mortgages and debts and disposing them to other banks and investment funds without the knowledge of the mortgagees or clients who found themselves caught up in a financial tsunami which swept away their homes and lives. People who thought they had a contractual liability to a respectable high street bank or mortgage company found themselves tied to unscrupulous and nebulous funds who had no hesitation in evicting families without any consideration to their situation.

The banks convinced governments to allow them to set up a "bad bank" to take over the so-called toxic assets and eliminate the debt from their balance sheets. This was a clever move to enable the banks to appear financially sound and post higher earnings. And the so-called "bad bank" could sell off the assets to other funds or dealers at knock down prices with little consideration for families in difficulty.

However, in most cases this fancy financial engineering to protect the original lender did not relieve the borrower from his original debt. The whole system was designed to protect the banks while ignoring the plight of the borrowers. Many occupied properties have been packaged up and sold off to other banks or investment companies at a knockdown price only for the new owners to offer them at higher prices to the same occupiers.

It would have been more ethical and possibly cheaper for the government to have required the banks to simply extend the loan period or reduce the monthly outgoing during a time of hardship leaving people in their homes or for the original lender to have sold them off to the occupiers at a fair price instead of allowing other banks, who are acting as middlemen, make a profit from people's misery. The banks' response is that they do not have the expertise or staff to deal with negotiating and refinancing loans for thousands of homeowners in difficulty and it is better to let a specialist company handle it.

Investors have begun once again to look at real estate in many countries where property values have collapsed since the outset of the financial crisis. But it is unacceptable to see the banking sector, which forced millions out of their homes, now cashing in by selling their mortgaged properties to vulture funds well below the market value.

Despite the crisis and calls for wage restraint, the bankers and corporate bosses continue to help themselves to astronomical salaries, bonuses, free stock options, pensions and golden parachutes regardless of the damage they caused or the financial situation or performance of their companies.

There is no moral or economic justification in the practice of awarding golden parachutes or watertight contracts and severance pay for chief executives. Described as incentives for retaining talent they are really insurance policies for many executives to ensure that regardless of success or results, they can collect fortunes when they leave or are removed. Huge amounts of shareholders' funds are allocated for loss of office of the boardroom directors even when they choose to leave or immediately find another position. There are so many abuses of the system it is odd that there are not more revolts by shareholders into these unethical practices.

Why have governments done little or nothing to stop the greed of the privileged elite in the City while the vast majority of the population endures harsh austerity measures? Why have top civil servants and university chancellors been allowed to award themselves such generous salaries and pensions? The answer is that members of the so-called independent bodies, which fix earnings, are all from the same privileged elite. It is the members of the remuneration committees, who determine the level of boardroom earnings. But has anyone considered just who sits on these committees handing out millions in salaries, bonuses, stock options and pensions regardless of performance? Often they are made up of chairmen and directors from other City financial institutions and corporations exchanging favours and acting as if it were a private club distributing shareholders' funds or taxpayer's savings among the members. This band of brothers makes sure everyone can win the lottery with the winning ticket handed out in advance. It does not need talent, risk or effort.

Despite the huge bank losses and bailouts, political leaders have protected the bankers' huge earnings and bonuses by arguing that they have legal contracts, which are binding and cannot be rescinded. However when it comes to public or private employees, who also have contracts, there is no compunction in tearing up their contractual agreements to reduce their wages, alter their conditions or even dismiss them. Proposing an eleven percent increase for British MPs while the rest of the population struggles on lower wages was both insensitive and immoral and demonstrates how our political and corporate leaders are so distant from reality.

Corporate boardrooms have become the playground for the elite who exchange chairs in a perpetual merry-go-round. Chairmen, CEOs and directors all collect fat pay cheques for sitting in their leather chairs. But just how useful are the non executive directors who collect substantial sums for a few hours a week sitting in boardrooms? In the vast majority they are male and come from the same cozy City establishment. Does their presence really justify their remuneration packages?

They are either fellow directors from other major corporations or ex-politicians rewarded for previous favours and offered a means to supplement their pension. Too often the boardroom members are appointed to rubber stamp the decisions of the CEOs rather than provide independent advice.

There has been criticism over the lack of women in boardrooms who, it is suggested, would bring a sense of justice and fairness to corporate practices. It will be difficult for women to break down the barriers of the male dominated city boardrooms and their political allies. One of the reasons is that women, in general, have not been brought up in the same elite schools and clubs, which are the preserve of the establishment. This is changing, albeit slowly, but it would be wrong, in my view, to introduce quotas. Governments seem intent on wanting to enforce quotas in every facet of our lives based on ethnic origins, sexual leanings, religion, age etc., etc. This will neither improve efficiency nor lead to a fairer society. Advancement has to be based on merit, not gender or the colour of one's skin.

Politicians invariably find a seat in the boardrooms when they leave office with similar high earnings and perks to go with it. Timothy Geithner left the Obama administration to become president of a major Wall Street private equity firm, Warburg Pincus. Tony Blair is a prime example, showing his true colours with a highly paid unspecified role – estimated at more than two million pounds a year – with J.P. Morgan as well as other wealthy patrons. France's ex-president, Nicolas Sarkozy, is well remunerated for his speech making conferences. Rewards for services rendered, is perhaps a polite way to describe this practice, known as revolving doors, which operates in every country. The conflict of interest is inescapable. It is intolerable to stand by and watch the bankers and corporate bosses plundering the coffers while the government does little or nothing to prevent what can only be described as bank robbery or corporate theft on a massive scale by insiders while the rest of the population struggles to survive.

The world's stock markets, once the realm of huge industrial conglomerates have been transformed by the growth of the service sector and new technology. The FTSE 100, CAC 40, Dow Jones, Hang Seng, Nikkei etc. are dominated by banks, financial institutions, technology companies, real estate groups and the privatized energy, utility and telecommunications sectors. Many of the newcomers listed such as Facebook, Google and Twitter did not exist twenty years ago and it is likely that during the next decade there will be many companies listed which do not exist today. Technological developments such as 3D printing will open up new opportunities. The global economy and liberalization of markets have allowed too many people without any particular talent to become wealthy through simply sitting in boardrooms with a widening wealth gap between those at the top and employees. What seems morally wrong is how the chairmen, CEOs and executives of the privatized corporations and banks, after a career as managers and without taking any personal financial risk, can walk off with excessive severance and retirement packages which they cannot spend in a lifetime, as well as benefitting from generous tax breaks in order to keep their wealth. But does anybody consider that these fortunes are ultimately passed on to the family and heirs, people who have done nothing whatsoever to deserve this transfer of unearned wealth. We are creating a future generation of mega rich people who have not worked to earn their wealth but whose influence, due to it, will be of significant importance.

More democracy in the boardrooms is needed to restrict the amount of severance payments when leaving office. Too many boardroom directors or sports managers receive massive sums when they leave or are sacked while employees have to make do with a few weeks' salary. The granting of stock options has led to an abuse by many CEOs and board directors. The aim today is to obtain a flotation on the stock market as fast as possible to make fortunes from the sale of shares. They are handed options for shares for nothing or at a low price and make fortunes by disposing of them within a short space of time at a higher price with no effort or work required. Often they have watertight contracts to guarantee substantial pay offs and pensions regardless of their performance. Where is the motivation or incentives to be successful when corporate bosses can walk off with fortunes in less than a year just for turning up for work?

Dishonesty, negligence or incompetence are also highly rewarded. The bankers are award winners in this category, with Fred Goodwin winning the Oscar. Just behind is the Phoenix 4, described above, as well as people like Rebekah Brooks. The former editor of the News of the World, who resigned from the Murdoch Group after the phone hacking scandal which she claims not to have known about, and has since been cleared by the court, walked away with a pay off estimated to be in excess of one and a half million pounds. The employees did not receive the same treatment. They were merely discarded by Rupert Murdoch, who shut down the newspaper. After a dreadful first season in charge, Manchester United manager, David Moyes, was sacked and walked off with several million pounds as a reward for his lack of success. More often than not these people find new highly paid jobs relatively quickly as opposed to most employees who might face years out of work.

This is a distant world to the one where entrepreneurs created their businesses using their own money, talent and hard work. There is little chance of building industrial giants such as Ford, Michelin, General Motors, Dow Chemicals, Boeing, Proctor and Gamble or Nestle today. The cost is too great and it takes long-term commitment. Given the huge rewards for sitting in boardrooms and taking no personal risk, it is not worth the hard work or effort required.

The rot set in during the seventies when the service sector began to overtake manufacturing industries, which actually made and produced goods. Companies like Slater Walker became the darlings of the stock market. They cottoned on to the fact that the value of the land on which stood factories or warehouses used by manufacturing companies was worth more than the actual business.

Real estate assets could be redeveloped as offices, apartment blocks or shopping centres. Asset stripping became a household word and the people behind the schemes, which shut down manufacturing operations and left thousands out of work, became very wealthy without actually making anything.

This was the beginning of the transformation of the Western economies from manufacturing to financial services and the belief that financial markets could be left to regulate themselves, which ultimately led to the crisis. Mergers and takeovers became the new game in town creating powerful corporations, which loathe competition. Corporate democracy evaporated; Capitalism was transformed into an international jungle in which only the strongest survive.

In the technological age, the protection of intellectual property has become a lawyer's paradise to maintain control – and the money – over the intangible rights of literary, musical and artistic works. The controversy relates to when works should enter the public domain. Is it fair that copyright lasts for 70 years after the death of the creator, enabling the heirs and families of composers, singers, writers, movies and other creative works, or the companies which acquired the rights, to continue to be the only beneficiaries even though they had little or nothing to do with the original work?

The world's stock markets have become casinos where a company's future can be decided in minutes; the game plan being to strip out as much profit as possible in the shortest possible time. Although it is supposed to be illegal, the fact is only those with insider knowledge can possibly survive and make gains in the global jungle. Professional investors do not stick pins on to a board, they have to know all there is to know about a company and this requires insider information. The small investor can no longer trust the markets or advisors who are out of their depth competing with vulture funds, which dominate the markets.

Major organizations like Enron, Anderson, WorldCom, financial institutions like Behrings, Bear Stearns and Lehman and powerful industrialists like Robert Maxwell succumbed to corporate greed, speculation or just plain fraudulent dealings leaving the taxpayer to pick up the tab.

When RBS, the British bank which needed massive government aid to survive, has been accused of deliberately forcing viable companies to go to the wall in order to profit from the sale of their real estate premises, it shows how capitalism has failed to learn any lessons.

The Forbes list represents a handful of people worth billions but few have actually created their companies. Many have profited from political friends granting them control over oil, energy telecommunications, utilities and transport companies; public monopolies transformed into private monopolies or cartels run by the new oligarchs able to benefit from favourable tax status and so powerful they can make or break governments.

The largest conglomerates tend not to be industrial manufacturing organizations but service operators whose income is generated from captive consumers who have to use water, electricity, petrol, gas, telephones, transport, roads, car parks, airports and now hospital services. These have simply become cash machines for the new breed of the privileged corporate elite, growing wealthy at the expense of consumers and often at the expense of employees. One of the effects of increased competition and the drive to achieve more corporate profitability is the stress it imposes on employees. The danger only came to light in France after the suicide of several France Telecom workers. It shocked the company into altering its policies on work rate, its goals and especially human relations within the organization, which had reached a low point with much of the staff uncertain about its future.

Some governments have finally woken up to the abuse of power, treatment of employees and lack of competition. The President of Mexico, Enrique Pena Nieto, has promised to end the virtual monopolies of the country's telecom and television companies. At present Grupo Televisa has 70% of the market while Carlos Slim's America Movil controls 84% of the country's telecom and Internet sector. Under new laws to open up markets to competition, no one company will be allowed to own more than 50%.

Thanks to corrupt regimes, powerful mining conglomerates have simply exploited the developing nations, stripping out their natural or mineral resources for private gain to the detriment of the indigenous population; compare the profits of mining companies like DeBeers and Glencore/Xstrata with the earnings and working condition of thousands of indigenous workers who risk their lives in extreme conditions extracting the minerals.

Governments have not only pandered to these wealthy and powerful corporate bosses allowing them to plunder national assets but in addition have granted them advantageous tax exemptions. The result has been that companies use whatever means at their disposal to reduce the number of employees and workers, who have become modern day slaves to be discarded at will with minimum legal protection purely to satisfy the insatiable appetites of these oligarchs and major shareholders.

Mergers and takeovers are now the prerogative of mega investment funds with billions at their disposal. Household names have become toys for these, often opaque, sovereign or offshore funds which bear no loyalty to employees. It is a far cry from the paternal industrial entrepreneurs who built their empires while looking after their employees like a family. Employees were once proud to work for these corporations.

Great family-run businesses have succumbed to the harsh reality of the global economy. Fiat, which is intrinsically linked to Italy, caused a bombshell when it announced that following its merger with Chrysler it was transferring its corporate headquarters to Holland with its tax base in the UK. While the company's fortunes have benefitted so has the wealth of its CEO, Sergio Marchionne, who moved to the US and last year is believed to have taken home in excess of thirty million dollars in earnings. Chinese motor giant, Dongfeng, has taken a major stake in French automobile company, Peugeot, which has been losing market share and money.

Whether this will result in a loss of local jobs remains to be seen. But today there is no loyalty left and trust and confidence in the workplace have gone out of the window. It is all about the bottom line. It has become common practice to see new larger merged corporations worse off once the bankers and advisors have taken out their multimillion dollar fees. Consider the AOL-Time Warner deal, which destroyed billions of dollars of value as well as tens of thousands of jobs. Mergers and acquisitions are now back in fashion as corporations with cash are looking to buy competitors in debt or take advantage of the current very low interest rates to borrow funds. It is doubtful that many of these mergers, friendly or hostile, are necessary or justified as the result is usually reduced competition and, once again, a loss of jobs.

The international expansion of leading quoted corporations has been made possible through leveraging and increasing debt to unsustainable levels in balance sheets. The media reports may paint a rosy picture and the bosses may be on Forbes' list, but does the share price reflect the accurate balance sheet and market value of many corporations or is it a house of cards, which could fall apart at any moment? Glory is so fleeting as Tesco found out to its cost.

The big four accounting firms, Price Waterhouse, Deloitte, Ernst and Young and KPMG have come under increasing criticism for the power they wield. Where were they before the crisis erupted? They have a clear professional duty to investigate the financial situation of the banks and major corporations, yet none warned of any problems or irregularities or the extent of debt or toxic assets. They are reluctant to pass up the colossal fees they earn, which have led to an unacceptable conflict of interest. It is no surprise that they are often cited in cases of fraud or professional negligence.

The folly of the savings banks, real estate developments, empty airports and motorways in Spain, are perfect examples of how political and business corruption can lead to ruin when there is a lack of real economic planning or thinking behind the project.

Spain's autonomous Regions each have their own parliaments. Each created its own savings banks as well as local TV stations. During the property boom the local authorities engaged in dubious transactions allegedly selling land to developers at agricultural prices before changing the zoning and granting them planning permission. The increase in value enabled the developers to borrow from the savings banks to develop housing estates, apartment and retail complexes, and buyers were able to obtain mortgages from the savings banks. The regions were run by megalomaniacs with little vision and even less economic sense. Motorways were built where there were no cars, airports where there were no aircraft and privatized public services were awarded to close business acquaintances. In the town of Cuidad Real, less than two hundred kilometres from Madrid, the brand new expensive, and empty, airport was appropriately named Don Quijote. The building of Spain's railway network has led to accusations of false accounting and fraudulent increases in the price of contracts. All these projects were part of a cosy, incestuous system with bribes and commissions being distributed all round until the crisis ended the party.

The saving banks and developers became hugely indebted. The massive overspending led to the Regions facing huge financial debts and their situation opened up a world of fraudulent operations. Magistrates began to pursue politicians and businessmen for corruption and fraud on an unprecedented scale. The bankrupt savings bank directors were found to have dubiously awarded themselves massive watertight remuneration packages and pensions just prior to the crash, which the courts are now trying to recover. It is hard to accept that in a major democratic European nation, institutionalized corruption is so endemic. Yet despite the almost daily disclosures of corruption scandals, remarkably few politicians, bankers or corporate bosses have resigned or been sent for trial. The only victims have been the investigating magistrates, pressured into dropping cases or in the case of Judge Baltasar Garzon, being removed from office by those in the judiciary whose primary interest seems to be protecting the elite. The courageous judge from Andalucia, Mercedes Alaya, has so far refused to bow to pressure from the political establishment. She has been investigating a political scandal in Andalucia for years attempting to ascertain the whereabouts of over eight hundred million euros of public money, which disappeared between 2000 and 2012, implicating a number of high profile regional politicians.

I have detailed the present Spanish problems since they never cease to end. But Spain is not alone. I have already mentioned the Italian banking scandals and there is no need to repeat Berlusconi's battles with the courts. Too many countries use public works contracts to inflate prices for either political purposes or just personal gain. Whatever the reasons it shows how corporate and financial corruption is institutionalized throughout Europe and many parts of the world.

Faulty or negligent construction procedures are believed to be the cause of several high profile scandals In Italy. The most recent case concerned the collapse of a viaduct on the Palermo-Catania motorway in Sicily effectively cutting the island in two. It added to a long list of incidents which includes the collapse of ceilings in many schools, one of which resulted in the death of a pupil. On a visit to Sicily infrastructure Minister Graziano Delrio said, "While Brunelleschi's 15th century Dome still dominates the Florence skyline, drivers have to pray every time they cross a viaduct." Perhaps he should also introduce helmets for schoolchildren. The damage to the Sicilian viaduct prompted the Government to shelve a large number of major building works whose viability appeared suspect.

The proposal to build a high-speed train tunnel beneath the city of Florence is one of the most controversial decisions facing the government. According to opponents of the scheme, it would put at risk many historical buildings and monuments. The project, designed to by-pass the existing rail terminal, includes an underground station, designed by Norman Foster and seven kilometres of track beneath the city costing an estimated three billion euros. Environmental groups have calculated that the massive underground concrete walls of the station and tunnels would act like a dam leading to contraction of the ground and damage to buildings above. Apart from the arrest of several politicians and businessmen accused of overpricing contracts, engineers from Florence University have come up with an alternative proposal which would entail the transformation of one of Florence's five other stations and two kilometres of new track at ground level at a cost of two hundred million euros. Given that there would be virtually no gain in time by trains using the tunnel, surely Matteo Renzi, as ex-mayor of the city, will shelve this pharaonic scheme and save one of Europe's most beautiful cities from potential disaster.

More and more goods are now being produced in countries where manufacturing costs, rents and taxes are lower in Eastern Europe and Asia. North and Sub Saharan Africa have seen a huge increase in investment from China but so far it has achieved little to improve the living standards of the indigenous people and led to resentment as many of the jobs created are actually filled by Chinese workers. French farmers regularly block the country's southern border to prevent Spanish and Moroccan products entering the country accusing them of dumping. They are caught in a pincer between cheaper competition and the low prices paid to them by the major retail groups, which they claim makes it impossible to survive. And when French farmers get angry, the government tends to listen.

In the Congo, a country rich in mineral resources, with a long history of colonial occupation, Chinese money has been flooding in. But working conditions are still primitive. Long distance truck drivers who transport goods between the major towns along congested, unmade roads on a 1200 kilometre journey, can be away from their homes for up to four weeks if bad weather turns the roads into impassable bogs. All they earn is one hundred and forty euros a month and they are lucky if they see their families more than three or four times a year.

Recently Qatar, one of the wealthiest states in the world, has been accused of inhuman treatment of Asian workers, forced to live and work in slave conditions on building sites, where some have lost their lives. Singapore, which has built up an enviable reputation as a stable, financially sound democratic state, has been accused of ill-treating its largely Indian workforce, forced to work for low wages.

Food retailers pay peanuts to the workers who produce their nuts while profiting from massive mark ups in their stores. Mining groups use slave labour in the gold, copper, tin or coal mines while the traders make fortunes. The fashion industry makes many of its products cheaply in Asia yet still charges astronomical prices for its products. Using slave or child labour does not seem to touch the conscience of the food, pharmaceutical, mining or luxury brand industries.

Nike has come under criticism for producing most of its products overseas while still charging up to three hundred dollars for a pair of sports shoes. The Bangladesh factory tragedies highlighted the unacceptable working conditions of many workers and although this did lead to Zara's Spanish president, Amancio Ortega, reviewing the company's manufacturing policy, which is a welcome start, few other companies appear to have followed his example or have been prepared to compensate workers or their families for the tragedy. The Turkish mining disaster was another example of the exploitation of cheap labour with little regulation.

Vandana Shiva is an Indian academic and a leading feminist. Born in 1952 she has devoted forty years protecting the interests of poor Indian workers using Ghandi's method of peaceful civil disobedience. Her refusal to allow multinationals to exploit the country's natural resources and workers, resulted in massive demonstrations and her winning several court cases against multinational companies like Monsanto and Coca Cola. Unfortunately Haiti, one of the world's poorest nations, does not have a Vandana Shiva and its gold reserves were handed over to a Canadian mining company. In a recent case, Philip Morris has actually taken Uruguay to court over the Government's ruling to remove brand names from packets. To combat the global economy takes courage and time. It is thirty years since the Bhopal disaster and there are still thousands of victims awaiting justice and compensation.

Francisco Van der Hoff is a Dutch missionary who runs the Union de Comunidades Indigenas de la Region de Istmo (UCIRI). Founded in Mexico in 1988, its aim is to expand the concept of equitable commerce and fair trade by engaging in a North-South partnership to export local produce including coffee, rice, tea, cotton, sugar, bananas and cacao. The idea is to eliminate the number of middlemen involved in the production and distribution process. Instead of the traditional system of producer-local intermediary-transformer-exporter-agent-importer-distributor, retailer and finally the consumer, the equitable route is to limit the number of operators to producer-cooperative-importer-distributor-retailer-consumer.

This way a greater proportion of the financial benefits would remain with the producers. From its origins in Mexico this fair-trade concept has grown in importance throughout Central and Latin America under the brand Max Havelaar. In France Artisans du Monde is a concept started by French missionary l'Abbe Pierre, who died in 2007 and who called for aid to Bangladesh when the country was affected by famine and civil war. The first store opened in 1974 selling products made by local craftsmen. It has grown into an association with affiliates and producers in more than forty four countries selling a wide range of products in competition with the major brands

At the other end of the scale is the relatively recent concept of *Vanity capital* described as catering for the mega rich. The mega rich go for mega yachts, a boon to shipbuilding companies. They are usually moored in exclusive ports, like Cannes, Monaco or Saint Tropez creating a backdrop but are rarely used for sea trips. The luxury brand industry has gone from strength to strength but one of the mysteries is how they find customers. Despite an increase in shopping tourism from the rich Arab states of the Middle East and increasingly from China, whose wealthy population is addicted to brand names and can buy goods in Europe or the USA cheaper than at home, walk past the beautifully designed shop windows of major brand name store in the smart streets of Western cities. The only people to be seen are security guards at the door and the sales staff folding goods or standing behind the counter. This is in total contrast to Asia, now their leading market, where vast shopping centres cater for luxury brand stores with lengthy queues lining outside.

But is "luxury" really an illusion, nothing more than a gigantic propaganda machine designed to brainwash customers into paying more? The only apparent difference in terms of comfort between hotel rooms or suites of three and four star hotels costing one or two hundred pounds and five star establishments charging five hundred to several thousand pounds a night, is that clients can ring a bell for room service, and sometimes other more dubious services. How can some restaurants charge twenty-five pounds for a good quality menu while "chic" establishments, with renowned chefs, charge hundreds of pounds for microscopic, albeit well presented dishes. Why are there so many sushi bars and restaurants? Is it a healthy way to eat or can it be that it is the mark up for serving tiny bits of raw salmon and a few grains of rice that is so mouthwatering? Is a "croque monsieur" or welsh rarebit (a toasted ham and melted cheese sandwich) costing nineteen euros in a Champs Elysees café, a luxury item or a rip off? Top chefs seem to compete to see who can conjure up the tiniest dish at the most exorbitant price. The biggest names now run restaurants around the world as international businesses. But since they cannot be in more than one kitchen at a time they can be compared to the great classic artists with disciples who copy their creations with varying results. France has recently decided to clamp down on restaurants which simply heat up prepared dishes, something we can all do at home, rather than actually make it in their kitchens. Establishments complying with the ruling will be able to display a sign to show that all dishes are freshly prepared.

Wines too have improved in quality and it is debatable whether the massive mark up in the elitist establishments is justified even if the bottles are carefully opened and served by a sommelier. One of the worst habits is when waiters fill wine glasses to the brim in the expectation of selling an extra bottle. Being pampered by an army of waiters or hotel staff or the thought of being exclusive is the difference for which some people believe is worth paying the price – the snobbery factor. I never reserve a table in the fashionable "in" restaurants with a supposedly three-month waiting list where clients rarely go for the cuisine but to be seen. I turn up and if there are no tables available take my custom next door. It is always amusing to walk into a half empty restaurant and be asked if I have booked. Fortunately many successful restaurants are run on a first come first served basis and refuse bookings in advance.

Once upon a time fashion designers made clothes for elegant women. Now they make clothes for men, perfumes, sunglasses, hats, watches, bags, cases, leather goods and anything that might sell with their name stamped on it. Even soccer players and actors and actresses are becoming fashion designers using their names to sell their own brands. And their goods must be expensive to preserve the prestige of the brand name. Look at the windows of some of the designer stores. They have men's jackets and trousers which seem to have been screwed up and trodden on and do not look as if they will fit, for sale at more than a thousand euros. They sell sunglasses at two hundred and fifty euros, ripped pairs of jeans at one hundred and fifty euros, or leather shoes for five hundred euros, which appear to be made for people with deformed feet. Why do celebrities spend a fortune on shoes yet seemingly can't afford a pair of socks? Delicately made women's shoes often priced at more than two hundred euros look so fragile it would be inadvisable to wear them in the rain. In contrast companies which provide quality at reasonable prices like Zara, Mango, H&M and Desigual are experiencing massive growth.

There are whole page advertisements in newspapers and magazines for watches and expensive cars, invariably endorsed by a celebrity, who probably never wears or drives them. There is a plethora of very costly watch brands, which appear to do everything except tell the time, unless it is under water. But do people actually need or wear time pieces today when mobile phones do the job? And one thing which surprises me is that despite almost everybody in the world carrying a mobile phone, their stores, which have taken over entire high streets, are always full of people. What are they all doing?

To be fair fashion designers' ladies fashions can look stunning and might justify the expensive price tag but apart from the catwalk, women are rarely seen wearing any of these clothes and the celebrities, when not attending film premiers or awards ceremonies, are usually seen wearing ripped jeans or very short skirts or shorts and sneakers.

What would the luxury brand industry do without celebrities? With their endorsement to wear branded goods the companies give them an aura of exclusivity. Adidas has been accused of increasing the price of its footwear by adding Pharrell Williams name on its products, adding to his wealth and the company's profits. Paradoxically those who can most afford branded goods often get to wear or use them for free. They can also gain access to nightclubs and sporting events free. Only the public is obliged to pay the full price to see them. But why pay the full price for clothes when huge reductions are usually offered in sales or at the fashion discount retail parks, at prices which simply suggest they were overpriced to begin with? The moral issue is whether these companies overcharge when much of the production comes from low paid workers in Asian sweat shops.

La Salada in Buenos Aires is reputed to be Latin America's largest shopping mall as well as the biggest counterfeit goods market in the world, offering branded products at unbeatable prices. Twenty thousand people flock to the site twice a week to seek out locally produced goods or false branded items. The local authorities consider it a social need, where poor children can fulfil their dream of being able to afford soccer shirts and boots worn by their idols. It is tolerated because nobody is being cheated. Everybody is aware that many of the goods are counterfeit and buyers know what they are getting. So are the real fraudsters the luxury brand corporations with their astronomic prices or the cheap counterfeit goods producers?

Supermodels have become some of the world's highest paid "workers" and young girls are naturally attracted to the agencies which specialize in finding the new "face" or "body" to adorn the covers of fashion magazines. A select few actors and actresses and sports stars have also been seduced – by lots of money – to appear on posters, in magazines and on packaging projecting the image of the brand they are promoting. The sight of Christian Ronaldo prancing around with his torso exposed at the stadium in Lisbon during the 2014 European Championship final after scoring a penalty was not a spontaneous burst of joy but an example of deliberately orchestrated publicity. It is a world of hype, which does not seem to have any logic. Invariably the published photos of models have been retouched so many times the models could have been created artificially using computers. I consider myself to be a competent photographer and notice many unknown pretty young girls who, in my view, could easily replace many of the top models without anybody noticing. With the computer technology available to create, airbrush and alter photographs why do advertisers pay models so much and engage in expensive contracts with stars? They could even save money and use computerized images. Consider the alleged forty million dollar contract believed to have been signed with actor, Robert Downey Jnr, for another version of Ironman. Given the special effects and costumes making it virtually impossible to recognize the actor behind the mask, why didn't the producers get an unknown for the role? Or even a robot?

The endorsement by sports stars and celebrities in the promotion of luxury real estate developments, golf courses and other projects is another popular marketing ploy to entice buyers, dreaming they could become neighbours of famous people in exclusive surroundings with top class restaurants run, of course, by three star chefs, cocktail bars, luxury shops and sports facilities etc. The only drawback is that it is never certain whether the "names" ever set foot in these places, some of which are in far off locations and which may never even be built.

The plethora of products on the market has made buying a complicated process, especially when it comes to hi-tech items such as mobile phones, computers, iPads or cameras. With manufacturers constantly changing models and designs it has become a minefield to know what to choose. People do not usually change their cars every year yet it seems car manufacturers bring out new models every month, offering more sophisticated technology. We live in an age where there is a risk that as soon as a product is purchased it is out of date before it leaves the store or showroom. The motor industry has adapted to this new world by not actually selling cars. They are offering renting or leasing arrangements for a monthly payment, rather like a mortgage, taking care of insurance and maintenance and the possibility of exchange. This way they hope to ensure the loyalty of their clients and of course, like the banks and utilities, sit back and collect the regular monthly payments.

Swedish furniture company IKEA has become a worldwide phenomenon. In every country where the large blue and yellow store is present they are full of families with children all following the maze-like alleys zigzagging around the vast array of products on display. The first lesson is to find the short cuts to avoid being caught up in a mass of suburban families who use the stores like theme parks for their children clogging up the alleys with prams and caddies. Choosing and buying the flat pack, furniture items and collecting them from their storage shelves is an art, requiring practice. And actually opening the packs at home and fathoming out how to put together kitchen units, wardrobes, tables and beds requires training. Whoever packs the items in the factory with the dozens of different tiny screws and fittings, must be a masochist since failure to follow the instructions precisely leads to panic and some pretty odd shaped furniture. There should be university courses with an IKEA sponsored diploma in do-it-yourself technology.

While on the topic of homes I must mention illumination – in the electricity sense. Once upon a time there were cheap light bulbs with either screw or bayonet fittings. In the name of energy conservation these have virtually disappeared to be replaced by designer lighting. Changing a bulb often means rewiring the whole home and installing costly modern, high tech lights which come in a vast range of different sizes and types. What was a straightforward simple operation is now a highly complex matter requiring knowledge and a considerable amount of time to learn how they work.

Another phenomenon is how the new breed of oligarch or billionaire has become an avid art collector, a perfect example of *Vanity capital.* These new mega rich acquire works of art regardless of the price and consequently values have reached stratospheric levels. They are not very original either paying for artists' signatures rather than the artistic value or the work itself. It is noticeable that the collectors or investors all go after works by the same few artists recommended by art experts and dealers even if the result happens to consist of a blank canvas, a mattress with dirty sheets and ladies underwear, a box of empty pharmacy bottles, a plastic cow, a phallic symbol or a pile of bricks. The latest favourite of the auction houses, is Sheika Al Mayassa of Qatar who has unlimited funds to spend in order to fill her new museum. Given the huge fees from both buyers and sellers, the only clear winners are the dealers and auction houses. Frank Lloyd, founder of the influential art gallery, Marlborough, was reputed to have said, "I collect money, not art." This simple truth explains what the art market is about. Protected to date by cultural lobbies, there is a strong case to introduce taxes on all works of art, now an international trading business like so many others. Often the buyers hide behind middlemen and there are always myths of megalomaniacs paying criminals to steal major works for them to hide in their cellars to view privately. I do not see the point of this secrecy when everybody can visit the world's major art galleries and museums to peruse their favourite works at little or no cost.

Wines and spirits too have become a collector's dream. But it is a game of pass the parcel. Even if the bottles are carefully kept in cellars at a constant temperature, the price goes up and up at each sale so long as nobody opens the bottle to actually taste whether the contents are what they are hyped up to be, corked or reduced to vinegar. Only when the bottles are finally opened can the collector learn whether his investment has been worthwhile and then the wine ceases to be an investment.

Is there a correlation between luxury brands, art and real estate prices? As already mentioned, in prime locations the cost of acquiring property has reached astronomic levels catering for the mega rich awash with cash. But at the same time it has created a serious social problem making it increasingly difficult for the majority of the young to get on to the housing ladder.

France, as could be expected in a country where solidarity is part of their culture, has chosen to legislate in order to stabilize rents and provide reasonably priced accommodation to the detriment of landlords and real estate investors. But equally in a country with a huge civil service, it is fraught with complicated new rules, which are open to interpretation, complicated to understand and ultimately help nobody leading to uncertainty, which adversely affects the property market.

Governments have realised that property is a sure way to obtain tax revenues since it can't be moved offshore. The cost of buying and selling real estate is becoming prohibitive taking into account stamp duty, estate agent and legal fees and removal charges. Estate agents have been major beneficiaries of spiraling prices as their fees are usually based on a percentage of the sale price. After bankers, they come a close second on most people's list of undesirables. They do no more work than before but have seen fees double or treble just for introducing a purchaser. They not only fix the values but negotiate the sale and have been some of the largest beneficiaries of rising prices. London's leading firms work as a closely-knit cartel fixing their fees and conditions among themselves charging around 2-3% of the sale price. On every one million pound sale they make twenty to thirty thousand pounds. This pales into insignificance when large houses change hands for over five million pounds, giving agents one hundred thousand pounds or more. Considering that the agents merely introduce purchasers while solicitors handle all the vital time consuming legal work for less than five thousand pounds, estate agents are grossly overpaid.

Over the past decade there have been several mergers and many of the leading agents have become global corporations. They have turned their attention to the growing demand from wealthy Russians, Asians and Arabs for Western real estate and have set up offices in the Middle East and Asia to promote developments in Europe's capitals and sophisticated resorts exacerbating the housing problem.

Not only are they are criticized for the way they earn their commissions and fees, but are at the centre of many consumer complaints, primarily with regard to letting fees. The famous

"Foxtons" ruling in the UK called for a change in the terms and conditions which letting agents generally use, ending an abuse, which has been allowed to operate for years.

A few major firms dominate the letting market imposing their terms and conditions on landlords and owners. One of the most controversial points relates to the renewal fees where agents do nothing but collect a share of the rent regardless of how long a tenant remains in occupation. They have become in effect silent partners.

Regrettably the Office of Fair Trading failed to obtain a clear ruling on this point from the court, leaving future complaints to rely on a judge's interpretation of the terms and conditions of each contract. The renewal issue needs addressing further with a new law to clarify the situation. So far the "Foxtons" ruling has not made any significant dent in the agents' pockets and they are doing everything to camouflage ways of making up for any loss of income. Although it is true to say that most UK agents are professional and practice according to the rules of the Royal Institution of Chartered Surveyors, fees are now unrelated to the work involved and there is still a lack of genuine competition.

The main threat to the Estate Agents monopoly position is coming from the Internet and the growth of online companies dealing directly with purchasers and vendors. This competition is likely to lead to a considerable reduction in fees. In most European countries many vendors prefer to deal direct, due to a traditional distrust of agents, although most are now professional and regulated. Nevertheless estate agents still only handle around fifty per cent of residential transactions, likely to be reduced even further as people learn how to handle transactions direct through the Internet.

The lack of competition applies particularly to the major privatized organizations in the energy, utilities, health, telecommunications and transport sectors and especially the financial sector. They can increase prices at will without the consumer being able to do anything about it. And without class action cases permitted as there is in the USA, the public has to rely on the government to keep unfair selling, price increases and charges under control. Europe is considering changing the rules in this respect, which can only be good news for consumers.

With the increase in population, immigration and growing demands for more competition and jobs, comes the problem of how to deal with closed shops or regulated sectors of the economy. Should we allow unfettered competition?

Some Governments have declared war on Airbnb attempting to prevent the short term rental of private homes which they say creates unfair competition for the highly regulated hotel industry. France and Spain have introduced laws making it illegal for owners to let their homes on a daily or weekly basis. France's argument is the lack of housing for a growing population in certain cities, especially Paris. Spain, with an estimated one hundred and twenty thousand properties on the coast providing extra income for their owners, is concerned about the black economy. In the UK there is actually a law dating from 1973 under the GLC making it unlawful to let a property for less than 90 days without change of use. However to help provide reasonably priced accommodation in the capital new proposals have been put forward to allow private letting for up to a maximum of 90 days in any calendar year. Despite regulations it is difficult to see how local authorities will be able to prevent owners from letting their homes unless they put a police officer on every street corner.

Taxis have to pay substantial sums for their license and do not want competition, which they argue is unfair, from mini cabs, limousines for hire or via unregulated Internet companies like Uber or drivers offering car sharing. While I am sympathetic to their arguments over the regulation and tax burden it has to be said that taxis tend to be too expensive. Their monopoly position often means it is difficult to find a taxi at peak times or whenever it rains. This may be because they are all queuing at airports. I never understand how hundreds of taxis can sit in interminable lines for hours at airports and stations. It suggests that the charge for transporting passengers to their city centre hotels or homes, often in excess of fifty pounds, is too lucrative. It is also prohibitive for many people. A taxi driver is someone who either refuses to take you where you want to go or, if they do, makes it seem as if they are doing you a favour. If they want to survive they will need to review their pricing structure and client relation strategy.

Pharmacies, bars and tobacconists in many countries are also regulated by governments to ensure they provide an adequate service for a given population. France's new finance minister has suggested that the country's notaires – solicitors, in our language – who are state controlled, should be open to competition. Naturally his idea has been met with a torrent of protests from the legal profession. The increase in immigration has led to the proliferation of ethnic businesses, many in the catering and mini cab sectors. But can so many bakeries, opticians, fast food restaurants, kebab vendors, cafes, florists, hairdressers, estate agents etc. all survive without some form of regulation? Just how many professions, trades or businesses are necessary for a given population to enable everyone to make a decent living? I can remember the ice cream turf wars of the eighties in Glasgow when dubious elements of society used to fight each other in the streets to reserve space for their vans, all in the name of fair competition. And they did not throw vanilla cornettos at each other.

The crisis has thrown up the injustice and unfair treatment of clients by the banking sector. One of the paradoxes of our societies is that the rich, who do not need loans, are able to raise money far more cheaply and effortlessly than the poor, who need to borrow but can't afford it and who are invariably refused credit. Experian credit ratings can ruin people's lives. This, of course, is also what happens to nation states when they go to the bond markets. It reinforces the adage that a banker is someone who hands out umbrellas when it shines and takes them back when it rains. Thousands of families unable to keep up with mortgage payments with less than one hundred thousand dollar debts had their homes taken by the banks with no qualms about leaving them on the streets. But quoted corporations which were virtually bankrupt with billion pound debts, were able to renegotiate terms and extend the repayment period. Of course the bosses also maintained their high salaries as if nothing had happened. Consider the fate of the Caesar's Palace Group, owner of the flagship Las Vegas hotel complex with over three thousand rooms as well as over forty hotels and casinos. It has sought bankruptcy protection with a twenty-eight billion dollar debt.

The crisis has also allowed the so-called payday lenders to expand at a fast rate, charging extortionate rates of interest for short-term loans to those unable to borrow from the major high street banks. There have been cases of these lenders being able to access their clients' bank accounts to recover loans. Unfortunately, despite the effect of the austerity measures on a growing segment of the population with families falling into debt at an alarming rate, the government has failed to deal with this growing problem remaining unsympathetic to the plight of thousands of families.

In a democratic society there should be legislation which forces loan companies, whether a high street bank or payday lender to limit interest to a maximum of say five percent over base for all credit, overdrafts, debts or loans. It cannot be right for the financial sector to make exorbitant profits out of human misery or rip off customers. The dramatic situation has led some UK retailers to group together to offer credit at fair rates in an attempt to end this insidious practice.

The pharmaceutical industry has often been accused of putting its profits and shareholders before the provision of new medicines and treatment, opposing the introduction of generic products or supplying treatment at an affordable price to the children and poor in the developing countries, leaving charities or foundations such as that created by Bill and Melinda Gates to fill the gap. The Ebola outbreak has woken up many governments to the risk of contagion and might lead to more funding for the supply of cheaper medicines. Given the amount of health products being advertised, there also needs to be a review of whether all these medicines are actually beneficial for our health or aimed solely at making profits.

The electronic age has been a boon to the gambling industry. There has been an explosion in sports betting with punters enticed to place bets on results, goal scorers etc., and if allowing sophisticated slot machines in betting shops and bars is not bad enough, governments have turned a blind eye to high stakes gambling which has resulted in addiction and the financial ruin of many families while allowing gambling companies and criminal gangs to cash in.

We live in the age of big data which has opened up enormous opportunities for corporations to be able to use the latest technology to determine the right segment of market, pinpoint and communicate with their customers on a personal basis through Facebook, Twitter etc. They can tailor precisely a customer's desires and demands with the aim of reducing costs and making more profits. Telephone callers at all times of the day and night have become a curse trying to entice consumers with their new offers and deals, a practice which some governments are trying to curtail. To attract potential customers companies make it easy to make contact with glossy brochures and promotional material, usually with an image of a smiling celebrity, expounding their product or service's virtues. What they want is to hook the customer into twelve or twenty-month contracts with regular direct debit payments. This way the money just rolls in effortlessly.

Yet paradoxically when customers need to communicate with the vendors of services or products regarding cancellation of contracts, refund of goods, complaints or other matters, it is virtually impossible. It is one-way traffic and there is no way out. There are no fixed telephone lines, only premium numbers directed to call centres. After listening to all the available options, which requires a great deal of patience, the voices of the staff employed to respond tend to be incomprehensible even if they emanate from the same country, which is not always the case. There are no high street stores to make a personal visit and usually no address to write to. Often emails are used to send clients promotions but there is no way to reply. All this makes it a minefield to obtain any information or redress when necessary. Another ruse is to automatically renew agreements for telephones, TV channels, insurance etc., forcing the customer to remember to take action or face another year of payment. It is time governments legislated to ensure that the onus is on companies to request renewal and operate transparent and efficient client services and technical advice at no cost using standard rate telephone numbers.

In June 2013 I waited over five hours at Pisa Airport in glorious sunshine for a delayed or cancelled RyanAir flight, due, according to the company, to fog! I asked Refund.Me to claim my right to compensation in the Irish courts, which is the sole jurisdiction and at the time of publication, almost two years on, I am still waiting for the court to reach a decision. This is what client services does for customers.

Things are not always so bad. During a recent summer trip to Stockholm my train arrived more than two hours late. I was handed a form, in Swedish, to fill out, which I did with the help of a kind Swedish passenger, to return to the rail administrative office, since it appeared I was entitled to a refund. Presumably to deter personal visits, the office was conveniently based in the town of Ostersund close to the Arctic Circle. On my return I tried to contact Swedish Rail (SJAB) by telephone but if you think English options are hard to understand, try listening to Swedish. Not to be daunted I wrote to the Swedish tourist office in Stockholm explaining the situation and threatening never to shop at Ikea again. I received a reply from a very nice lady who agreed to assist. After several months exchanging emails I finally received the money from Swedish Rail. Persistence sometimes pays.

The governments of our democratic societies cannot continue to allow corporations to continue to shed jobs purely to maintain profits, dividends and, increasingly, the remuneration packages of the boardroom bosses. When the privatized energy, utility, transport and telecommunications corporations as well as banks, vital to the country, start to lay off employees purely to maintain their earnings, there is also a case for governments to limit the amount of profit they make. The creation of PPP structures (public, private partnerships) to manage public sector activities such as health and water services on fixed term contracts, has led to huge additional costs for the state and massive earnings for the companies, their directors and shareholders. After a less than successful arrangement, which cost the taxpayer an estimated two billion pounds, in 2010, the government had to take back control of the London Underground; a classic example of government incompetence and corporate greed.

For organizations which were once public bodies, surely it would be preferable both morally and economically to agree with the private sector a fair return on capital and a reasonable percentage of profit for shareholders in order to keep people in their jobs rather than unemployed benefit seekers.

Madrid's medical profession with huge public support recently won a victory to prevent the city from privatizing six major hospitals. It took two years of demonstrations to convince the Regional Authority that it was unacceptable to outsource people's health for private profit.

While in power, Luis Inacio Lula de Silva, the ex-Brazilian president instigated a major plan to eradicate poverty in his country through financial assistance, which is beginning to bear fruit although there are still major hurdles to overcome. In contrast since 2008 the US and European Governments have injected ten thousand billion dollars into the banking sector. A tiny percentage of this money would have gone a long away to eradicate world poverty and generate economic growth.

While politicians and the media tend to concentrate on the activities of the major international quoted corporations, the fact is that all our economies rely on the hundreds of thousands of small companies. They provide seventy-five to eighty percent of wealth generated and are by far the main job creators. Far more attention is needed to help small businesses.

What is certain is that we live in an interconnected world where corporations are going to have to adapt to innovative changes rapidly to survive and individuals are more than ever reliant on their smartphones, which will become the only means to communicate with the outside world exchanging information with stores, banks, motor vehicles, doctors, energy and transport companies and government departments as well as friends and family; a brave new world..

There has to be a political will for change. The excess of boardroom greed has finally led to shareholders demanding more power in the selection of CEOs and board directors as well as revolting against excessive remuneration packages.

Nobody expects equal pay for all. There will always be a need and justification for highly qualified people or those with exceptional talent to legitimately earn more than others. But the gap and the rewards have reached unprecedented and immoral proportions, and the whole earnings and tax structures need readjustment. It is part of a change of thinking and a growing need for the financial and business sector as a whole to alter its short-term policies and accept more corporate social responsibility.

Tax Morality

What should be done if there is famine and not enough money in the government?

Why don't you apply the Che method and impose a 10% taxation?

A 20% taxation is hardly enough. How can I apply the Che method of 10%?

Cut the taxation and limit your expenses allowing the people to raise their standard of living first. Then you will have no worries about shortage.

If the people are not rich what can a ruler do to deal with a shortage?

Chinese proverb of Confucius school

We live in a world of the privileged; Wall Street and the City of London are producing not just rich people, but a new generation of mega rich, whose wealth is not only unmatched but made virtually overnight. This new elite, some wealthier than entire nation states, can dictate their terms to governments. And one of their conditions is that they do not want to pay taxes because they are rich.

Lower down the list, but still in the first division of wealth, stars do not want to pay taxes because they are celebrities, football clubs and players don't want to pay taxes because they are the opium of the people, bankers and corporate bosses don't want to pay taxes because they are talented and it would be difficult to attract the best and they would leave the country. Euro MPs, who are quick to criticise anyone who avoids tax, are themselves beneficiaries of special low tax regimes. In short, everyone thinks he or she deserves special treatment. And governments have lent the privileged their full support leaving the majority to bear the burden of taxes, cutbacks and austerity measures. F. Scott Fitzgerald was purported to have said, "The very rich are different from you and me." He was right; they avoid tax.

Globalization, the removal of monetary controls, bank deregulation and the Internet have been a boon to anybody seeking to avoid paying taxes. Billions can be transferred around the world at the click of a mouse. And without currency controls Treasury departments have lost control over the movement of money, legal or illegal. Tax regimes will have to adapt to this changing world.

One of the consequences of the crisis is that governments are not only losing tax revenue due to less VAT and sales tax, but are faced with increased housing and social benefits from the growing number of unemployed; a Catch-22 situation. Hence a sudden desire to close the loopholes and recover untaxed funds in tax havens. According to the Tax Justice Network more than thirteen trillion dollars is sitting in offshore banks, while Oxfam, whose aim is to eliminate poverty and reduce inequality, claims that the poor countries lose in excess of fifty billion dollars every year.

The privileged elite does not like taxes and has always been able to avoid paying thanks to political friends in power. Governments have encouraged offshore banking and tax havens to flourish as a sop to the wealthy. The British Government actually runs many of these small states while the European continent contains many of the world's most sophisticated tax havens.

After the success of the Spanish Podemos (We Can) party, its leader, Pablo Iglesias and associate, Jiminez Villearejo were elected as Euro MPs. They have compiled a list of major banks, which they say hold billions of dollars and euros in tax havens, which if repatriated could solve the world's economic crisis. They include ABN Amro, Bank of America, Barclays, BNP Paribas, City Group, Credit Agricole, Credit Suisse, Deutsche Bank, Goldman Sachs, HSBC, Julius Baer, J.P. Morgan Chase, Lombard Odier & Cie, Merrill Lynch, Pictet & Cie, Societe Generale, and UBS; household names, which project an aura of respectability yet act more like organized criminal organizations. The major scandal involving HSBC, accused of deliberately aiding wealthy personalities to escape their tax liability through secret accounts in Switzerland, is the tip of the iceberg. What makes this case so disturbing is that it exposed the close links between ex-HSBC boss, Stephen Green, the politicians who appointed him as Trade Minister, and HMRC which did nothing to prevent the loss of tax revenue.

The unpalatable fact is that in a global economy tax havens are used to divert taxable earnings creating an uneven tax playing field and allowing a privileged group of corporations, wealthy individuals, corrupt political leaders and criminals to escape their tax obligations. The close links, which have always existed between politics and the financial and corporate world, have developed into a corrupt and incestuous relationship.

So long as the economy prospered, people thought little about the antics of a few wealthy individuals to protect their assets, some even became celebrities. The wealthy Vestey family, owners of Dewhursts and cousins of the Queen, were reputed to have avoided tax for years thanks to a myriad of trusts, all legal but totally immoral. Although the Queen of England has been paying tax since 1992, the Vatican, Greek shipowners and the Orthodox Church still possess very favourable tax arrangements.

Cases like this highlighted the fact that many rich and successful families have not actually earned their wealth through their talent or hard work but through avoiding tax, owning trusts, farms, woodland and real estate or shares, through inheritance or simply hiding their wealth in tax havens. And the more they earn the less tax they want to pay.

Obsessed by money and riches, politicians from all sides have pampered these masters of the universe, the non doms, or erstwhile legal residents of Monaco, Jersey or other so-called independent states, granting them all kinds of tax advantages – even knighthoods and peerages – succumbing to the same old threat, *"We are the wealth creators, if we leave there will be a loss of jobs."*

As people's wealth grew, wealth management became a major fee earner for the financial sector. But it is also a code word for tax evasion. There have never been so many complex schemes invented to reduce the tax liability of the rich. And what is astonishing is that despite a growing loss of tax revenue, they come with government approval. All the loopholes such as calling income loans or capital gains or soccer players having image rights or investments in specialist real estate companies, should be abolished as they serve no other purpose than to avoid taxes.

This anomaly came to light in Spain over the earnings of soccer star, Leo Messi. It seems Messi senior had been hiding sponsorship earnings and image rights of Messi junior offshore to avoid Spanish taxes. The Barcelona player incurred a massive fine. And then the club too faced a huge tax bill following an investigation into the ramifications of the transfer of Brazilian star, Neymar. The huge amount of money involved in the movement of overseas players involving agents and some of the major European soccer clubs has often been associated with accusations of fraud.

The Madoff and Stanford scandals demonstrated how otherwise intelligent and wise people could be seduced by high returns and ways to avoid tax through investing blindly in opaque funds located in Luxembourg, Switzerland, Liechtenstein, Jersey, Cyprus, Bermuda, the Cayman Islands, and other exotic locations, which now hold hundreds of billions of dollars, much of which comes from dubious origins.

We now face a world war – the 1% against the 99%. Germany made the first move against these fortresses by a blitz on Liechtenstein, followed by the US threat to Switzerland. The drawbridges are being pulled up in tax havens everywhere but can they withstand a long drawn out siege?

Switzerland has entered into tax agreements with the US and European Union to protect the Swiss based assets of its wealthy, non-resident population. It entails deducting tax but without disclosing the name of the account holder. The tax evaders therefore remain anonymous, which is not a way to level the tax playing field. Spain wants to end the status of Gibraltar. Although Spain argues it is one of Europe's tax havens, their opposition is clearly linked to its claim to regain sovereignty over the Rock. The UK and the USA have put pressure on the Cayman Islands and other Caribbean islands to disclose their foreign account holders. Barack Obama has spoken about a building in the Cayman Island with twelve thousand corporations which he says is either the largest building in the world or the biggest tax scam in the world.

The loss of revenue is so great there is a growing consensus in the present crisis that tax havens will have to go. Every day we hear of financial scandals involving the world's privileged elite, corrupt politicians and dictators. The leak of the dubious financial transfers of some of China's top political families has made it even more urgent to deal with what is becoming not only immoral but a danger to the future of our democracies. There are too many of these opaque tax havens and too much revenue is at stake to allow billions of dollars to remain out of reach of State treasury departments. The Bahamas, Bermuda, the Cayman Islands and West Indies used to be havens for pirates who plied the Caribbean. Today they are still used by pirates only this time they do not use galleons to plunder or transport treasures but computers to set up opaque companies, open bank accounts, create trust funds, and transfer billions of dollars.

The collapse of the Cyprus banks demonstrated how Russian oligarchs as well as multinational corporations have been using the Eurozone to either escape tax or launder illicit funds with the connivance of politicians. Now it seems they may have shifted their attention to the USA. More recently it was Ukraine's turn to be under the spotlight as its political and corporate elite were accused of plundering billions from the State to bank accounts in tax havens. The Crimean crisis has led to a massive flight of capital from Russia, presumably to Western banks and real estate. The volatility and ease with which huge sums can be injected into a country's banking system, and then removed by foreign investors or sovereign funds poses a serious threat to governments.

While the hunt is on for wealthy individuals' bank accounts, more attention should be paid to the activities of offshore subsidiaries of multinational corporations. The practice of transfer pricing whereby most of the profits are retained by subsidiaries established in the most advantageous tax havens, is estimated to cost governments billions of dollars a year.

One potentially useful side effect of bringing transparency to offshore bank accounts would be to discover the whereabouts of the proceeds of organized crime, fraud and unsavory dictators, making illicit gains easier to recover and tougher to hide.

Cracking down on tax evasion and recovering revenue would enable governments to engage in urgent reforms of the tax regimes to reduce the overall tax burden. By creating a more equitable tax structure and lowering rates, the wealthy might accept that it is hardly worth the effort or cost to look for ways to escape the tax net.

However governments need to put their houses in order first. Despite all the talk, the rich nations will always face resistance from the legal and financial fraternity to introduce any changes, which are likely to increase the tax for them and their wealthy clients and reduce their earnings. Tax authorities have been accused of granting tax exemptions to major banks and corporations at a huge cost to the state.

Possibly the worst example of how governments protect the rich is through tax amnesty. This has allowed thousands of the wealthiest people as well as organized crime syndicates, who have evaded tax for years, to declare hidden untaxed cash in exchange for paying a tiny percentage of the tax owed. This is an affront to all honest taxpaying citizens.

The Madrid authorities called a halt to negotiations with casino magnate Sheldon Adelson, who wanted to build a massive multimillion euro leisure complex with hotels, casinos and shopping centres on the outskirts of Madrid at Alcorcon. Called Eurovegas it was to be developed and run by the Las Vegas Sands group whose interests range from Las Vegas to Singapore and Macao. But their demands to changes in planning, smoking, drinking and employment laws in addition to favourable tax breaks, went too far. The project would have created a virtual tax free zone in the heart of the country, which was simply unacceptable to many Spanish politicians and a large segment of the population.

Increasing VAT is considered by most governments to be a simple method to raise tax revenue but they do not seem to realize it only leads to increased fraud and a thriving black market. Governments are now beginning to find ways to increase taxes on the wealthy through taxing assets – the so-called wealth tax, but this is penalizing the upper middle class more than those at whom the tax is aimed. Spain has introduced a requirement for all residents to declare their foreign assets over fifty thousand euros. It has led to droves of retired foreign expats from northern Europe with low incomes leaving the country. These taxes are self defeating; the main objective should be to reduce, not increase, taxes on the vast majority of the middle and lower class in order to increase spending power and provide a higher standard of living for the people, which is vital to the economic well being of every nation.

The crisis has led to governments seeking any means at their disposal to raise taxes to compensate for the huge national debts and loss of tax revenue. But tax collection today needs international cooperation. Governments have to realize that in a global economy no country can operate independently.

At the same time companies and wealthy individuals abuse their obligations by creating structures or engaging in financial engineering to reduce their tax liability. Schemes designed solely to avoid tax without any commercial justification should simply be ignored by the taxman.

The publicity surrounding Facebook, Apple, Google, Starbucks and Ryan Air, which are the tip of the iceberg, show how corporations play one country off against another to reduce their tax bill and demonstrates just why Europe and ideally the USA, should harmonize financial dealings and tax regimes.

The French government's proposal to tax earnings above one million euros at 75% was one of the more controversial proposals. It said much for France's commitment to socialist ideals and had its merits. It was a radical move but could never work if implemented solely by France. Instead of the highly paid directors seeing their net income slashed their employers were liable for the extra tax. Since most high earners tend to work for quoted banks and multinationals, they were not going to have any sleepless nights, as the shareholders would end up paying. But lobbying by the corporate elite has forced the government to backtrack and it has already had to back down. France's socialist principles also seem to have been forgotten in its dealings with Qatar, a major client for its arms industry. The Qataris are granted exemption from capital gains tax on their real estate transactions.

Sport is another activity facing pressure to put its tax affairs in order as mentioned above. The soccer industry has become one of the most opaque businesses in the world; secret negotiations, illicit payments, offshore companies etc. are the norm to evade taxes for clubs, agents, players and an army of intermediaries.

The French Government faced opposition from the French football league to its seventy-five per cent tax, which would hit clubs and not players. The clubs argued that many could not afford it. There is also the case of Monaco's football club, which wants to maintain its privileged tax haven status instead of being obliged to set up a legal entity in France where it would have to pay charges and taxes like all the French clubs.

There is a never-ending list of taxpayers demanding special treatment. At present Luxembourg, Holland and Ireland offer special tax status for holding companies, Spain has different rules for its Autonomous Regions demonstrating the inequality in the treatment of its citizens. France and Spain are virtually alone in implementing a wealth tax, and although Berlusconi abolished Italian inheritance tax, the new government may well reintroduce some form of tax on the transfer of estates.

In addition each European country fixes different rates for corporation tax, income tax, capital gains tax, inheritance tax and VAT, and of course Europe possesses numerous tax havens, tolerated by all the major countries' governments. It has become a minefield. Europe simply cannot function with different rules if it expects to retain its role as an economic power. A perfect example of tax hypocrisy is Luxembourg, where the government has announced the creation of a tax free trade commercial centre as a sop to the luxury brands industry in the heart of the European Union while allowing multinationals to benefit from low taxes. Where does Jean Claude Junckers stand on this?

Why do the wealthy make their lives complicated by attempting to avoid or evade tax? I would suggest that the reasons have more to do with inheritance tax (death duties) and wealth tax than income tax.

The purpose of introducing inheritance tax or death duty is to spread wealth. If that is the case how is it that the world's wealthiest families somehow manage to become wealthier generation after generation while middle class families constantly face a lower standard of living?

Something is wrong with a tax system, which operates under two rules; one for the privileged elite with close links to political friends, one for the people. Herve Falciani, a computer analyst with HSBC brought to light the anomalies which exist and how wealthy people are above the law. His list of foreign clients with Swiss bank accounts was disclosed to European and US Governments but while Mr Falciani was treated as a criminal, there has either been a cover up or the rich people named have been granted an amnesty allowing them to get off with minimum damage to their wealth. Antoine Deltour is a whistleblower who worked for an auditing firm and disclosed the existence of a secret tax agreement between the Luxembourg authorities and multinational companies aimed at avoiding tax. The Luxleaks scandal as it is known has resulted in Mr Deltour facing trial. A balance needs to be restored.

When people have spent a lifetime working, saving and paying tax, it is natural that those who have accumulated assets in the hope of passing them to their children are reluctant to hand them over to the state. In today's precarious and uncertain world it is also self-defeating. By allowing more people to pass on assets to their children it would lead to more prosperous future generations with greater spending power and thus stimulate the economy as well as reduce the need for state assistance. Why should a frugal family looking after the interests of their children be targeted while profligate spenders avoid being penalized when they pass away? The British Government's recent plan to tax family trusts has been met with a storm of protest from financial advisors and City institutions, which earn substantial fees from arranging the tax affairs of the wealthy. Instead perhaps Britain could envisage adopting the Latin countries' laws with regard to the rights of heirs. To protect the family, a spouse has a right to a quarter of the estate and direct heirs, i.e. a child, an automatic right to half of the estate (two thirds if there are two children) before any other beneficiary, and regardless of what is written in a will.

The whole principle of taxation is that it should be a levy on earnings and real gains from transactions rather than on the hypothetical value of unsold assets, which in practice have already been taxed. It is also supposed to be fair and apply to everyone. But whenever a government introduces new taxes it invariably leaves loopholes to ensure that the wealthy elite can avoid paying.

How can governments ask audit firms to advise on tax, paying them substantial fees, when they are instrumental in arranging tax avoidance schemes for their clients? Clearly there is a conflict of interest. The desire to avoid tax has created a huge financial services industry whose sole aim is to protect people's assets from the state.

One tax which needs abolishing is the so-called wealth tax which France and Spain currently impose. The inequity of taxing assets was clearly illustrated by Laurent Fabius, ex-French Prime Minister and present Foreign Minister. He is credited with creating the wealth tax based on the value of every citizen's net assets. But as he and his family are believed to possess a valuable art collection, he ensured that works of art and shares held by directors in their companies were exempt thus allowing the wealthiest French families to escape the net. Where it became absurd is that families have to declare the value of their Ikea furniture, while those with valuable antiques are exempt. The tax, called ISF, (Impot sur La Fortune) has led to an exodus of talent from France, many moving to London or Brussels, where no doubt they can buy their Ikea furniture without worry, and a disincentive for foreign business people, stars or sports personalities thinking about living in France. There are more French citizens now living in London than in many towns and cities in France. In Spain each Region has its own tax laws thus creating different levels of tax depending on where people live. This makes a mockery of the conception of the nation state where all the people are supposed to be equal before the law. The crisis which has left many of Spain's regions in debt has led to a major rethink into how to deal with tax issues. With legislative elections planned for the end of the year the incumbent government is planning a long overdue radical overhaul of the tax regimes, aimed at creating a more harmonious system across the country.

But the strongest argument is that the wealth tax penalizes many middle class families who have saved for their retirement. No thought was given to families who are asset rich but with low annual incomes. In France, instead of the wealthy, the burden falls on many ordinary people. Many families face having to sell assets, even their homes, to pay the annual tax. This being France it did not take long for those most affected to take to the streets, led by fishermen from the Ile de Rey, pensioners and widows, who became the main protestors. These categories found that they were caught in the tax net due to the increase in value of their properties. But their relatively low earnings meant they could end up paying 75% of their incomes in tax.

It is clearly an inequitable tax and Spain is toying with the idea of abolishing it. The mansion tax being considered in the UK will probably be shelved by the new government. It is discriminatory and one which could lead to the Court of Human Rights declaring it abusive and an attack on privacy since the tax is assessed on residents' assets regardless of the country where they are held, where different tax laws apply.

Yet despite all the exemptions, many wealthy entrepreneurs, artists and sports people still choose voluntary exile in Monaco, Switzerland and even Belgium showing a distrust of governments which keep moving the goalposts at every election. Interestingly the French cannot benefit from Monaco's advantageous tax regimes since De Gaulle threatened to blockade the principality so there is no reason why the rest of Europe cannot follow suit and put the tiny state and its sister tax havens off limits. One way to level the playing field would be for Europe's nations to follow the

American system and make all citizens liable for tax regardless of where they are resident or living in the world with double taxation treaties set up. This would mean, for example, that foreign residents of Monaco would pay tax on their worldwide earnings in their country of origin, less tax paid in Monaco. Of the thirty-six thousand residents in the Principality only eight thousand are believed to be true Monagasques. If this system was introduced it could lead to a fairer tax regime and make tax havens obsolete. Sports stars like Lewis Hamilton would be obliged to pay most of his earnings in the UK so long as he remained a British citizen.

But in a changing world there is a growing requirement to reform the tax regimes. Governments have realized that with Europe's ageing population there is a pension time bomb on the horizon. There are not enough people working to provide a decent pension for a population living much longer lives. It is one of the arguments given for increasing immigration. But this is now being reviewed in the light of the increase in the number of potential workers from Eastern Europe coupled with illegal immigration, which is leading to social problems. Lower wages and unemployment brought about since the outset of the crisis, resulting in a reduction in spending power, have been major factors in the loss of tax revenues. This is a double whammy since those without work rely on benefits increasing the cost of social security and the national debt. But raising taxes does not help the economy either since increasing taxes on the majority of the population only results in less spending power, more hardship and recession.

There have to be ways to find alternative sources of raising tax revenue and they require a radical reform of the tax systems. The most obvious is to recover the billions of euros, dollars and pounds, which escape the tax net each year. Governments must crack down on the use of tax havens and review the transfer pricing methods of the multinationals to ensure they pay their fair share in the countries where they operate. The foreign exchange market, Forex, is run like a private club with little regulation, yet it trades more than four trillion dollars a day. Top of the currency table is of course the US dollar followed by the euro and Japanese yen. The Swiss franc is sixth and Chinese RMB ninth, for the moment. The margin for traders is clearly very small but I would have thought there is room to fix a tiny percentage tax to raise revenue given the colossal amounts being traded.

The fairest and most equitable way to raise new tax revenue is to finally introduce the plan devised by US economist James Tobin years ago, but which was tucked away in the archives. There are already duties imposed on share transactions in many countries so it is not revolutionary. Tobin's plan, to impose a tiny duty on each and every daily transaction in the financial markets, would raise billions. When the foreign exchange markets handle two trillion pounds a day, the arguments are compelling for the introduction of the appropriately named, Robin Hood Tax. The plan should include transactions on the stock market, currency and commodity exchanges. The standard reaction from bankers is that any increase in duty or taxes would harm the markets and push talented traders and companies overseas. That is why plans to introduce this tax require international cooperation and agreement, which is going to be difficult to achieve.

The Tobin tax should not be seen as a kind of penalty or punishment but a logical means to raise tax from the sector most able to contribute to society. Governments were quick to realize that road users should pay congestion charges for using their vehicles in city centres, so why shouldn't the financial markets, which do not actually produce anything, pay a duty on the daily movement of money or commodities?

The amount raised, estimated at tens of billions of dollars, would hardly cause a ripple in the financial pond but would revolutionize tax collection. It should enable governments to raise enough revenue to reduce their deficits, invest in education, social services and infrastructure projects, lower tax on the poor and middle class and be able to afford to pay out state pensions. The money raised could also be used to invest in the poorer nations to improve their schools, hospitals, housing, infrastructure and economic development and alleviate poverty, which has to be one of the most urgent and important challenges facing the world.

There is no excuse for this tax to be ignored any longer. Computer technology makes it simple to implement. Making the financial markets contribute would be universally acceptable given the damage they have caused and reduce the risk of further crisis. Eleven European countries have agreed to introduce the tax from 2016, but to work, and to avoid what worries economists – the flight of capital overseas – it really needs the agreement of all the European member states, especially the UK, as well as the USA and Canada. It is encouraging that the G20 nations have promised to clamp down on unfair tax practices. This was reinforced at a meeting in Berlin in October 2014 when many nations finally agreed to exchange information relating to tax evasion. How this can be put into effect without the cooperation of banks and an end to bank secrecy remains to be seen.

I would put forward the following proposals for a more equitable system:

1. Introduce the US system in all Western economies whereby a nation's citizens are taxable wherever they happen to live in the world with double taxation agreements set up.

2. Ignore all structures or financial engineering designed solely to avoid tax.

3. A total clampdown on the use of tax havens making offshore accounts, trusts, corporate ownership and company transfer pricing fully transparent and subject to the same tax laws as everywhere else.

4. Introduce a Tobin-type tax of say 0.1% on daily financial transactions in the currency exchange, commodity and stock markets.

5. Abolish wealth taxes and reduce income tax for all employed corporate executives and CEOs to 20% on salaries up to five hundred thousand pounds, 50% to a million and 75% above with all earnings treated the same whether salaries, dividends, stock options or bonuses.

6. Following the initiative in Switzerland, all remuneration packages to CEOs and directors of banks and quoted corporations should be limited to twenty times the average company salary.

7. Bonuses, if justified by performance, should be limited to ten percent of salary per year and divided among all employees, similar to the scheme run by British store group, John Lewis. Free or preferential stock options should be abolished and instead directors and employees should be able to purchase shares in their companies as a long-term incentive rather than a gift which only increases short-term speculation.

8. Risk taking entrepreneurs who own their own business should be granted more favourable tax treatment on earnings, their share holdings and capital gains to encourage the creation of private businesses.

The case for abolishing or reducing inheritance tax.

1. Inheritance tax or death duties, originally conceived as a means of creating a fairer society and reducing inequality has become one of the most inequitable measures of raising revenue. It was originally introduced at a time when the welfare state guaranteed free health and education and a state pension for all.

2. During the past three decades rising real estate prices and increased wealth among the middle class has meant that hundreds of thousands of hard working people are falling into the net each year; people who have strived to make a better life for themselves and their families, paid taxes and now find

they need accountants and advisors to protect their homes and savings.

3. At the same time the wealthiest segment of the population, at whom the tax is aimed, simply avoids the tax through fancy avoidance schemes conjured up by the financial services industry and approved by governments. The present rules are unfair and unjust and need abolishing.

4. Instead of the desired concept of a more equal society, inheritance tax has actually widened the wealth gap. In the global unregulated economy the wealthy have been able to set up trusts and companies offshore, building up considerable fortunes tax-free at the expense of the majority of the population. In every Western country the wealthiest families seem to become wealthier at each passing generation while the middle and poorer classes grow poorer as their assets and savings are confiscated.

5. Assuming the heirs of a deceased person worth one hundred million pounds paid the full forty percent rate imposed in the UK, they would still be left with around sixty million pounds, which would not affect their lifestyle. In contrast, a family with one million pounds would need to find around three hundred thousand pounds, which they may not have without selling the family home and be forced to substantially lower their standard of living.

6. There is a strong moral argument that for anyone who has acquired assets and saved during a lifetime's work and has already paid taxes to society, inheritance tax is a double imposition penalizing the hard working, frugal or wise investor whose prime concern is to look after the family's future. .

7. It is accepted that life expectancy is increasing and it is not unusual for families to comprise both grandchildren and great grandchildren. Pensions are unlikely to provide financial security in an ever more precarious world in which job security no longer exists and education and health are no longer entirely free. It makes economic sense to allow the older generation to hand down assets and savings to their

offspring to enable them to provide for themselves without recourse to the state, leading to a more prosperous society. Implementing the Latin countries' inheritance tax laws to protect the family would assist this transition.

8. My objective would be for governments to level the playing field by abolishing all the exempt trusts, companies and avoidance schemes and impose a flat rate of ten percent of net assets above a threshold of say half a million pounds, excluding the family home. Net assets over one hundred million pounds should be taxed at fifty percent to avoid heirs becoming obscenely wealthy through no effort. It would simplify collection and the government would probably raise more revenue. One side effect would be that the wealthy might consider it a fair amount to contribute to society rather than engage in avoidance schemes or move overseas.

Adopting such a wide range of measures would naturally be unpopular with the wealth management industry of bankers, lawyers and advisors who would no doubt engage in serious lobbying in the same way the NRA in the US lobbies for arms sales. But this would be a small price to pay to enable the majority of the population to pass away peacefully knowing that their families would be left with greater financial security.

Environmental Morality

Only after the last tree has been cut down
Only when the last river has been poisoned
Only after the last fish has been caught
Only then will you find money cannot be eaten.

Cree Indian proverb

The high plains Indians would have been devastated to see what we are doing to the earth today; overdevelopment, deforestation, contamination, pollution and the destruction of our cultural heritage. The World Health Organization has calculated that seven million people die each year through contamination of the air we breathe. Yet despite the evidence of rising atmospheric temperatures and sea levels and a reduction in snow and ice caps, negation of climate change is preventing action. "A situation which will cost far more if ignored," warned Ban Ki-Moon, UN Secretary General.

Deforestation in Brazil, described as the earth's lungs, has led to the Amazon forest disappearing at an alarming rate. In spite of humanitarian and charity organizations demanding international aid and intervention, unscrupulous companies are expropriating, or even killing, the indigenous population. According to the ONG Global Witness over nine hundred environmentalists and ecologists have been murdered – four hundred and fifty in Brazil alone – during the past few years. Peru has been facing demonstrations from its indigenous people who want to prevent mining corporations from transforming and polluting the earth and rivers and forcing them off their land. Illegal gold mining has become a source of contention as the local people, who strive to make a precarious living, engage in conflicts with both the government and international mining companies who want to take control over its extraction. Several countries of South and Central America as well as Africa face similar threats from guerrilla groups, drug gangs and paramilitary forces under the orders of their corrupt government. The poaching and killing of wildlife for their ivory or skin and overfishing are putting many species in peril of extinction with quotas often ignored. Wild Aid is a non-profit organization whose aim is to spread awareness and persuade governments to act in order to end the slaughter and ensure the survival of threatened species. It is estimated that every year twenty-five thousand elephants, eight hundred rhinos, seventy million sharks and three thousand tigers are killed. Around the world, people's lives and the environment are not considered as important as extracting natural or mineral resources or protecting wildlife

Many countries face devastating earthquakes, forest fires, hurricanes, tsunamis, tornadoes, floods or droughts every year as well as the destruction of their cultural heritage. Several of Southern Europe's forest fires are started deliberately with pyromaniacs acting alone or aimed at persuading local authorities to grant building licenses. What is happening in Syria, Mali, Afghanistan and many other countries, where temples, statues and monuments are being destroyed for religious or financial reasons, is an irreplaceable loss for future generations. Closer to home Italy has been guilty of neglecting the ruins of Pompeii and Venice is constantly investigating ways of keeping the water at bay. In this precarious world, where climate change is at the top of every political agenda, energy conservation must be given priority to reduce pollution and provide a better, cheaper and healthier lifestyle for future generations. It has been calculated that forty percent of the total consumption of energy is in the home and that proper insulation could reduce this substantially.

Electricity and gas consumption will need to become more efficient and water and waste will need to be recycled. Energy and utility corporations will have to come to terms with a new world where technology will be available to insulate, power and heat homes with little or no cost to the occupiers. These sectors provide considerable opportunities for the creation of new industries as the age of fossil fuels draws to a close

Governments have a duty to ensure that planning laws are respected to avoid over building, that mineral resources are not exploited and prevent the destruction of forests, the killing of species facing extinction and ensure the protection of natural parks.

The 2013-14 winter floods in the UK highlighted the problem of protecting the soil and how the richest farmers, who receive huge subsidies, are not doing enough to protect or cultivate their land to provide more agricultural produce. Given the problems of floods and droughts, which create shortages, more planning is needed to increase food production without the use of pesticides. The question always asked is whether there will be enough for the world's growing population? Can it be justified to ship produce around the globe all year round or should we return to the idea of buying and consuming local produce in season and stop buying food out of season? Fishing quotas have led to fishing wars as each country attempts to protect its own industry, and the food industries in developing nations have been accused of unfair competition through an absence of health and safety laws and the exploitation of workers, which allow them to ship goods at cheaper prices. The Fair-Trade concept mentioned in another chapter is addressing this problem.

It has been estimated that almost a billion people suffer from malnutrition and feeding the planet is going to be one of the major challenges facing the world's agriculture industry. Migration from rural areas to cities by millions of people in Africa and Asia is leading to a reduction in small farms and agricultural workers. It is increasingly difficult to persuade the young generation to take over their parents' holdings when the conditions are harsh, earnings are low, strict regulations apply and stress is a constant factor. Climate change is also affecting food production. Agriculture needs water, lots of water, and it has become fundamental to reduce the amount of water required in the production process. Technology is the answer and it is going to play a major factor in optimising food production and distribution which is increasingly concentrated among the world's largest food processing corporations. Leaving the production of food in the hands of the multinationals and private investors whose aim is maximising profits may not reduce malnutrition or famine where it is needed and governments and NGOs will have to monitor their activities.

Another practice which needs to be addressed is the disposal of food products by supermarket chains simply because they are past their sale-by-date. The waste of food in the rich countries is abominable and unnecessary when there are so many people living on or below the poverty level and whose families could live quite healthily on what is thrown away. France has taken the initiative by requiring stores to distribute safe but out of date food to charities. Households too can make an effort not to over shop which results in a massive amount of food ending up in bins.

Too many countries have been stripped of their natural resources and strategic assets through privatization, a consequence of the unhealthy relationship between politics and big business. It is inconceivable that mining, transport, roads, water, gas, electricity, education and health, vital to our economic survival and well being, are being taken over by the private sector, which now includes foreign investors. A nation could find its future mortgaged to a sovereign fund or rely on vital energy supplies from a foreign state and be under the influence of a foreign government. This is precisely the situation in which Western Europe finds itself with its reliance on gas from Russia. Any long-term opposition against Russia for its intervention in the Crimea and Ukraine could boomerang. Spain could provide the solution. The country already has pipelines connected to Algeria and these could be extended through France into central Europe. However, in order to reduce imports of foreign oil and gas supplies there is no alternative but to concentrate on alternative energy sources. Do we really need to build thousands of kilometres of pipelines across Europe or beneath the sea when alternative sources and technology exist in the form of nuclear energy, wind farms and solar energy? Nuclear power is clean and could provide a long-term solution but it has become a source of controversy and many countries' attitudes have changed following the Fukushima disaster in Japan.

Fracking is suddenly seen as the solution bringing with it major environmental problems as well as dubious land transactions reminiscent of the Wild West. In northern Spain foreign mining companies have been attempting to beguile local farmers into selling them their land, threatening them with compulsory purchase. It reminded me of the legend of Jesse James. His career as an outlaw started after individuals claiming to represent the railroad companies warned his family and other farmers that if they did not sell to them at knock down prices they would face compulsory purchase and receive no compensation at all. The US with its vast underdeveloped territory is the new El Dorado for this new source of energy but the jury is still out on whether it is environmentally safe or a threat to the earth.

Governments have been guilty of selling the family silver and ignoring long-term strategic interests. Handing over the running of the energy, utilities and transport sectors to the private sector has simply been an opportunity for those with political connections to make fortunes at the expense of consumers: public monopolies have been transformed into private monopolies or cartels.

Some are successful. Norway has a prosperous and efficient sovereign wealth fund to look after its oil revenues. Scotland argued that if it became independent it would follow suit. But has anyone in Britain wondered where all the wealth generated from North Sea Oil has gone? The oil bonanza was a unique opportunity for the Thatcher Government to

163

modernize schools, hospitals, transport and the infrastructure of the country. But in one of the largest asset stripping operations in history, the money simply disappeared and has been squandered leaving the country still needing major public sector investment.

Privatization of energy, water, transport and telecommunications simply enabled the energy and utility suppliers, transport and telecommunications companies to constantly increase prices. And while consumers are forced to bear the burden the only beneficiaries seem to be private company directors and shareholders.

Spain fumed after Argentina took back control over oil company, YPF, from Spanish giant, Repsol and Bolivia nationalized the airports, taking them back from Spanish operator Albertis. Both countries' presidents claimed that the Spanish companies were stripping out profits rather than investing. These cases have been resolved but it is a sign of the changing relationship being forged between the old colonies and their once colonial powers.

Rafael Correa, the President of Ecuador has called for an end to exploitation and a more equitable sharing of its natural wealth. "I want to send a warning to all companies which do not abide by laws or evade taxes or take into account environmental factors." He has accused petrol companies of profiteering. "Out of every five barrels, one stays in Ecuador and four go to the USA."

For this reason there is a strong case for either returning the production and supply of such vital resources to state ownership or exercising strict control over suppliers of energy and utilities as well as transport. Many road and rail operators are now owned by foreign entities only interested in generating profits.

The comparisons between the UK rail network and the French state owned SNCF are interesting. The French Government invested billions to run efficient, modern high speed trains which charge reasonable prices in order for people to travel to work, run their businesses or take vacations, while the UK has expensive and inefficient services run for the benefit of directors and shareholders. They make the profits while Network Rail, i.e. the taxpayer, picks up the tab for operating, repairing and maintaining the tracks. Spain, which has invested massively, claims to have the most extensive high-speed rail network in the world, although it could be overtaken by China, now at the forefront of rail expansion, creating a high speed rail network throughout the country for its long-term economic benefit. Japan Rail's Shinkansen high-speed rail network is still the envy of the world; linking the country's major cities, it is an example of comfort, cleanliness and efficiency. Nevertheless Brussels is hell bent on opening up Europe's railways to competition, which will ultimately lead to confusion, shutting down of services, loss of jobs and higher prices. It has led to strikes in France as the SNCF has become concerned about safety following several mortal accidents after cut backs in personnel. Before any decisions are made Europe's transport commissioners should take a look at the UK to study the adverse effects of competition.

Open spaces and parks in our cities rightfully belong to the people. They are maintained by local authorities, play an important role in society and are free. Of course we all pay towards their upkeep through local taxes. Imagine then if one day we were suddenly confronted with manned or automatic gates, charged a fee to enter and learnt that the government had granted concessions to private investors. Clearly nobody would accept it. Yet this is precisely what has happened to major road networks in many countries.

While Europe has been removing barriers at its borders it has been erecting them on highways across the continent. Many of the original motorways have more than recouped their initial investment but when governments handed over to the private sector our public energy, utilities, telecommunications, and transport monopolies, they included in this bargain disposal of national assets many of the motorways. These were given new corporate status and shared out to companies, often run by businessmen with close political connections who obtained concessions on favourable terms to manage the network. We were now in a different ball game; one which illustrates perfectly why capitalism has gone wrong, permitting privileged groups with government backing to grab national assets for private gain. The relationship between investors and constructors seems a natural partnership since motorways need to be financed, built and maintained. But given the colossal sums involved it is a system open to corruption involving political parties, banks and building companies. Private concession holders are only interested in making money for directors and shareholders. By reducing manned tollgates and replacing them with automated machines taking cash or credit cards and electronic telepasses, motorways have become a cash-generating machine for major corporations around the world. Across Europe handing over toll roads to the private sector has led to a constant increase in toll charges. Major construction firms have queued up to build and operate toll motorways around the world. Oil companies have been allowed to charge more for fuel at motorway service stations than on ordinary roads. Why?

Giorgio Ragazzi, an economist at Bergamo University, wrote a book, "I signore delle autostrade" (the rulers of the motorways) describing how Italy's motorways, built during the 1960s and 70s, were sold off to corporations, which make huge profits from roads which the Italians have paid for several times over. Given the country's geography, they simply cannot be by-passed. Traffic is very heavy and often saturated on the network of northern motorways. Berlusconi's government granted Benetton a concession until 2048 to run more than three thousand kilometres of Italy's motorways through its subsidiary Atlantia. In 2010 its turnover was four billion euros and the company posted profits of seven hundred million euros. Back in 2006 there was a projected merger between Atlantia and Spanish conglomerate, Albertis, but it was blocked by the government.

The aborted merger raised the issue of foreign ownership of national road networks and showed the close links between multinational building groups and investors. One of the largest shareholders in Albertis with a twenty-six percent stake is ACS, Spain's largest construction group, whose CEO is Florentino Perez, president of soccer club, Real Madrid. Albertis is one of Europe's largest operators managing more than six thousand, seven hundred kilometres of motorways in Greece, Austria, and France.

Only in Spain have concession holders recently learnt that the streets are not always paved with gold. The Spanish government offered concessions to private construction groups to provide five new toll motorways around Madrid. They were eager to take up the concessions creating separate corporate entities. Clever accounting enabled them to extract the profits from the road building leaving the newly formed concession holders to manage the running of the motorways. But Spanish motorists have not been tempted to desert the excellent free "autovias" to use the private "autopistas". Instead of money simply pouring into their pockets from motorists, the concession holders have found their automated toll gates virtually deserted despite a total investment of some four billion euros.

This has led to several of the large quoted construction companies queuing outside government offices claiming compensation on the grounds that they paid too much. I doubt they would have been unhappy if traffic projections had been underestimated rather than overestimated. Why should the taxpayer pay for the poor commercial judgment of the contractors? This is another example of the practice of private gains and public losses. Their latest proposal is make all of Spain's free autovias, toll roads, and the government is actually considering it. But with a general election on the horizon it would need a brave politician to raise this issue during the present crisis. Instead the Spanish government should recover the motorways, tear down the tollgates and give the roads back to the people. Portugal should follow suit. Following the 2014 European soccer championship final in Lisbon thousands of supporters travelling back to Madrid found themselves trapped in a monster traffic jam at the toll near the Spanish border. Demands to open the barriers to relieve the congestion were refused by the operators on the grounds that, "This is a commercial venture." So much for the joy of driving.

Taking into account national debts imagine how much tax revenue governments and taxpayers are losing while the private investors make fortunes from road users. In France, ecology minister, Segolene Royal, has called for the free use of motorways on weekends and a ten percent reduction in tolls to reduce the profits of the private companies holding the concessions. This privileged club includes corporations such as French operators Vinci and Eiffage, as well as Albertis. They control almost ten thousand kilometres of France's toll motorways and have been accused of increasing charges by more than twenty percent over ten years. Shedding staff to incorporate automatic gates has enabled them to increase annual returns to between twenty and twenty-five percent a year. The money just rolls in. Unacceptable says Mrs Royal. France's socialist government has shown where its interests lie by shelving her proposals.

There has also been criticism from environmental groups, which seek to reduce the influence of the road lobbies. They claim motorways are so saturated the tolls cause massive jams at peak times leading to an increase in pollution and petrol consumption due to braking, accelerating and waiting in line to reach the toll gate. Whenever there is bad weather or an accident motorists can remain prisoners for hours unable to exit, which defeats the object of reaching destinations quickly and safely and hinders economic activity.

Toll motorways also have a negative economic impact on many small towns and villages, which have faced isolation and economic decline due to the lack of exits, often thirty or more kilometres apart. One casualty has been the chain of small country hotels – Logis de France – family run establishments renowned for excellent accommodation and food. Motorways have left many stranded in villages facing competition from the no-frill hotels, which have sprouted up by motorway exits close to shopping centres. One way to reduce traffic is to expand national bus services and astonishingly this sector has been blocked in France until now. Finance Minister, Emmanuel Macron, has announced plans to allow the private sector to operate a network of routes linking major cities as in most other European countries, which operate fast motorway coach services at competitive prices compared to the cost of rail and air transport. It has been estimated that by carrying around fifty passengers, each coach could eliminate up to twenty-five car journeys resulting in less accidents, congestion and pollution.

Germany has few toll motorways and is blessed with regular exits serving villages and towns. The country's economy seems to manage pretty well without tolls. The latest proposals to introduce tolls for foreign vehicles using German roads in a tit for tat exercise, is regrettable. France dropped its proposed Eco tax but in exchange is considering implementing taxes on foreign vehicles. These are examples of European folly when one country tries to implement rules unilaterally without consulting other member states.

Europe encourages the free movement of people but not vehicles. There are compelling arguments to dismantle all road tolls and introduce annual road taxes based on the size of vehicle. I would also force the operators to refund motorists who face serious delays through accidents or road works, as airlines are supposed to do when flights are delayed or cancelled. It is time to give the roads back to the people.

Does Heathrow really need a third runway? With five terminals surely it has reached saturation point and it would be wiser to consider increasing space at London's other airports or build a new airport as Boris Johnson has advocated in the Thames Estuary.

I believe that it would make sense to consider a major European Hub somewhere in northern France near Calais with the investment shared between Britain, France, Belgium and the EU. Being located near the sea and with abundant land and labour available, pollution and noise would be greatly reduced.

The airport would be linked to the three capitals by Eurostar, which already operates an efficient train service, or by high-speed buses. With less need or use for taxis and car transport it would be more cost effective and environmentally friendly. The cost would also be shared between three countries together with the European Union. The only handicap might be fog during the winter months but the problem of visibility applies to many major hubs including those in the Emirate States where sand storms can shut down its airports.

Airports are now shopping centres with runways. The decision to expand or build airports has less to do with making travel easier and more with filling duty free shops, restaurants and car parks for the benefit of private companies, which have been allowed to operate them. Passengers cannot fail to notice in their Internet ticket reservations the disparity between the seat price and airport taxes which are the main cause of high travel costs. It is either lack of foresight on the part of politicians or selfish interests on the part of the private organizations running our airports since the loss of passengers will lead to a loss in business and tourism. The UK has actually begun to reduce airport taxes on many long haul flights.

In Adolfo Suarez Madrid Barajas, the operator, Aena, has been losing money and passengers due to the huge cost and underutilization of building Terminal 4 coupled with the financial problems of the main carrier, Iberia. It is being forced to reduce its airport taxes and open up slots to additional carriers. Fortunately it has the capacity to do so. Madrid is one of Europe's traveller-friendly airports. While it has its share of duty free shops, car parks, and taxi ranks, it is served by the city's public bus and metro systems providing fast and cheap travel to the city centre. This is something all airports should strive to achieve.

Easy Jet and Ryan Air have been pioneers in the attempt to bring down air travel by using smaller airports to save money. Recently Ryan Air has been forced to reduce flights or shut down some of its bases, but not its flights, in several European airports including Marseille in France and Bilbao in Spain, following increases in airport taxes. This seems a shortsighted view on the part of the authorities. Given the growth in the number of potential passengers and destinations across Europe, it is hoped that governments will realize that the advantages of increasing the number of visitors is more important than the profits of airport operators. Ryan Air must have obtained an advantageous arrangement to become the first user of the ghost airport at Castellon, near Valencia, which is a relief for the Valencia authorities, which built the airport four years ago during its era of reckless spending on mega projects.

Housing is perhaps the one area needing a radical new approach. According to 2013 government statistics, there are over eleven million empty homes in the European Union. The countries with the most unoccupied properties are:

Spain: 3.4 million
France: 2.4 million
Italy: 2 million
Germany: 1.8 million
Portugal: 750,000
UK: 700,000
Ireland: 300,000
Greece: 300,000

Many of these properties are in towns and villages, which are no longer in desired locations and have suffered from factory closures, or lack of transport communications. In Spain the boom led to the abuse of planning consents and building for profit without any thought of the economic or social need for homes. It is my view, as mentioned above, that toll motorways or absence of adequate transport have exacerbated the problem by isolating too many towns and villages.

France has recently announced the dismantling of military bases around the country. The effect on several medium and small towns will be devastating. The loss of thousands of military personnel and their families will lead to the closure of shops and services and leave empty housing with a consequent reduction of property values. Can Europe afford blighted towns and cities so prevalent in the United States where the traditional industrial cities such as Detroit have faced decline and bankruptcy?

Today we have to take into account changing social patterns. There are more single families and single people needing homes and with people growing older and likely to live alone at some point, there is a case to increase the number of smaller units. At the same time older people should think carefully before moving into a holiday cottage or to a dream villa or apartment overseas. Too many people have regretted settling into new homes in rural locations with a shortage of public transport, shops, pharmacies, and hospitals, which they might eventually need should their health deteriorate as the years pass.

The nineteen sixties and seventies saw the suburbs of many cities and towns transformed by high-rise housing estates using prefabricated building techniques, which have not achieved their goal of creating or uniting communities. The poor quality of many of these buildings, lack of maintenance, shopping, leisure and transport facilities turned many of these suburbs and inner cities into ethnic ghettos often filled with poor people or immigrants who found themselves alienated from the rest of the population. The most deprived suburban areas can end up as no go areas for police and fire services and become notorious for crime, delinquency and drugs. This tendency is a growing world problem concerning Africa and Central and South America. Reports from environmental study groups point to an increase in gang violence in many cities due to political corruption and lack of law enforcement. The massive movement of the population from rural regions in search of jobs has led to the growth of mega cities where whole sectors have been transformed into urban ghettos and fortresses. Fortunately some of these errors have been corrected and many of these estates have been demolished to create new urban housing with open spaces.

The problem today is how to restrict the use of motor vehicles after years of building suburban housing estates for the middle class. Town planners are now reconsidering the wisdom of building in rural areas far from urban centres. New out of town housing estates, shopping centres or business parks require road construction, parking, public transport and an increase in the use of vehicles bringing with it a consequent rise in infrastructure investment, pollution and travelling time. These mega projects have led to a plague of advertising billboards, posters and neon signs along the major routes, which blight the environment. However, the crisis has altered people's shopping habits. The large out of town supermarket groups have seen a dramatic fall in customers and profits as shoppers turn to smaller local discount supermarkets. Choice may be limited but they are cheaper and more convenient. Another indirect casualty of the crisis due to the increase in the cost of fuel and road tolls is the fashion outlet centres located far from cities. It remains to be seen whether the recent fall in petrol prices will alter people's habits. The increasing use of the Internet for online purchases is likely to have a profound effect on the future of department stores and shopping centres. To combat the growing threat from this new form of shopping as more and more companies offer their goods and services online, the major store groups have been forced to adapt by offering more services, becoming leisure centres for families with restaurants as well as a place to shop. Even before the crisis, the traditional high streets were in decline for many years as small family stores closed down to be replaced by chains of banks, estate agents, betting shops and fast food groups. The popularity of cafes with terraces has been the catalyst to reverse this trend and bring life back to town centres.

It makes sense for new building to be concentrated in existing urban areas where there is a supply of obsolete industrial sites or government owned land ripe for development – the so-called brownfield sites. Whether this means building upwards is debatable. In Paris the authorities have chosen to allow high rise buildings around the periphery of the city in answer to the city's housing demand thus leaving the centre with its unique skyline. London has always spread outwards and horizontal into the suburbs and while the Shard has become a landmark, it is hardly designed to alleviate the country's housing shortage.

The same can be said for London's latest urban development regeneration programme taking place south of the river Thames in Wandsworth and Lambeth. The Battersea Power Station and Nine Elms projects with their spectacular modern glass fronted buildings and towers comprising several thousand apartments, retail space and offices, are being developed by Asian development companies. Although completion is not expected before 2016 the marketing and sales campaigns, organized in many major Asian cities, have been targeting Asian investors with a view to selling the apartments off plan. There has been a rush of buyers hoping to benefit from an increase in value before the properties are completed and make a profit by selling on their contracts. The developers are offering a lifestyle, not a home. The buildings come complete with a club, gym, public space and restaurant and the interiors appear to have been designed by the same designers giving the impression of apart-hotel rooms for short-term rental rather than somewhere to live.

It is pure unfettered property speculation, described by some as the purchase of safe deposit boxes for wealthy foreign investors. It has nothing to do with providing homes for Londoners, most of whom could not afford the substantial service charges. Having been raised in London I have always thought of the power station as an ugly monstrosity from a by-gone age. And despite it being part of Shanghai on Thames my view has not changed. It stands for what is wrong with the property market, which has shifted from building family homes to be lived in, to become investment vehicles for foreign speculators. While many of these schemes are undoubtedly improving London's skyline, are these foreign owned developments a boon or a curse since they move the capital further out of reach of the average purchaser? Whether they will ever be lived in to create what the developers call "a vibrant new community" remains to be seen. The government has already introduced capital gains tax from 2015 for non residents to stem price rises, but these mega projects raise the issue of whether we need regulation to reduce speculation by blocking the sale of contracts and making buyers complete on a purchase before disposal.

Arguably the most visible symbol of the real estate bubble is the uncompleted forty-seven storey, two hundred metre high tower in Benidorm, Spain. Vaunted as Europe's highest residential building, it ended up in the hands of the Sareb, the company created by the Spanish Government to take over and dispose of toxic bank property assets, after the developer became insolvent. With its parallel towers joined at the summit by a strange cone-like structure, the gleaming, glass facade overlooks the Mediterranean and stands as a monument to the folly of high rise urban development. So far the only high rise towers in Madrid are located to the north of the city on the old training ground of Real Madrid soccer club comprising offices and a luxury hotel. They stand out against the city skyline but may soon be joined by other office and residential buildings if the two-billion euro Chamartin project on nearby railway land is approved. Given the abundance of virgin land available around the city, several satellite towns have been built to cater for the increase in population. But this required a massive investment to extend the metro system, which indebted the Spanish capital. Italy is an exception in that town centre redevelopment is heavily restricted due to the historical nature of so many towns and cities, which possess a unique cultural heritage. The only alternative is to extend development into new suburbs or build new towns. Many German cities tend to be modern, rebuilt after the Second World War, which made the planning and redevelopment process simpler. In cities such as Dresden, totally destroyed during the war, the city centre has been painstakingly rebuilt with low-rise construction and architecture to reflect the city's past heritage.

Western governments should take an interest in how the Middle East and Asia deals with their housing needs. Nearly every city has allowed high rise buildings to cater for large population growth with contrasting results. Many cheaply built tower blocks have created creating almost inhuman living conditions for the majority of the population, while at the same time mega projects catering for a wealthy international clientele have enabled several of the world's most renowned architects to test their creative and technological capability to the limits.. Norman Foster, Richard Rogers, Renzo Piano, Frank Gehry, I. M. Pei, Zaha Hadid, Herzog and Meuron are among the current names producing eye catching, futuristic, energy saving and environmentally friendly buildings which will have as lasting an impact on our societies as have the buildings of Corbusier, Frank Lloyd Wright and Oscar Niemeyer.

Italy's prime minister warned his fellow citizens, "Non c'è piu posto fisso" literally meaning that there are no more secure jobs. In today's mobile environment job insecurity has become a fact of life. Whether we like it or not people need to relocate to where jobs are available, across town, in another city or even in another country. In this changing world the whole question of home ownership may need to be reconsidered.

Given the changes in employment opportunities with mobility becoming necessary to seek jobs and the difficulties for the young to buy, there is a strong case for increasing the stock of affordable rented accommodation. Since the 1960s home ownership has enabled millions to obtain financial security through the rise in house prices. But it is possible that the golden era of home ownership is ending.

Not just because it is becoming harder to step on to the housing ladder due to the ever increasing cost of buying property, but because for the young, increasingly mobile population, a twenty-five year mortgage will hinder moving home to a new job in another town or even overseas.

It cannot make sense for families to engage in long-term mortgage commitments to own property in areas where they might find it difficult to find buyers. This generally means many smaller provincial towns and villages where job opportunities are limited.

France and Spain, for example, with substantial agricultural communities scattered across their large countries have a substantial number of isolated small towns and villages. Many rely on one or two employers and when these shut down or relocate, as has been the case, the communities face economic and social decline.

More rented accommodation would not only alleviate the housing shortage but stabilize or even lower rents to affordable levels in our cities. Germany has always relied on a reasonably priced rental market to house its citizens without the population being obsessed by house prices. Enabling families to move into and out of accommodation more easily would benefit the economy. Of course this would mean a change of mentality and a break with the notion that a home is an investment. And the class divisions will be hard to break down. Every city in the world is divided into sectors either for the upper class, the middle class and working class, immortalized by John Cleese, Ronnie Barker and Ronnie Corbett in one of their most famous comedy sketches. With property prices playing such an important part of our lives it is natural that people who have paid a great deal of money to live somewhere do not want to see a fall in the value of their homes or a change in the make up of their neighbourhood.

They have a legitimate argument. Our cities are divided into sectors each with a different lifestyle and everyone has been free to choose where they wish to live according to their means. Where prices are high, buildings tend to be of a higher quality with more services. In addition the surrounding environment tends to be of a higher standard, with more exclusive shops, schools, restaurants, parks etc. Why, therefore, should someone without the necessary financial resources or who has not earned the money to move to a larger, more expensive property, benefit from living in the most exclusive areas?

But it is equally clear that city centres cannot remain a bastion of the rich and privileged elite. Hospital staff, police, council workers, teachers and firefighters have to be near their place of work and need reasonably priced housing to enable a city to function. Students also require affordable accommodation close to their universities.

In France the government introduced laws to force local authorities to provide up to twenty of its stock for social housing to create what they see as a fairer mix of the population. Not surprisingly in the smarter areas this is being resisted, as residents fear a reduction in the value of their homes and more crime. Neuilly, an affluent Parisian suburb, is a perfect example of an extremely rich and exclusive borough whose mayor argues it does not have the space to create social housing, which would obviously alter its image and perhaps the lifestyle of its privileged residents. Its population agreed to pay the fines imposed rather than see more social housing. This thinking, now being considered by Islington Council in London, is reminiscent of the Russian revolution where large private homes were confiscated and divided into smaller units for the poor. Why not force four and five star hotels to reserve twenty percent of their rooms for people who cannot afford the rates, or make luxury car dealers hand over twenty percent of their vehicles to people with no money? It is a naïve look at life. If there is a lack of affordable housing, governments should encourage the building of more homes on the fringes of cities. To improve the environment, it usually makes more sense to gentrify poor neighbourhoods. During the past forty years many run down urban areas have been transformed as the middle class moved in renovating properties encouraging the arrival of higher quality shops and services. It is true that increased real estate values often forced poorer families out but this can be checked through government intervention. The problem affecting many of the poorest Paris suburbs – les banlieues – is political. Run by the communist or socialist parties they do not want to see a loss of their electorate, which would result from the arrival of more affluent residents. And of course moving the poor and immigrant population to affluent areas to create a social mix would perhaps provide them with votes. Exacerbated by the economic crisis, there has been a gradual deterioration of the quality of life and an increase in violence from a largely impoverished, immigrant population, and moving them to the more expensive suburbs in town centres is not going to resolve the main problem, which is a lack of integration, education and jobs. To reduce the problem of the banlieues, the government has come up with a cunning plan- eliminate them. Incorporating the suburbs into what will become known as Le Grand Paris, will, they believe, give the population the feeling of being part of the capital.

Another phenomenon is the growth in second homes. There has been a construction boom in coastal areas and many rural or mountain villages facing extinction have been given a new lease of life thanks to foreign investors who undertake the refurbishment of old country properties. But the demand during the past thirty years has led to overdevelopment in many rural and coastal regions in southern Europe and irreparable damage to the environment.

Spain is an example of what not to do and it is only now changing its planning laws regarding building in the countryside or close to the sea. But astonishingly instead of calling for the demolition of all illegally built properties, it has granted many exemptions and, ignoring all environmental considerations, reduced the distance where building can be permitted from one hundred metres to just twenty metres from the coast in certain areas not already ruined from overbuilding.

The end of the real estate bubble has left hundreds of thousands of empty properties across Spain, especially on the Mediterranean coast. An example of the folly is the Castellon region where a municipality with a population of just seven thousand granted planning permission for more than thirty thousand units to house one hundred and twenty thousand people as well as a new airport mentioned above.

Many of these properties stand not only empty but incomplete, derelict, concrete skeletons. Given the virtually impossible task of achieving sales in the foreseeable future and lacking the funds to complete the buildings, developers are considering demolishing these eyesores as it would be cheaper than paying local taxes. Spain has recently seen a phenomenon of whole villages, which have become derelict, being offered for sale although most are isolated and comprise a few abandoned homes requiring total renovation. The problem has been to locate the owners long gone.

Nevertheless, despite the current crisis and unsold stock, the second home market is going to remain an attractive investment and it could make sense for young families to consider purchasing a second home as an income producing investment to provide security for retirement while renting their main town residence. This would allow for more mobility during a person's working life should either partner in a relationship need to relocate for professional reasons. The USA is used to its population being mobile. Around twenty-million families live in trailer parks scattered across the country, which does not have a shortage of land. In theory the timber-built single story dwellings can be towed from site to site depending on where the family wishes to live and where there is employment. The trailer parks are private and regulated. The problem is that while families own their homes they do not own the land and should the owner want to sell to a developer, they can be evicted and forced to find a new park.

What will determine future development is how to deal with the use of motor vehicles. The metro strike in Sao Paolo aimed at disrupting Brazil's World Cup preparations or the daily gridlock in Beijing are visions of what the future holds. Car ownership, of course, is a consequence of suburban life. As families moved out of city centres into houses with gardens, a car became essential. The spread of suburbs and dormitory towns coupled with the increased affluence of the population led to families owning two or three cars. But jobs tend to be located in city centres requiring longer and longer journeys to reach work. The result is that too many cities have reached saturation point. It is generally accepted that there has to be a reduction in the number of cars in urban areas coupled with a consequent improvement in cheap and efficient public transport. Our city streets are littered with parked vehicles, many of which do not move for days or weeks. They hinder short-term parking as well as loading and unloading. Japan has created an environment where cities have no street parking at all and it will be interesting to see how Paris copes with a proposal to ban older vehicles, which pollute and increase the number of pedestrian streets. In a radical move to end the reliance on cars in order to reduce pollution, several city authorities are proposing free public transport on certain days. Of course this will not apply to the privileged class, which owns or will no doubt buy an extra car creating even more inequality in the land of fraternity.

The age of the electric car is coming. Norway seems to have taken a lead but the problem remains one of recharging batteries. Their use in city centres over short distances will certainly reduce pollution. A European wide network of recharging outlets is on the cards but I question whether long distance car travel will be worthwhile when high-speed trains and low cost airlines now make road travel uncompetitive and almost unaffordable.

Several local authorities have been introducing urban bicycles and electric cars for rent which can be taken from and parked in secured, allocated spaces. They have met with considerable success but finding a bike available and then a space to leave it can be time consuming as there are only a limited number of spaces in the most sought after locations of the city, where most people want to go. It is noticeable that everywhere where pedestrian streets or squares have been introduced it has led to an increase in footfall, as retailers call it, with a consequent improvement in the environment and growth in retail and restaurant businesses with their outdoor terraces. Italy's historic cities have had to adapt to save their unique heritage despite the Italians' love of driving everywhere and parking anywhere. There is a saying that Italians find angles to park unknown to geometry. Venice, of course, does not have a car problem but the city authorities decided to restrict the entry into the lagoon of cruise ships, which posed a threat to the city's fragile environ. These gigantic ships are more like floating apartment or hotel blocks with up to five thousand passengers on board and the waves they generate hit the fragile foundations of buildings like tsunamis. However the port, concerned about the potential loss of revenue, objected and the ruling has been overturned for the moment.

The downside of car free urban centres is that pedestrian areas have led to the building of ugly multistorey or underground car parks, which entail delicate steering up or down endless spiral ramps and then manoeuvring between rows of columns to find a space. Drivers then face being ripped off by extortionate parking charges. Far more environmentally friendly is the provision of car parks at the periphery of towns with free public transport to the centre. Like parking meters, these are seen as a vital contribution to local authorities' coffers. The lack of space has created a market for private car parks and in many large cities the price of buying a car park space is almost as much as an apartment suggesting that housing a car is more important than a family.

There is a strong case for giving up owning a car. Most of the time they just sit in the road, in garages or car parks and what is worse, in traffic jams. Humps, detested by every motorist, are another reason. Aimed at reducing speed in urban areas they can ruin brakes and the suspension. When the cost of insurance, petrol, tax, tyres, repairs, maintenance, depreciation and time lost just sitting in traffic jams are taken into account, the car is not a wise investment for most people and can become a major liability. It makes more sense to hire a car for weekends or holidays. But common sense or logic will not prevail until the concept of the car as a status symbol is eradicated. The paradox is that while there is a need to reduce traffic congestion, cars are the lifeblood of our economies. Despite the congestion and anti-vehicle policies in towns and cities, the press, radio and TV pump out advertisements for cars.

One hundred years ago the motor industry was reserved for the USA and Europe. The 1950s and 60s was the golden age of motoring. Nobody had to worry about petrol consumption, size, the use of leather or lots of polished chrome and magnificent cars were produced. To see the classic American cars today a visit to Cuba is a must, but don't wait too long. Competition has changed the rules. The British motor industry was virtually wiped out and Italy and France face plant closures. Only Germany retains its position. Japan conquered the world and more recently, South Korea, China and India and many smaller nations have all established plants to build vehicles for their growing, more affluent population who all want to own a car. In these countries the car has become a symbol of having arrived. Only the traffic has become so dense they can no longer arrive anywhere.

Our roads have become multicultural melting pots. There are saloon cars, sports cars, off road cars (which never go off road), luxury limos, old bangers, taxis, mini cabs, coaches, buses, caravans, campers, heavy goods vehicles, white vans, motorbikes, pizza delivery bikes, scooters and bicycles all competing to use the same narrow stretch of tarmac; there are slow drivers, hell drivers, white van drivers, drivers who own the road, old drivers, boy racers, women drivers, Italian drivers, drivers without licenses, and uninsured drivers. The only common link is that they all think they have right of way. Someone someday is going to have to realize that this state of affairs cannot continue. And with the risk of more traffic accidents involving pedestrians, people and motor vehicles are going to have to be segregated. However in order to get people to leave their cars behind every city needs safe, modern, efficient and cheap public transport.

During the next few years while the West reduces its reliance on the car, Asia and possibly Africa will see hundreds of millions of new road users. Statistics point to China having just thirty-five cars per thousand population today, estimated to rise to two hundred per thousand by 2023. This can be compared to the USA, with four hundred and thirty-nine vehicles per thousand. Many of Asia's mega poles are already notorious for traffic congestion and pollution. How can we reduce polluting the atmosphere when the motor industry is such an important part of a nation's economy? It is not just about assembly lines but thousands of suppliers of equipment and spare parts, dealers and garages. It provides jobs for hundreds of thousands of workers and vital revenue from exports. A reduction in car manufacturing and use of the car will lead to less demand for petrol and road building and result in a dramatic effect on world economies. In the meantime China is pressing on with its own vehicle production and when it starts to export its cars, made in China, the US and Europe are going to catch pneumonia.

The motor and construction industries are vital to our economies providing jobs, which for politicians translates into support for their election campaigns. We are therefore going to have to come to terms with living in an endless state of road works and building sites, enduring all the inconvenience and pollution they bring. Cranes will become a permanent feature of city skylines and children will ask their parents. "Daddy, where do cones come from?"

Recent statistics have illustrated the enormous waste and cost of transporting goods by road. The report found that trucks are only productive for around ten percent of the time. The remaining time is divided between unloading, loading, waiting or travelling empty with consequent damage to the environment. By using the Internet to monitor movements there is scope to increase efficiency and profits. Meanwhile the road lobbies are calling for an increase in the size of trucks. Not content with forty ton vehicles they want to see forty-four ton juggernauts with trailers on our saturated roads to increase their profits. The use of rail transport for long distances has been considered for years but has yet to gain acceptance, especially with the truckers' unions. Has anyone considered the advantages of using the Mediterranean to ship trucks and containers to and from Spain, France, Italy and Greece saving thousands of miles of long distance motorway driving?

It is quite possible that an alternative to the internal combustion engine has been available for decades but the oil industry is so powerful it has been doing everything to conceal new technology to preserve its interests. However, it is inevitable that the petrol or diesel engine vehicle is ultimately destined for the scrap yard, to be replaced by smaller electric vehicles if we are to save the planet. Who knows? Perhaps water or solar energy could power vehicles?

The US and China are the world's leading polluters and have finally accepted that they have to deal with climate change. Their cities can no longer cope with traffic and pollution and they are finally making an effort to deal with the problem through more efficient vehicles, cleaner fuel and gradual transformation to renewable energies. But given the size of China and its population it is likely to be a long-term commitment.

Dan Brown's novel, Inferno, incorporated his usual complex symbols and warnings on how to save the planet from powerful opaque organizations and megalomaniacs. But it really had little to do with Dante and everything to do with the issue of population growth and the very survival of humanity. Despite birth control methods and medicine, the world is reproducing at an ever-faster rate, doubling each century. Will it cope with the estimated nine billion people on the planet? The disparity between the wealthy one percent and the remaining ninety-nine percent has reached unsustainable proportions. With the birth rate in the Western countries declining and that of Africa and Asia increasing, unless there are major improvements in education, health and living standards, it poses the risk of a poor and less educated population pursuing their dream to emigrate to the Western countries which can no longer cope, the risk of the spread of contagious diseases and ultimately to a nightmare world where anarchy and chaos will reign.

Ease of travel has led to problems of massive traffic jams on our roads, overcrowding at airports and railway stations and even mountains and beaches. The massive increase in the number of mountaineers or tourists in Nepal wanting to climb Everest has created tensions and restrictions given the amount of rubbish left on the mountainside and the authorities are considering ways to restrict access while at the same time not wishing to lose the financial benefits. The earthquake and its tragic consequences has obviously reduced considerably the number of visitors for the foreseeable future as the country recovers.

The development of beach resorts like Cancun, with its huge hotel complexes providing everything for the tourist has caused environmental and economic damage to the surrounding region, which sees no benefit from the thousands of foreign visitors. During the peak holiday period, Europe's major beach resorts are packed with sun worshippers all competing for beach space while their motor vehicles compete for parking spaces. Hemingway would not recognise Pamplona today. The San Fermin festival has turned into an overcrowded eight day, drunken orgy with thousands of foreign visitors cramming the narrow streets of the old town. There is far less risk of being gored by a bull than being trampled to death by humans. When tourists criss-crossed Europe in their old Volkswagen camper vans stopping wherever they pleased nobody objected. But during the past decade the sheer number of the latest much larger camper vehicles, which come complete with bikes, surfboards, satellite dishes and TVs, parked in streets or along the beach front forced many towns to declare war on the infringement of municipal space and removed them to sites on the edge of their towns. Being stuck behind these slow moving enemies of the people on country or mountain roads during the summer tests every motorist's patience.

Beaches have become a source of controversy in Italy. Traditionally they have been cordoned off into privately run sections managed by concession holders, who charge for deck chairs, parasols, changing rooms, showers, games and snack bars. Sometimes hotels have their own section of beach reserved for their guests. While this system ensures a clean and tidy sea front, protestors claim the fenced off, gated and guarded beaches prevent access and visibility to the sea front which by law should be freely available to every citizen. For people who do not wish to pay the daily or weekly charge, local authorities do provide free public beach areas. However changes in holiday patterns with less people taking a two-week vacation by the sea, the relatively short summer season as well as bad weather, are having an effect on the survival of many of these private beaches. Should they all be scrapped in the name of freedom of movement?

China, with its huge population and rapid economic growth, faces overcrowding in its mega cities, while the Chinese New Year sees railways stations totally saturated as millions head home to their villages. Another example of the problem with the sheer number of people is the fad for lovers to lock padlocks on bridges. The security of the famous pedestrian Pont des Arts in Paris is now at risk from the sheer weight of thousands of these metal locks placed there by tourists and they may have to be removed. There will simply come a time when governments will be unable to cope with overpopulation and mass tourism. Barcelona's new mayor may have started a trend by publicly announcing that she wants to put an end to mass tourism, which brings unruly behaviour and alcohol abuse.

Minerals such as gold and silver have always been considered as valuable commodities. But the world's most precious resource is taken for granted, at least until recently – water. It may account for seventy percent of the earth's surface but a growing world population is using it, consuming it and wasting it in ever growing quantities. It is also poorly distributed with the rich developed nations monopolizing its use and consumption, while a quarter of the world's population lacks basic supplies. Will we have enough fresh water, food, jobs or money for every human being on the planet? It is clear that the West will have to reduce its consumption and waste or living conditions in Western mega cities will become worse than they already are. California faces a serious drought problem which could affect the lifestyle of much of the population used to pristine lawns and golf greens as well as over consumption, who will have to come to terms with saving water.

One novel idea to reduce waste is to reintroduce the concept of charging customers for bottles in the same way that supermarkets charge for plastic bags. I remember when this was common practice in France. Bottles of wine were charged for and to obtain a refund, empty bottles had to be returned to the store. This would be a useful way to recycle glass and end the discarding of thousands of empty bottles by the roadside or the sea.

Yet despite the urgency in dealing with all these issues ratified under the Kyoto protocol, the 2013 climate conference, which took place in Warsaw, ended in stalemate as some delegates walked out following the refusal of leading nations to ratify measures which need implementing. Other conferences have come and gone and Paris will host the conference in November 2015. Decisions on climate change and the environment are too important to defer and cannot be ignored by governments. It is one of the major challenges for the survival of humanity.

We do not inherit the earth from our ancestors, we borrow it from our children.

Ancient Cree proverb.

Social Morality

All our problems are man-made. Which means they can be resolved by man. And our most basic common link is that we all inhabit this small planet, we all breathe the same air, we all cherish our children's future and we are all mortal.

John F. Kennedy, 10 June 1963

Since the end of the Second World War most Western countries have veered from left to right in successive elections. But the thirty glorious years of economic growth brought more prosperity regardless of which party was in power. Reaganism and Thatcherism were deemed a blessing by half of the population, freeing them from the shackles of socialism and bringing the unions to heel. But it was also a watershed as far as social equality was concerned.

Their legacy has been globalization, the removal of monetary controls and banking regulation, the elimination of labour laws and a return to the unfettered capitalism of the 19th century, which after years of reducing the gap between rich and poor, has led to an unprecedented transfer of wealth through corporate and financial greed. The result was the crisis of 2007/8.

But instead of learning the lessons and returning to a fairer society, the crisis gave too many corporations the opportunity to shed jobs by the thousands, relocating overseas to countries with cheaper labour or encouraging immigration to keep wages down just to maintain boardroom salaries, bonuses and/or shareholder dividends. Despite a massive increase in economic wealth all we have achieved is a shift from *Cathy Come Home* to *Benefits Streets*. French comic, Coluche, created the "Restos du Coeur", a charity aimed at helping the homeless in 1985. At the outset it catered for less than one hundred thousand people. Today it helps over one million people, damning evidence of how our democratic societies are in decline.

And one of the reasons is tax evasion or avoidance. There is sufficient evidence to demonstrate that profits and earnings have been, and still are, being diverted to subsidiaries in tax havens leading to a serious loss of tax revenue. These short-term selfish goals are not in the national interest.

To justify high remuneration packages for bankers, lawyers and corporate directors, the argument of supply and demand is always put forward. However when, as at present, we lack nurses or other essential workers, governments never suggest increasing wages, but prefer to rely on cheap immigrant labour.

Governments must consider the consequences of corporate layoffs while businesses are still profitable. They should legislate to avoid what would be more unemployment, an increase in the cost of social security benefits and ultimately the risk of social disorder from a population facing poverty.

It requires a change of mentality, which would require boardrooms and shareholders to consider the interests of employees as well as themselves; in other words a new form of shared capitalism where employees are not treated like objects to be discarded at leisure.

This is especially relevant in the light of the tragic deaths resulting from what can only be described as slave labour in Asia but which also include mining operations in Africa and Latin America. Apart from the abominable low wages, conditions are appalling and too many Western corporations turn a blind eye to the actions of their subcontractors. Chinese corporations too are finding that their expansion overseas is not always welcome. In Vietnam, Chinese factories have been obliged to repatriate workers after their premises were burned by local workers unable to find jobs. And closer to home in the Tuscan city of Prato, in Italy, Chinese workshops, which seem to operate with little or no regulation, have been mysteriously burned down with loss of life.

Clearly corruption plays a role and there needs to be international agreement and regulations on how to provide decent wages and conditions in the developing nations while at the same time guaranteeing well made and reasonably priced goods for consumers in the richer countries.

Surely the directors and shareholders of the major brand names, whose mark up is massive, could accept a reduction in the amount of their profits to give the poor a better standard of living. There is also a need to reduce the number of sub contractors and middlemen who drive the prices up unnecessarily which the Free Trade movement is attempting to resolve.

It is to be hoped that the bad publicity and actions of consumer groups to bring the worst cases of exploitation to the public, thanks to the use of social networks, will have an effect and bring about changes. Those brands failing to take action will find that their lack of concern will cost them dearly in the long run.

Coca Cola, which through its advertising campaigns has created a worldwide image of social responsibility, came unstuck in India where it was accused of polluting hundreds of acres of land, as well as in Spain following the decision to rationalize its bottling plants and reduce staff. It led to a revolt, strikes, blockages and a severe dent to its image from which it is trying to recover.

However, despite the crisis and the plight of millions of poor workers, governments seem more concerned about banks than jobs or equality. The return to profitability and massive bonus pay outs by banks so quickly after the bail outs suggests that instead of pumping money into the financial sector it would have been more sensible to engage in job-creating public works or energy saving industries, or, as the economist, Steve Keen suggested, instead of bailing out the banks, governments should have nationalized the financial system and given the money to the people to pay off debts.

Corporations are often allowed to write off debts and renegotiate short-term refinancing arrangements. If the same rules were applied to families with mortgage debts, enabling them to extend the loan period and reduce their monthly outgoings, perhaps thousands could have been saved from eviction. When people lose their homes governments are invariably obliged to re-house them and pay social benefits. So it seems more sensible to let people remain in their homes with state aid until they find employment. And instead of spending millions to house people in bedsits or hotels surely it would be more economical in the long run to build more new homes.

Spain has recently announced new laws to prevent unruly social behaviour by imposing heavy fines, especially when any demonstrations touch politicians or public buildings. Following the massive demonstration of the March of Dignity, earlier this year, which resulted in violence by extremist groups, politicians called for a ban on public protests in the street, which are a fundamental right written in the constitution. What governments fail to acknowledge is that if there were less greed and corruption by the ruling elite and less austerity measures, which affect the majority of the population, there would be less social unrest.

On the one hand corrupt public officials and bankers indicted for fraud or large-scale tax evasion remain untouchable and fraudsters are lauded rather than punished, while on the other, demonstrators, who have lost their jobs or homes and have little or no money, are heavily fined. Some, like Herve Falciani and Antoine Deltour, who disclosed tax evaders to the authorities, are treated like criminals. What future can there be for justice and democracy in such a distorted world?

To begin social change and justice we can start by banning premium telephone numbers. The use of these telephone numbers is symptomatic of the greed society we live in and it is unacceptable that companies or public services are allowed to overcharge in this way. There is no justification to charge extra for telephone calls, a ruse designed to make money for nothing from users.

Consumers are being exploited by utility and energy firms, the banks, telephone operators and other companies who have all found that keeping customers hanging on pays. The media have also jumped on to the bandwagon. They invent competitions in which prizes go to those who telephone a specific number with the correct answer to a question, usually so simple a two-year-old would know.

Naturally the prizes in no way reflect the amount of money made from the callers who hang on for several minutes believing they have a real chance, forgetting all the while that the price of the call rapidly mounts up. All premium numbers should simply be outlawed.

The Telecom companies are making a mockery of European laws by lobbying for the retention of roaming charges, which should also be banned. It is another example of how the free movement of goods and services does not apply to powerful multinational corporations when it suits them.

The media too, forced to adapt to the growing power of the Internet, blogs and twitters, is undergoing a mea culpa following the phone hacking scandals which exposed the links between big business and politics and a lack of ethics which permeates newsrooms. Truth and transparency were the objectives behind Julian Assange's WikiLeaks publishing confidential information and Edward Snowden's exposure of the NSA mass surveillance programme, which rocked the American Government. State secrets might never be the same again.

Social networks are a boon to people living alone who are able to connect with the outside world. But the downside is that spending too much time sitting in front of the screen can lead to people becoming more introvert with less physical contact and personal relationships leading to isolation from society. The Internet and social networks have also brought with them danger for adults and especially children, subjected to sex films or violent video games. Steps are being taken to block access of many illicit videos with paedophile or pornographic content but little seems to be done to reduce the increasingly violent video games, which sell by the thousands to young people. Does the ease with which computerized sophisticated weapons kill enemy targets in these games lead to disturbed young people being responsible for some of the violent mass killings America has faced or the conversion to Islamic terrorist groups? I believe it does.

One of the most damaging factors facing society over the last fifty years is how TV and the press have gradually been reducing the publication of serious news and pursued a policy of dumbing down in the race to expose scandals among royalty, celebrities and football stars or promote soap operas. It is a phenomenon contaminating the world.

Fictitious characters in soap operas have been elevated to cult status as if they are real people. News stories on the Internet actually announce what is happening in these shows as if they are actually happening. Can people really believe they are real? Even the Internet providers' news content has now been infected with headlines of stars in bikinis or no bikinis, lurid and smutty stories and irrelevant celebrity gossip.

Serious journalism ended the day Rupert Murdoch took over the Times newspaper group. The Sunday Times was renowned for its powerful news stories. Wherever I travelled I made sure that I found a copy. *Sunday isn't Sunday without the Sunday Times* was certainly true for me. But editor Harold Evans resigned and photographer Don McCullin was forced to leave. The new editorial policy was aimed at pandering to advertisers of luxury goods, who Murdoch believed did not wish to see photographs of starving children or bodies in its newspapers. The age of the celebrity began. Today only the

New York Times, Washington Post, Le Monde and Spanish daily, El Pais, come near in terms of serious journalism.

We live in the age of awards. Once upon a time there was the annual Oscar ceremony and Cannes Film Festival. I have seen the reality behind the facade of the red carpet. While the public only sees the stars in their borrowed designer clothes and jewellery on the steps, the festival is a market and a hard slog for anyone trying to promote or sell their screenplays or movies.

Today there is hardly a city without its own film, theatre, music or TV festival handing out prizes after the suspense of announcing the nominations. We are confronted with award winning cars, airlines, towns, beaches, restaurants, wines and even plumbers, although nobody really knows just what they are for or who awards the awards. Festivals and sporting events also come with "official" cars, beer, balls, strip, and anything else the organizers can get sponsors to pay for to give them a sense of exclusiveness.

This is the age of lifestyle: we no longer buy a home, but a lifestyle; we do not wear clothes so much as a lifestyle; we do not drive cars, but a lifestyle. TV advertisements for cars show happy, beautiful people cruising along empty roads, when the reality is crawling through congested streets polluting the atmosphere. There are even lifestyle experts, whoever they are, as if it is a new profession, which comes with a university qualification to be able to practice. One of the words I hate most is *Celebrity*. It is generally reserved for the unknown aspiring star whose talent and intelligence is as superficial as their dress or lack of it. They have become icons, with their, often very ordinary lives, as well as their bodies, given full public exposure. And bodies now come complete with a variety of tattoos, which, while I find them ugly, have become another fashion item, only rather more difficult to discard. Body piercing is no longer restricted to ears. Both sexes fix rings on their eyebrows, noses, lips or private parts. A couple engaged in a deep kiss could need a locksmith to separate them. Stars, celebrities and sports personalities have become a boon to writers and journalists who often "ghost" their autobiographies churning out unreadable books. They have also become money machines for corporations as well as themselves. The fame of celebrities is guaranteed regardless of their conduct since whenever anything distasteful is mentioned or their bodies are exposed on the Internet, their lawyers start legal actions providing them with even more media coverage.

Can someone explain the interest in the Kardashian family and their rise to cult status? To my knowledge they can't act, sing, dance, write, run, swim, kick a ball, play tennis or cook. Yet when disaster strikes, such as a pimple on a nose, TV and radio programmes are interrupted with news bulletins and the paparazzi take out their ultra long telephoto lenses.

Nobody is safe from the prying eyes of the paparazzi, as Diana and now Catherine, William and Harry have learnt. Politicians are also fair game and do their best to cover up their private and public lives, which are not always in keeping with their image as ex-French head of the IMF, Dominique Strauss Kahn, found out to his cost. Somewhere in the chase for scoops, truth and genuine news has been lost. There is a saying that what interests the public may not be in the public interest. What is in the public interest, are family values, education and health.

Our priorities are wrong. We pay obscene sums of money to celebrities, fashion models and their photographers, whose contribution to society is questionable, while people vital to our daily lives, such as nurses, transport workers, garbage collectors, firefighters, fishermen, farmers etc. survive on meager earnings. Without these workers our societies collapse. Once upon a time nursing and teaching were respected, sought after professions. Today our youth dream of becoming actors, models or soccer and pop stars or, for those with little talent, famous celebrities. Of course nobody denies that talented people will always justify higher earnings but the inequality has grown to unacceptable proportions.

Priority needs to be given to the basic needs of the people. The USA is considered the world's richest nation yet forty-five percent of the population lives below the poverty line and the country's infrastructure has been neglected. President Obama has called for huge investment in the country's crumbling roads and bridges in urgent need of maintenance and upgrading. I first visited the United States in my late teens. My American dream was shattered before I set foot in the country. It was 23rd November 1964, less than twenty-four hours after President Kennedy, had been assassinated. When I disembarked from the transatlantic liner in the port of New York, the city was cold, with a bitter wind and the streets deserted. During my year long stay, which took me from the East coast to the West coast, I was shocked at the contrast between the extreme wealth in certain areas of the country and the abundance of run down, deprived urban areas coupled with the segregation of the black and white population. Half a century later little has changed. Whilst perhaps not on the same scale, there are a considerable number of important environmental, social and infrastructure projects needed in Europe to improve the education, health, housing and energy sectors.

The London Underground, the oldest in the world, is showing its age and requires major investment. But the low curved tunnels and trains can never remove the claustrophobic effect of travelling below the city. In Paris architects have drawn up proposals for the regeneration of several poor suburban districts as well as new transport links around the capital. All these projects will not only require public money but also create thousands of jobs.

One of the most damaging and far-reaching psychological issues of the crisis is foreclosure or repossession of family homes. Through no fault of their own many homeowners find themselves with a double whammy; repayments they cannot afford at a time when they have negative equity in their property.

Equally disturbing is the situation where tenants who pay their rent find themselves caught in a conflict between their landlords and banks. In both situations families with children are forced out on the streets. Financial difficulties can lead to the breakup of families. These situations are a burden to local government faced with providing housing or benefits at a high cost to the taxpayer.

Empty properties help neither the owner nor lender since they tend to become vandalized and depreciate further in value. As already mentioned the solution is to leave families in their homes and persuade lenders to reduce repayments or extend the loan period with the government providing temporary financial help for those in most need until they can afford to pay more.

Instead, governments seem more concerned about protecting the banks than people. The creation of bad banks to remove toxic assets from their balance sheets and reduce their debt has allowed the banks to sell off properties cheap so foreign speculators can buy them and make a profit to the detriment of the original homeowners. Meanwhile these same banks have negotiated with major real estate developers with unsold stock, to write off millions of euros of debt and or extend their loans over a long period of time. Why could they not consider the same favourable treatment with homeowners in difficulty?

It would reduce personal hardship, be more cost effective, make the banks accept responsibility for granting mortgages in the first place and ensure that properties are maintained until prices rise when they can be put on to the market. As the number of homeless rises, governments are faced with the problem of how to deal with people, sometimes families and children, sleeping in doorways, public open spaces or parked vehicles. Illegal immigration has exacerbated the problem as thousands of undocumented foreigners without resources have little choice where they live. Naturally councils are facing pressure to remove what most people find unsightly and degrading and some local authorities are actually deliberately fixing obstacles to prevent the homeless from sleeping on benches or in parks. Can this be tolerated in wealthy democratic nations or should the homeless be housed in local authority accommodation? As more and more families are affected by the crisis, governments have a moral duty to act and reduce the injustices and inequality in our society.

In Spain repossessions have become a major source of political and social conflict. It is estimated that hundreds of thousands of people have been evicted due to unemployment and their inability to cover their mortgage payments. The government has been slow to end repossessions by the banks, which have been putting properties up for auction at very low prices, leaving the borrower liable not only for the difference between the price and loan but also higher interest payments. Since 2013 more than one hundred thousand families have been evicted from their homes and twenty-five percent of the population is believed to be facing poverty.

One of the most abhorrent practices in Spain is where the banks insist on a guarantor when the borrower is unable to provide sufficient collateral. The guarantors usually consist of family members, who do not realize the risk they are taking. When a borrower runs into difficulty repaying the mortgage, the banks simply go after the guarantors, who find themselves in an equally precarious debt situation from which they can never escape. Instead of just the borrower losing his home, several people's lives can be ruined while the bank retains the property and then sells it off at a knock down price to speculators.

The government is finally bowing to pressure from street demonstrations, the courts, which are becoming reluctant to grant expulsion notices, and even the police who do not want to break down doors and drag wives and children from their homes. A Moroccan worker, Mohamed Aziz from Barcelona, actually achieved fame by taking his case to Brussels where he gained victory in the Court of Human Rights, which considered the clauses in small print inserted into his mortgage contract to be abusive. Spain's government has been forced to follow the ruling which is giving thousands more the chance to escape being evicted and is considering a law making repossession of the property, where justified, the end of a borrower's liability. But it is a tale without a happy ending. The judgment came too late to save Mr Aziz who had been evicted before the law came into force. His debt? Just eighty-five thousand Euros. Protecting families from eviction was the major platform of Ada Colau in her campaign to become mayor of Barcelona.

In the UK there have been reports that thousands of homeowners with interest only loans will face similar problems if they do not set aside funds to cover the capital at the end of the loan period. While borrowers should plan ahead, if they do not have enough to pay off the capital, surely after ten or twenty years, the value will have increased and the capital would represent a smaller percentage of the value enabling the borrower to extend the loan rather than face repossession. Where borrowers are of good faith and the project is financially viable, lenders must learn to be more flexible.

A reliable, trustworthy and efficient public service is what makes our democracies function. Housing, education and health services are the backbone of our societies and should not be considered as pure profit making enterprises. Suitable living accommodation, the health of the nation and education of our children are paramount to reduce or end poverty and for economic survival in an increasingly uncertain and precarious world.

Investment in France and Spain's public health services has always been at the forefront of their respective government's policy, but the crisis has regrettably led to cut backs in vital services. It seems inconceivable that Europe plans to follow the American way with its health services. Privatizing hospitals and selling off the nation's health to the highest bidder must be one of the most immoral ideas any government can contemplate. The crisis has led to many cases of people not being able to afford medical treatment with the risk of failing health and leading to more expensive treatment in order to cure serious illnesses. This is particularly relevant in the poorer nations where millions of people have little or no access to a health system and cannot afford the price of medicines.

Private health is a choice, which the rich can afford. But in our democratic societies, the majority of the people and the country need a modern and efficient health service. A healthy population is the basis of a prosperous society and economy. Prevention is better than cure, is a well-known adage and also makes economic sense since it is likely to save more costly treatment at a later stage. Annual medical tests should be obligatory to diagnose health problems in order for treatment to be provided at the earliest possible stage. Programmes aimed at children to warn of the dangers of smoking, alcohol, drugs etc., while exhorting the importance of healthy food should be part of every government's health service.

Naturally all this comes at a cost. And this cost could be born in part by the pharmaceutical industry, which makes massive profits from its drugs and has profited from privatization. Clearly these companies have to invest in costly research, which is fundamental to finding new drugs but, like in other sectors of the economy, we need to find a balance between making reasonable profits and the public interest.

This is something Tullio Simoncini, an Italian doctor, has learnt to his cost. After years of research he is credited with diagnosing that cancer could be caused by a fungus, which, in his view, can be eradicated by using sodium bicarbonate. Not surprisingly he was hounded by the pharmaceutical industry, which derided his findings and he was removed from the Italian medical list. He is now conducting his research in Japan. Whether his findings are right or not it demonstrates how big business will use its power to discredit anyone or anything likely to affect its profits.

In the USA, Michelle Obama has been working tirelessly for years to change the eating habits of her fellow citizens.

Her "Let's Move" initiative, similar to Jamie Oliver's goals in the UK, are aimed at switching the fast food culture in homes and schools across the country with a Mediterranean style diet. She is attempting to ban excessive use of sugar and salt, reduce the consumption of red meat, sweets and cakes and increase cereals, fruit and vegetables in everyone's diet. This is not just to make the people healthier but reduce the two hundred billion dollars the US spends each year on healthcare for treatment relating to excessive weight. Eastern and Northern Europe, with a similar food culture, is affected by alcohol related diseases while in southern Europe the Mediterranean diet linked to wine consumption has been proven to offer a longer and healthier life. While binge drinking has become one of the scourges of British society among both men and women of all ages, on the continent, cafes and bars are places to meet and mix, full of young men and women who also drink, but are rarely prone to end up drunk in the streets. The drinks industry has become too powerful. Through the use of advertising and marketing it has managed to convince consumers, especially the young, that alcohol consumption and lifestyle go together. Anyone ordering non alcoholic drinks in hotels, bars and restaurants is seen as an outcast with a personality disorder. .Perhaps it is time to consider adding nutrition courses to school curriculums in primary schools. This would teach children to take care of their health at an early age and encourage them to grow up on healthier diets and avoid dependence on alcohol.

Keeping fit is of course vital for our lives, but I fail to understand the fad of fitness centres and exercise clubs. Our lifestyle chasing population, which prefers to take elevators, drive or take taxis for short distances, seems prepared to spend a great deal of money to sacrifice themselves on machines, which look as if they were designed for medieval torture chambers, in order to get physical exercise, which can be provided by climbing stairs or just walking. Those with larger wallets even employ their own personal trainer.

Pensions are another source of conflict and a potential time bomb. The state simply cannot afford to pay for an ageing population with longer life expectancy and less working people able to contribute. Every Western government is facing the same situation. Many countries in Western Europe rely on state pensions, which the public does not want to see changed, believing it to be an essential part of their social security system. But demographics and the cost of running pension schemes means private pensions are going to have to become a necessity to enable people to have enough money to provide for retirement. There is an argument for early paid retirement for people in factories or engaged in physical and hazardous jobs, but the rest of the population should consider whether it is worthwhile ending their professional lives until they have enough funds set aside. Many professional and creative people actually expect to continue working, long after the official retirement age. Keeping active, mentally and physically, is considered vital for our health.

But the future of private pensions, which is a multi billion pound industry, could be at risk due to the globalization of the financial markets. Increased unregulated financial speculation has seen stocks rise and fall overnight while pension fund investors are investing over the long-term. More stability is needed to protect people's savings from another banking crisis. The UK has a long established pensions industry, which unfortunately has come under criticism due to the abuse in the management of many corporate pension funds due to high charges and fees and the rules constantly changing. One such arrangement is the creation of the QROPS (qualifying recognized overseas pension). This is a scheme, conjured up by the financial services industry, to enable non-UK resident pensioners to transfer their pension pot to an overseas, i.e. offshore jurisdiction, where the money will be invested on their behalf, less fees and charges of course, free of UK tax and most important, free of inheritance tax. And it is legal, approved by the British Government. British expats are therefore treated more favourably than UK resident pensioners. Explain to me the logical reason for this other than to benefit wealthy pensioners and offshore investment funds?

The British Government recently opened a breach in the financial wall with its decision to abolish annuities for pensioners. The insurance industry was shocked since it has been making a great deal of money from fees and charges managing all the pension contributions. On the face of it the decision seems to be a fair move enabling the holders of pension funds to exercise more control over their own savings. But the downside is a risk that with money in their pockets many people will simply spend their pensions and rely on the state to look after them when they run out of cash. Perhaps it was not a well thought out plan and needs more thought.

The social networks and mobile phones have perhaps been the catalyst for the most radical change in our society. People can communicate with each other instantaneously regardless of where they live in the world, exchanging messages, text and images. The adage of everyone having their fifteen minutes of fame has been shortened to ten seconds of fame. People have used modern technology to show and promote themselves as they go about their daily lives. "Selfies" is a new word to describe the narcissistic personality disorder of more and more people taking images of themselves. What used to be the preserve of professional photographers is now open to anybody who can take a picture, using their phone the moment something happens and then downloading it to the media.

The Internet has created a world in which there is no respite from the constant barrage of publicity and news on mobile phones, iPads and computers. It is twenty-four hours a day, seven days a week. But do we really need all the products and services available, many of which serve no real purpose.

People have become so dependent on their mobile phones it is like a drug. Waiting for a message to come through leads to anxiety and stress. Being able to communicate at all times has become so vital that panic sets in should a phone or computer fail to function. Psychologists have recommended that like Alcoholics Anonymous there is a need for group therapy for addicts to switch off and take a break from being connected.

However instead of leading to extended relationships and physical contact, the result of this technology and the digital age has been to isolate people more than ever. Studies have shown that young people tend to spend more time alone in front of their computers in a virtual world shutting themselves off from the real world. And the text and images they see are just as likely to have been modified or copied to the extent that the truth is becoming harder to detect.

I receive a constant barrage of email messages from social network sites trying to entice me to click on to their sites. Facebook announces – to use their favourite term – "you have notifications pending". These are supposed to be from my so-called "friends", most of whom I have never heard of. Why, if Facebook is so useful, do they need to send me emails to seduce me into clicking on to my site? I also admit to not being a twitter or tweeter, if that is how to describe users. I really cannot see any purpose in texting short comments and I seem to be able to get on with my life without any undue hardship. There are now too many intrusions of unwanted messages and I have learnt never to provide any personal information. If I want to send confidential messages I prefer to use my email provider. And learning that my messages might be intercepted by the NSA or hacked makes it even more necessary to change tactics. The rule is never to open unknown links, however enticing and never give bank details or send money to unknown sources

One of the most fundamental recent social changes has been the demands and introduction of laws to allow gay marriages and the conception and adoption of children. This shift in family values has divided people in every country whatever their religious and cultural traditions. In Ireland it needed a referendum to decide and despite being a strong catholic country the people voted overwhelmingly in favour. Whether governments are for or against these measures, they have been given far more attention than they deserve in parliament and especially in the media, taking into account the demands of such a small segment of the population. If gay men and women wish to live with each other it is their prerogative, but I believe that the concept of marriage should be reserved for husbands and wives to preserve the status of the family. This seems to be the current view of the majority of the population but the controversy also reflects the generation gap.

Couples used to build their lives together, for better or for worse. In today's ephemeral world there is simply not enough time. Relationships are no longer for life with couples changing partners on a regular basis. People expect too much from their partners whose image is more important than their personality or character. This is especially true among celebrities who marry on a whim rather than for genuine love and move on when their partner does not match their expectations, either financially, professionally or in bed. It gives rise to the notion that men and women are totally incompatible; the Venus and Mars syndrome. We are raised from childhood with totally different ideas which forge our identity. Toys are different, education is different, we dress differently – most of the time – think differently, have different eating and drinking habits, drive differently, have contrasting views on where to live and take vacations, women tend to love and men detest, shopping, we have different tastes on everything, enjoy different leisure and sporting pursuits and differ on how to educate and bring up kids. Whose idea was it to ever get men and women to live together?

The rise in the number of Western couples paying for and adopting babies from poor countries in Africa and Asia and the right of girls and women to undergo abortions are other controversial topics, which deal with personal situations. It is one of those issues where a country cannot fix its own laws as they are simply circumvented by going to another country. There needs to be agreement at international level.

Societies can only function if there is respect. Yet we live in a world with a growing lack of it. The West in contrast to

Asian society has little respect for older people and today young people have a tendency to ignore authority whether it is parental, school or the law. How often do young people give up their seats for ladies or the elderly? Modern society has created new forms of abuse. Mobile phone users are among the worst offenders, talking loudly on public transport, cinemas, theatres, restaurants etc., oblivious to other people. Noise is another contentious issue. Loud music and late night revelling in the streets have made residents in certain areas of our cities especially angry. In Madrid, which has a culture of late night eating and drinking, the local authority, bowing to pressure from residents, has been forcing some bars to close by 1a.m. If there is too much noise in the street it has something to do with cigarette laws, forcing smokers outdoors. Why do motorbikes make so much noise? Can't the government simply force manufacturers to fit silencers to reduce their impact? Road rage is another relatively recent phenomenon, incomprehensible in a civilized society. The problem has grown in proportion to the number of vehicles using the same streets or roads, their role as a status symbol, people's selfish thinking of how to drive and modern day stress. Pet owners too have become thoughtless by owning dangerous animals regardless of the risk to other people, especially babies and children. The treatment and abuse of women and children is a growing problem often linked to differences in cultures and religions as a result of massive immigration and a lack of education.

Respect for others comes not just from education, but ultimately from the behaviour of peer leaders and governments. And the lack of confidence and trust in our politicians and institutions explains why our society is failing.

Nowhere is this more evident than in the United States, the world's richest country yet one where poverty affects millions of its citizens. In 2008 on the eve of the Presidential Elections, I attended a Democrats Abroad event in Paris. It was filled with young black people whose faces were gleaming. The popularity of Barack Obama had given them hope and a dream for the future. But these were French citizens, not Americans and I thought what could they expect from a black US president? But it did not matter, for these young French people and for millions of black Americans, Obama was going to change their lives. The tragic events in Charleston, Ferguson, Missouri and shooting of police officers in New York, was a stark reminder that in his second term in office , Barack Obama has failed to address the problems or improve the economic situation of the black community and segregation still exists.

Despite politicians calling for education, education, education, governments have been constantly tinkering with the education system and they have become more unequal with flawed results. The adage, "if it ain't broke, don't fix it", is ignored. I remember when the eleven plus determined who went to grammar school or secondary school and the system seemed to function well. Most of us wore school uniforms as a sign of identity, loyalty and to instill a sense of discipline. Since then as our society has become more multicultural, governments have pandered to the requirements of immigrant populations and political correctness set in. Today's youth reject conformity. So instead of uniforms, boys wear baggy jeans and baseball caps back to front while girls prance around in torn jeans and bare midriffs – a new form of uniformity. The wealthier families still segregate their children from the rest of the population through private education, even in the poorest countries. France had a first class education system covering the whole country, but it has been allowed to deteriorate through excessive political interference. The recent proposals to modify the education system have been met with considerable opposition by parents and teachers. History is being rewritten to take into account religious affiliation and ethnic minorities. However the country still maintains its elite schools churning out top civil servants and government officials and a network of Lycees around the world, while Britain has a strange way of calling its top establishments, public schools, when they are strictly private.

The cost of university education is a source of contention. It is argued that university education does not always prepare students for those careers, where future job opportunities lie. The crisis has shown how the most educated youth in history is being forced to accept low paid part time work or jobs for which they have not been trained and thousands of Europe's young are emigrating to be replaced by unqualified immigrants; a recipe for economic and social disaster. University education must not be seen as a way to maintain an elitist education system. It has to be available to as many students as possible regardless of their wealth. More attention needs to be given to maths, science, languages, culture, art, literature and history. These subjects are the foundation of our societies and must not be neglected to satisfy cost saving measures.

The high cost of education is leading to more and more students dropping out through the double whammy of a lack of funds to finance their courses and being burdened with debt for years. Universities and colleges cannot be considered profit centres for a few academics and chancellors. In Great Britain UCAS has been criticized for the way it advertises and handles admissions. Governments must lower the cost to avoid putting our nation's future in jeopardy. The challenge is going to be to find the right jobs for students with degrees. And to find the right jobs the emphasis has to be on training, science and technology. Yet the privatization of education has led to the proliferation of too many courses, many of which are unregulated or downright fraudulent, awarding diplomas found to be worthless in the job markets. Perhaps more emphasis needs to be made on training and apprenticeships.

Erasmus has been one of the most successful creations of the European Union. Encouraging European students to live and study in another member state where they can learn the language and culture has been one of the most successful means of bringing Europeans together. It is a major advance and vital for the continent's economic, cultural and social future. Cuts will put our future in jeopardy and must be avoided. Education has to be the most valuable asset to pass down to our children.

As the world becomes smaller and the population of the developing countries increases, there is a growing necessity to educate our children. UN Organizations and the governments of the richer Western countries cannot fail to recognize that our own future economic and social prosperity is at stake. But governments cannot take over the role of parents. There has to be more parental responsibility. And this is becoming increasingly difficult in an age of children born out of wedlock, single parents, gay marriages, broken homes, unemployment, poverty, children born to immigrant families with different cultures and the addiction to social networks and violent videos. The common factor is a lack of authority and guidance.

We have to accept that in fifty years time our societies may well look totally unrecognizable. But whatever the future holds, preserving the family, housing, education and health services will need investment, and the money has to be found for what are the pillars of a democratic and prosperous world. Politicians should consider that a nation, which neglects the health and wellbeing of its people and fails to educate its children, is doomed.

Sexual Morality:

Morality, like art, means drawing a line someplace.

Oscar Wilde

The sex industry is one of the largest in the world, on a par with the arms and pharmaceutical sectors. Can anyone doubt that the increase in pregnancies, sex offences and abuse of women and children is not linked to the ease with which explicit sex is available in magazines, movies, the Internet and videos or openly available in sex shops? In addition schools have introduced sex education in the curriculum and there is a plethora of TV programmes and discussions coupled with endless magazine and newspaper articles about sex. I believe there is a correlation and governments should begin to crack down on the most violent video games and accessible pornographic material as well as attempt to reduce the amount of sex which is being fed to the people on a daily basis.

The recent admission by the British Government that prostitution alone generates £5 billion a year shows the amount of money involved. Sex has become vital for the media's financial survival. No day goes past without the publication of images of people's sex lives or showing where and with whom they hang out and more often than not, what they hang out. As already mentioned it used to be limited to the gutter press and tabloids but now even Internet providers have succumbed to the use of providing titillating irrelevant details of anyone who purports to be a celebrity, most of whom nobody has ever heard of. There is no escape.

Is it all really necessary? Female, and male, bodies have been used as models for artists ever since Adam and Eve met for lunch. The invention of photographic images during the Victorian era heralded a market for portraits of scantily clothed ladies. The 1950s was the age of the pin up, always discreet, until the breakthrough, if that is the right word, in the sixties, when Hugh Hefner brought his bunnies to the world. What followed was a plethora of sexy magazines with nudity gradually becoming more explicit until full frontal nudity became the norm filling whole shelves in newsagents. It is far removed from the page three girls baring their breasts, which sold the tabloids or the innocent comedy shows of Benny Hill with his sexual innuendos or Dick Emery whose sketches were full of gay characters, some of which might well upset gay groups today.

As taboos seemed to disappear, erotic movies and magazines became ever more adventurous until unfettered pornography took over with the proliferation of sex clubs, magazines, videos and the Internet. For years sex in early movies was restricted to a long embrace and then a cut to a couple smoking in bed, no need for explicit details. Today it is the smoking that gets censored. It seems directors compete to film the most erotic, artistic, sensuous love scene with their stars, who climb on top of each other and writhe about, always explaining at interviews for awards ceremonies that "It was necessary for the story."

Every young generation likes to believe that it invented sex. But it has been with us since long before the Greek and Roman era, which, as every cinemagoer knows, indulged in orgies. Between 100 and 800 AD, the Moche civilization in northern Peru educated its people through erotic, even pornographic, pottery and ceramics. Is this where the word "sexpot" originated? Little is known about what happened during the medieval age except for the alleged lust of the Vikings, but sex was definitely alive and thriving throughout the Renaissance in Italy, the Elizabethan and Regency periods, the French Court and through to the Victorian and Edwardian ages. The Kama Sutra originated in Asia, which may have something to do with the growth in their population. After the Second World War things were a little drab until the 1950s when Elvis Presley came along introducing rock and roll and vinyl pop records. Teddy Boys with their long coats and thick soled suede shoes hit the streets and the teenager era began. Then the world moved into the swinging sixties in London and the advent of the mini skirt and mini car. Soon after passing my driving test – miraculously at the first attempt – I became the lucky owner of a red mini thanks to the generosity of my grandmother who provided half of the five hundred pound purchase price adding to the hard earned savings I had managed to put aside. The Beatles and Rolling Stones took over the music scene, Kings Road became the centre of the world and I had a tiny pad in Chelsea to listen to Sgt Pepper's Lonely Hearts Club Band.

Everybody still alive believes this is when and where sex actually began. In reality swinging London was limited to a couple of discos and pubs in Chelsea and house prices and cars became the main topic of conservation at dinner parties. America then took back control over our love lives, due primarily to the California sound and the Vietnam War. The beach boys epitomized the romantic freedom of driving convertibles across the sand in the sun while the flower power, which hit San Francisco in the 70s, was designed to liberate our sexual inhibitions. *Make love not war* was the symbol for a whole generation. Great news for the young male population who flocked to California thinking they would find an abundant supply of female partners available for free sex but ended up in gay bars and clubs in Haight Ashbury.

Yet all this supposed freedom has resulted in an increase of sexual problems, disease, sex abuse, domestic violence and prostitution. When problems occur, and every relationship goes through difficult times, instead of proposing harmony between couples the so-called agony aunts advise people to engage in extra marital sex, have several partners, separate and even get divorced as a means to improve their sex lives as if sex is all that matters in a relationship. The result is often unhappier marriages and the unnecessary destruction of families with the consequent damaging effects on children. The increase in immigration from the sub continents of Africa and Asia coupled with an absence of integration policies has been a major factor in the abuse of women and children. Ethnic minority groups with different religions and cultures have failed to adapt to Western society and young immigrant men, faced with an abundance of pornographic or erotic material, do not seem to know where to draw the line.

Yet if sex is so freely available why is prostitution booming with a seemingly inexhaustible supply of clients? It does seem to confirm studies which suggest that whereas men want sex, women want something else. The problem is that not enough men seem to understand what that something else is. Human Rights groups rightly call for action against the rape of Indian girls, female genital mutilation and the abduction of Nigerian girls by extremist Islamic group, Boko Haram. But they do not seem concerned about the number of Nigerian prostitutes in the West enslaved by Nigerian or East European Mafia gangs, the domestic violence in Europe which kills hundreds of women every year, the abuse of children, paedophile cases, the sex scandals which erupted in Rotherham and other British cities or the revelations that over one hundred thousand girls are mutilated in the USA and in Europe. So where did we go wrong?

Today, if one reads the press and magazines, it seems we live in a world of frustrated men and women relying on sex therapy for their survival. Clinics provide help for premature ejaculation or erectile dysfunction, known in the trade as ED, or how to achieve orgasms, without which a woman's life is incomplete. In my day sex was trial and error, learning as you go and we seemed to get along with far less problems than today. It is a wonder that we do not have a European Sex Commissioner in Brussels to bring in EU norms with manuals of operation: what to do, when, how, where and with whom to do it.

With people living longer and not wanting to lose out, pharmacies can't find enough space to store Viagra. Pornography has become so mechanical it can be more erotic watching Texas oil pumps in operation. My solution to cure sex addicts or predators is to send them for a week to a German nudist camp. It would probably be far more effective in curbing their sexual urges than medical help.

Masturbation, which was once frowned on with warnings to men that it would fall off if touched, is now seen as a perfectly normal and healthy activity for both men and women. For anybody worried about the spread of sexually transmitted diseases this is certainly the safest way to have sex. There are gay men, lesbian women and bisexuals who have to be catered for. Even the Eurovision song contest finds them. Governments have caved in to the gay lobbies to permit gay marriages and adoption and we now have a plethora of gay clubs, bars and even festivals. But has anyone considered the legal ramifications when gay couples separate or want to divorce?

Sex tourism has become a growth sector. Amsterdam became notorious for its red light district, while the ease of travel made possible by long haul flights, led to Bangkok becoming a sought after sex destination where every taste was catered for. The age at which schools begin sex education gets lower and lower and people are surprised that a 12-year-old becomes a mother and 13-year-old a father: reduce the age to learn to drive and kids will want to drive. Teach kids sex and they will want to practice what they have been taught. It is natural.

The result of our obsession with sex is the rise in the number of court cases, or at least an increase in publicity, relating to sex abusers, rapists and paedophiles and political figures, pop stars and TV personalities forced to face up to their past being increasingly exposed. The Church too has been forced to admit its own failings with regard to paedophile cases. The murder, rape and abuse of women and children in wars have been receiving a great deal of media attention. But this is a direct consequence of the increase in conflicts in many poor areas of the world and the number of uneducated young men, even children, handed uniforms and weapons and given the power to use them against civilian victims. Prostitution may be thriving due perhaps to women suffering from these conflicts and economic hardship. There has been an influx of poor immigrant women from East Europe and Africa pushed towards Europe by trafficking gangs who keep them in slave-like conditions. So far the government's response has been to crack down on clients by imposing fines. Yet they seem to be unwilling or unable to remove the prostitutes from the streets or curb the violence despite the intervention of personalities such as Angelina Jolie.

Education from an early age is the only solution to achieve more respect for women, especially in those countries in Africa and the Muslim societies of North Africa and the Middle East, where women's rights are virtually inexistent. In India the violence and rape of women and children is a direct result of the caste system.

Perhaps there also needs to be more control over the content of films, magazines, videos and the Internet. But we could also change mentalities if women, and some men, stopped projecting or selling their bodies as sex objects. We definitely need to draw a line somewhere.

Military Morality

War is the massacre of people who do not know each other for the profit of people who know each other but do not massacre each other.

Paul Valery

2014 was the centennial anniversary of the First World War, which was arguably the most wasteful conflict the world has ever seen. Four years of stalemate during which millions of young men were sent to their death, mown down by enemy machine guns, blasted by artillery fire or choked by gas in a matter of minutes in a vain attempt to gain a few metres of territory. The people who gave the orders for this bloodbath were not there. They were sitting in huts or buildings far behind the front line busy peering over maps with lines, dots and models as if it were a game of chess, with no thought for the safety of the men under their command. In fact it is necessary to go back to the Battle of Solferino in 1859 to find kings and generals actually leading their troops into battle.

Those lucky enough to survive only benefited from a short period of peace, during which they had to face hardship during the great depression, before they were engulfed in another major world conflict, which tore Europe, and the world, apart. Nazi Germany engaged in the systematic mass murder of millions of families who happened to be of the Jewish faith, gypsies or any other people they disapproved of. The world discovered this unprecedented crime against humanity when the camps of Auschwitz, Buchenwald, Dachau, Mauthausen Treblinka etc. were liberated in 1945. France, which prides itself on its resistance movement, must also accept responsibility for the deportation of thousands of Jewish children to the death camps and for the poor treatment of Spanish republican refugees who crossed the Pyrenees and were placed in camps along the Languedoc coast.

The war ended the same year after Dresden was bombed to oblivion and Hiroshima and Nagasaki were destroyed by the atomic bomb and the world entered a new era. The legacy of the Second World War is the European Union, which united the continent and allowed future generations to live through a period of economic prosperity and peace. It also led to the annexation of Eastern Europe by Russia to create the USSR. In contrast, the legacy of the Korean War was a divided peninsula, which still exists today. In the age of air travel, satellite communications and the Internet it seems inconceivable that more than sixty years after the armistice was declared on the 38th parallel, that a nation – North Korea and its people – remain totally isolated from the rest of the world. The biggest threat to the West from North Korean leader, Kim Jong Un, is if he sets a trend for his hairstyle.

The 20th century was not only the most destructive in history in terms of lives lost but also one which saw the greatest advances in technology. The risk of a further war in Europe was averted due to the proliferation of atomic weapons, which divided the continent into two power blocks neither of which wished to be obliterated. The Cold War lasted until the fall of the Berlin War. The year 1989 was a watershed. While the nations of Western Europe were joined together in the then Common Market, the USSR disintegrated into separate independent nation states losing much of its empire. The gradual expansion of the European Union and NATO eastwards is one of the reasons for Russia's opposition to Ukraine's attachment to the West and its annexation of the Crimea and the conflict in East Ukraine. One hundred years ago any similar aggression would have resulted in another European war. Today, perhaps we are fortunate that the world is interconnected and it is financial and economic interests which prevail, although it has not prevented regional conflicts in the Balkans, Georgia and the use of arms in the Ukraine.

The cemeteries and war memorials scattered across northern France and in Belgium stand as a permanent reminder of the last wars in Europe. But have kings, queens, presidents, political and military leaders or governments learned the lessons of the massacres, the destruction, the injuries, hardship, and the displacement or exodus of thousands of refugees and economic damage caused by wars? Not yet. Many Nazis were allowed to escape punishment and Turkey still refuses to acknowledge the genocide of Armenians in 1915 while dictators with blood on their hands seem to end their days in comfortable retirement. The Lion Mound south of Brussels commemorates the battle of Waterloo fought exactly two hundred years ago. Napoleon, who lost the battle, is still revered by the French. But was he a great administrator and general or megalomaniac dictator whose dream of a European empire led to a decade of conflict between 1804 and 1815 costing the lives of between three and five million military personnel and civilians?

Since the end of the Second War there have been military conflicts fought every year somewhere in the world. Nowhere is this brought home more than in Washington. The Vietnam memorial has 58000 victims' names engraved on the black marble wall and in Arlington Cemetery, where the grounds have been extended, in section 60, recently erected crosses with engraved names of young men, stand as a poignant reminder of America's military involvement and sacrifice of its youth in Iraq and Afghanistan.

Little is said about the role of photojournalists and war photographers in changing the attitudes of the American people through the impact of their photographs. During the Spanish Civil War and 2nd World War photographers such as Robert Capa were praised for their action pictures, keeping a record of events which were often used for propaganda purposes. This all changed during the Vietnam War when

British photographer, Don McCullin, working for the Sunday Times, became world famous for his dramatic images of the conflict, which led to sometimes violent anti-war demonstrations across America. He also covered the violence in Cyprus, Northern Ireland and in Biafra, where his images of starving children shocked the world. Today while photojournalists still risk their lives in the world's hotspots, video coverage and mobile phones are able to provide an instant coverage of dramatic events. While Western Europe has seen an end to religious and political conflicts, which ravaged the continent for over 2000 years, it did not prevent the ethnic violence and genocide in the Balkans. There have been wars in Algeria, Biafra, Cambodia, Chechnya, Congo, the Falklands, Iraq, Israel, Lebanon, Libya, Mali, Rwanda, Somalia, Sudan, Yemen and Syria, which is now in its fourth year. In Nigeria the Boko Haram radical Islamic group has extended its conflict into Chad, Niger and Cameroun. This year is the twentieth anniversary of the genocide in Rwanda, which cost eight hundred thousand lives while the West watched. Ban Ki-moon, current secretary general of the UN, described it as "the shame of the United Nations".

If there is one single example of the futility of war it is the conflict in Syria. Nobody seems to know for sure who is fighting whom. The only result so far is that the country has been devastated with parts of towns and cities reduced to rubble and the economy ruined. Neighbouring countries have taken in millions of families, housing them in camps putting a strain on their own resources, while thousands are risking their lives to seek asylum in the West. Young European Muslims or those who have converted to Islam, are heading in the opposite direction to take up arms against the Assad regime or join radical groups. The West has been learning about the differences between Sunni and Shia, the two principal Muslim sects. Meanwhile while trying to appease Muslim communities in Europe, the West does nothing to help the persecuted Christian communities who have been living in the region for centuries and who face death or deportation. What will it achieve? There can be no winners, only losers – invariably families and children. While it is certain that Assad like so many dictators before him, will eventually be removed or step down, this could lead to an even worse situation with ethnic groups fighting each other for control of the country, or what is left of it. The West has been standing back not wishing to be embroiled in an unwinnable conflict, which due to the rise of the Islamic radical group, ISIS, could extend from Syria and Iraq to Lebanon and even Israel and Iran. The seemingly never ending conflict in Syria and Iraq has made the Middle East a powder keg as the Sunni, Shia and other religious groups linked to Al Qaida, fight each other, all intent on taking power. Iran has been seen as the principal nuclear threat by the USA, but the softening up of relations between the two countries is now seen as a threat by Saudi Arabia, intent on maintaining its influence in the Middle East. It is inconceivable that any state in the Middle East would contemplate using a nuclear weapon. In such a small area it would destroy every country. What cannot be ignored is that sixty percent of Iran's population was born after the revolution and the young population wishes to become part of the twenty first century. How long they will be prepared to remain subdued by the country's religious leaders? If France had not been so tolerant and naive with Ayatollah Khomeini perhaps there would have been a totally different outcome to the revolution.

Since the end of the Iraqi war, the Kurdish people seem to have been granted a measure of peace. But there has been little discussion about the creation of a Kurdistan nation encompassing territory in Turkey, Iraq and Iran, which seems just as valid as creating a Palestinian state. The never ending violence in Syria and breakdown of order in Iraq with the advance of ISIS, the ultra radical Islamic group, poses a renewed threat to the Kurds and has finally led to the gradual increase in military intervention by some of the Western powers. By attacking the Kurds, Turkey has made the situation even more confusing. While the overriding aim has to be to prevent the creation of an Islamic State in Iraq, the

US, of course, is preoccupied with defending its interests in the Kurdish controlled oil fields. The invasion of Iraq seems to have opened a Pandora's Box of ethnic violence, the scale of which could not have been foreseen by the Western allies. It only reinforces Oscar Wilde's comment: "It is easier to get into something, than to get out of it."

After fifty years, the Palestinian problem seems no closer to a solution. With its divided territory it will not be easy to create an independent state. And the reconciliation pact to form a unity government between the Fatah movement of Mahmoud Abbas on the left bank and Hamas, which maintains control of Gaza and still seeks the destruction of Israel, is unlikely to change Israel's stance. On the other hand Israel's policy of confiscating land on the left bank to build homes for Israeli settlers only exacerbates the problem. Despite the tunnels and the missiles used by Hamas, it seems inconceivable that a country which still laments the deportation and murder of millions of Jewish children during the holocaust, seems indifferent to the death of so many women and children in Palestine through its bombing campaign which is also leaving thousands of children with possibly, permanent psychological damage. While the bombing makes any progress towards peace or a Palestinian state more remote and every Palestinian death nurtures more hatred towards Israel, culminating with the spate of attacks within Israel, there are other factors to contend with. These are demographic, environmental and geographic issues. The territory of Gaza is limited and it is imperative to find more land to cope with a fast growing population. This is a logistical fact and if not resolved will lead to overcrowding and a consequent further deterioration of living standards for the Palestinian population with the potential risk of a social explosion and more violence. The Gaza strip faces the sea on one side and Israel on the other, so where can this extra territory be found?

Would it be possible to extend into Sinai with Egypt's agreement or is there any chance Israel would consider transferring part of the Negev desert in exchange for land on the West bank? Water is also at the heart of the problems which need resolving and perhaps overrides political and religious differences. The river Jordan which flows into the Red Sea has to provide water for Jordan, Lebanon, Palestine, Syria and Israel. Sharing this vital resource is something every country in the region needs to accept. The only certainty is that time is running out and a solution must be found to extend the Palestinian controlled territory if there is to be any chance of lasting peace in the region.

Jerusalem is another contentious issue with both Palestinians and Israelis claiming it as the capital. Given its religious significance, I believe the UN, which has been conspicuously absent from the current ISIS violence, should take over the running of the city as a world heritage site for people from all over the world whatever their faith. This would mean that the Al-Aqsa mosque and esplanade, churches, synagogues and the Wailing Wall would cease to be the preserve of followers of their respective religions; a naïve dream, perhaps, but one, which could reduce the conflict and lead to a peaceful settlement. Tzipi Livni, current Israeli Justice Minister, has stated that, "There is no way to resolve a religious war."

Regional conflicts have also erupted in Central and South America, Africa and Asia as one dictatorship is ousted for another. As in all wars the victims are the vast majority of the people while the leaders who oppose each other usually end up retiring to a life of luxury in a friendly state, which often means somewhere in the West.

The Crimean and Ukrainian conflict has exposed the weakness of NATO to react at a time when the economic crisis has forced many countries to reduce their defence budgets. More than twenty years ago I was invited to the US Naval Headquarters in Grosvenor Square, London to a geopolitical briefing on US military and economic strategy in Europe. At the time the region seen by the US as posing the greatest threat to Western interests, was the Caucasus. They have been proven right. The break up of the USSR created new states, Georgia, Azerbaijan, Armenia, Moldavia, Ukraine, Kazakhstan with vast oil and gas reserves around the Black, Aral and Caspian Seas. These new states together with Estonia, Lithuania and Latvia which joined the European Union were left with minority Russian populations bringing with it the rise of separatist movements, now backed by Moscow. The accusations levelled against Russia by the West of violating international law, rings hollow when recent historical events are taken into account. The West did not seek approval of the UN Security Council when it invaded Iraq, attacked Serbia, declared Kosovo independent, intervened in Afghanistan or sent drones over Pakistan. Lord Palmerston, the British prime minister, accurately summed up geo political reasoning which often leads to armed conflict. "We have no friends, only interests."

It seems inconceivable that in this century two European states – Russia and Ukraine – can engage in military conflict to resolve a regional political issue, which has resulted in the death of more than five thousand citizens. Who gave arms to gangs of thugs hell bent on killing and destruction and who callously blew up a civilian airline with two hundred and ninety-eight innocent passengers, which happened to be flying harmlessly over its territory? The Russians do not seem to be concerned about finding and arresting the perpetrators and the West is going to need all its negotiating powers to resolve the present crisis. Russia must take much of the blame but the sanctions imposed are unlikely to have any impact on Mr Putin, who controls the tap on Western Europe's gas supplies. The greatest risk to Russia is the fall in the price of oil below eighty dollars. The recent drop to around fifty dollars, makes its own extraction in the Siberian oil fields unprofitable. This applies to many oil producing nations in Latin America and Asia, which are facing economic problems due to the dramatic collapse in the price. Is this the result of market forces or a deliberate policy engineered by certain powerful interests as part of their long-term geopolitical strategy? For consumers, the law of oil is that when the price rises, so does the price at petrol stations, but a fall in the price never seems to reach the pumps quite as fast.

The majority of European nation states plus the USA, Canada and members of the NATO alliance, seem unable to reach agreement on the issues at stake. Europe is going to need a review of its defence policies if it is to retain its influence in world affairs. President Obama has pledged a substantial sum in an effort to help Europe and Nato make a greater contribution in dealing with the world's trouble spots; a message that Europe is going to have to become involved more often whether it wants to or not and may need to consider increasing its own defence budget, not reduce it. Europe's southern borders are a major risk. Middle Eastern and Asian migrants reach Greece via Turkey, and while Italy has been facing an invasion of thousands of migrants from North Africa, for years it has had to cope with criminal gangs crossing the Adriatic from Albania and the Balkan countries.

The growth in the Muslim population of Europe coupled with growing influence of radical Islam, poses the greatest threat to world peace. Western governments have been negligent in dealing with this situation, which has been simmering for decades, preferring to ignore the problem rather than take positive action. Even the terrorist bombing campaigns in Europe's capitals, of which the 2004 Madrid Atocha station bombing was by far the most destructive in terms of loss of life, has not led to a real crack down on radical groups often living in the deprived suburban areas of many Western cities. Populated by ethnic minorities and suffering from unemployment and crime, these suburbs have given rise to a new form of criminal – European terrorists. Instead of foreign operators we now face an increase in home grown terrorists, trained and radicalized by Salafist or Al Qaida leaders who operate in Europe. Incredibly, Salafist imams in Europe's mosques, Islamic schools and prisons have been allowed to preach their ideas and indoctrinate young Muslims, who for personal factors feel rejected by Western society, as well as disillusioned Europeans. Most young people find a need to belong to a group, but the granting of dual nationality and passports to immigrant families from Asia and Africa has resulted in a loss of roots and divided loyalty. Access to the Internet and social networks, has given young Muslims the opportunity to find a purpose within the Islamic movement leading to thousands leaving Europe for Syria and Iraq. Ceuta and Melilla, Spain's enclaves in Morocco, have become recruitment centres for jihadists with Islamic spiritual leaders openly indoctrinating unemployed young Muslims and illegal immigrants living in camps or the city's poorer areas, where the Muslim population tends to live. Even in Paris, before the Charlie Hebdo massacre, salafists were allowed to hand out copies of the Qur'an in the streets. It is hardly surprising that many of the prisoners released from Guantanamo have rejoined radical Islamic groups. The abuse, torture and humiliation they suffered could only instill a hatred of the West, which seems lost in what is a new ball game without rules, where terror, bombing, summary executions and the abduction of women and children have become commonplace. After the publication of Charlie Hebdo, there were mass demonstrations and riots in many Muslim countries but few if any of the demonstrators could ever have heard of the weekly newspaper or its content, evidence of how people are being manipulated for political or religious purposes and the chasm which divides the Occident from Islam.

Europe and North America have to face the hard truth and clamp down on the rise of Islamist extremists if they are to avoid the risk of more terrorism at home, even if this means deportation and stripping some people of their nationality. The "lone wolf" terrorist, often with no previous conviction and therefore hard to identity, poses perhaps the biggest threat to stability. We also need strict measures to combat illegal immigration which is bringing thousands of undocumented Asians and Africans to Europe without any idea of the number of potential terrorists in their midst. But there will be no end to the violence until we are all able to engage in dialogue with a tolerance and understanding of all religions. This applies to both the Western societies and particularly to the different

Islamic factions; the Shia, Sunni and other minority groups, which are waging war on each other across the Middle East and parts of Africa and Asia. Surely they must understand that their conflict is pointless and they must learn to live together in peace. Instead there is more violence from radical Islamic groups based in Afghanistan, Algeria, Chechnya, Libya, Malaysia, Mali, Morocco, Nigeria, Pakistan, Somalia, Sudan, Syria, Thailand and Yemen. These groups, all linked in one form or another to Al Qaida, some of whom with cells set up in Western Europe, pose the greatest threat to Europe and world peace. Algeria faces an uncertain future as the health of its ageing president, Abdelaziz Bouteflika, worsens with little or no plans for an orderly and peaceful succession. With over 65% of the largely Sunni Muslim population under thirty years old and more than 20% unemployed, the country could become a prime target for radical Islam and a potential threat on Europe's doorstep.

The role of the rich Arab states is ambiguous. The strong implantation of Wahhabism in Saudi Arabia and the Gulf States, seems to make their leaders reluctant to crack down on the radical factions in their midst and, even if not state funded, much of the financing of terrorist and radical groups originates from these countries. It would also be logical to think they would be the first to accept refugees from other Muslim countries and wish to become involved financially and politically as well as share the military task of trying to end the conflicts and bring peace to the region. So long as these Arab states remain important clients of the West, which happily sells arms and buys oil, spending money at Harrods, Louis Vuitton or Gucci, Western governments are reluctant to openly criticize them. The terrorist attack in Saudi Arabia could perhaps be the catalyst for a change in policy of the Saudi rulers suddenly faced with a serious threat within their own borders.

The major beneficiary from all the world's political and military conflicts is the arms industry, worth according to reports some one and a half trillion dollars a year, aided and abetted by the banking sector. The manufacture of powerful automatic weapons, aircraft, warships, submarines, all with advanced technology, satellite systems, radar, armoured vehicles, defence systems, sophisticated rockets, bombs and antipersonnel mines, are all produced by large corporations in the world's richest economies. Although they claim production is designed for defensive purposes, the export of arms is a highly lucrative, dangerous and immoral business. The Vietnam and Iraq conflicts made billions for US defence companies supplying weapons, bombs and aircraft causing the death of millions of military personnel, civilians and children. More bombs were dropped on Vietnam than during the whole of the Second World War. Mines left indiscriminately across South East Asia have been killing and maiming the population long after the ceasing of hostilities. Collateral damage has become a phrase to justify the death of innocent victims. Ilaria Alpi, an Italian journalist, was one of those victims. Killed in Somalia in 1994 together with a cameraman it is rumoured she had evidence of secret arms dealing involving the CIA or Italian military.

The USA leads the table of exporters followed by Russia, Germany, France, China and the UK. Not surprisingly the USA also has the largest defence budget, far ahead of China, Russia, UK, France and Japan. (see Appendix III) During the time I lived near Marseille, as a member of the US Navy League, I was regularly invited to visit warships of the US sixth fleet in port to take on supplies. Touring the ships and meeting the officers, crew and navy pilots, who too often risk their lives to protect the rest of us, was a unique opportunity to appreciate the military strength of the US.

However, so many weapons are being produced, transported and stored around the world by defence contractors as well as by unscrupulous international arms dealers, it has become increasingly difficult to control where they end up, and many terrorist groups have been able to get their hands on sophisticated weapons. Radical Islamists under the Al Qaida or ISIS banner have now made many regions of the world unstable and dangerous.

World peace cannot be taken for granted while governments allow defence contractors and military suppliers to continue to make and sell weapons of mass destruction regardless of the consequences in order to generate profits, and so long as geopolitical and economic interests are considered more important than the lives of the people.

Immigration Morality

We must learn to live together as brothers or perish together as fools.

Martin Luther King

Immigration and multiculturalism are taboo subjects, which politicians have always tried to avoid tackling. But the terrorist attack on the French weekly, Charlie Hebdo and kosher supermarket in Paris, which resulted in the death of 17 people, sent shockwaves across Europe. January 7, 2015 is a watershed. It was a wake-up call to deal with a growing problem, which can no longer be ignored. The failure of Western governments and the European Union to address the issues and establish clear policies has led to confusion, mass illegal immigration, the rise of ultra right wing parties and, regrettably, too many tragic incidents and loss of life. It is an issue high on the agenda at every election. And the questions, which need to be asked by Western governments are whether there is any need for more immigrants and shouldn't we be concentrating on improving the quality of life in the developing nations rather than face the gradual decline of our own nations into Third World countries? Fortress Europe may have to become a reality to preserve our way of life and security.

Immigration to Western Europe and the USA, which have historically been considered the ultimate goal for immigrants, has been based on two factors: 1: Refugees and asylum seekers escaping despotic regimes and 2: The need for workers. Today, these have been replaced by a new category of undocumented immigrants able to take advantage of global communication, ease of travel, the Internet and the opening of, or manned but porous, national borders. The vast majority are people without any resources, who simply like the idea of living in the richer Western economies rather than their own. They are not attracted to Europe as a whole, just Western Europe. And it has set off a potential time bomb.

People cross borders without papers, with forged or stolen documents, making a mockery of our laws and customs controls as well as fortunes for Mafia gangs and officials in transit countries, who are oblivious to their plight. Nobody can be certain how many die before reaching their chosen country and increasingly nobody knows how many actually succeed in evading what is left of our immigration controls and evaporate into Europe's towns and cities.

The mystery relating to the missing Malaysian Aircraft highlighted the problem of millions of missing or stolen passports, which can end up in the hands of criminals or illegal immigrants. How many people travel and are living under false identities? Airport customs officers neglect checking the data base of Interpol, which must be taken more seriously. Reports confirm that European passports were used for the Malaysian flight by people of Asian appearance. This is hardly unusual given the multicultural societies in the West and increasing tendency of awarding nationality to people from other continents and cultures. David Cameron's admission that his Nepalese servant has British nationality is a case in point.

But the coveted destinations, which today also include Canada and Australia, and act as a magnet for the world's oppressed or poor, are no longer the El Dorado they once were, or were once thought to be. We are in a technological age when there is unlikely to be a return to full employment so the whole point of immigration needs reviewing. It is time the burden was shared with other nations whose economies and politics have made them richer.

It should be pointed out that there is no law, which grants rights to illegal immigrants or obliges any nation to take in immigrants or have an immigration policy. Every Government has the right to choose who should be allowed to settle in its country. During the 20th century up to, during and after the last world war, the USA and Western Europe welcomed hundreds of thousands of immigrants. But it was at a time when the population was much lower than today, there was a distinct likelihood of work or the people were escaping certain death. In addition, the immigrants, mainly of European origin, were accepted legally and despite some racism, were able to integrate. In America the infamous Ellis Island in New York was the entry point through which all immigrants had to pass and be checked. Both in Europe and the USA, within the space of two generations most immigrants had assimilated into their new country and many began to prosper.

The next wave of immigrants came from the colonies or ex-colonies seeking employment during the period of economic growth in the 1950s and 1960s. The new arrivals still faced racism and resistance but were gradually tolerated even if they did not always integrate fully into society and lived among their own communities creating enclaves of ethnic minority groups.

Excluding people from within the European Union, the more recent immigrants are invariably from other continents with totally different cultures, religions and traditions. They have come seeking a better life but with far less opportunity to find work. They have found it far more difficult to adapt to the more open and decadent Western society, especially at a time of economic recession and cut backs in social services and too many arrive illegally without papers.

Having handed over sovereignty to banks and multinationals who control our economies, Europe's political leaders have now transferred their customs and immigration departments to the people traffickers in Turkey and Libya who not only decide who is going to travel and be allowed to stay in Europe, but charge a hefty fee. Unfortunately the only way to stop this trade is to prevent the boats leaving North Africa and the Middle East and warn that there will be no asylum for anyone entering Europe illegally.

I am not convinced by the many arguments that immigration is beneficial. It has taken 2000 years of armed conflicts, whether for religious, economic or political reasons, with millions of lives lost, for Europe to have finally found peace. Seventy years after the end of the Second World War, Western Europeans accept each other's cultural and language differences and have forged a united and prosperous continent.

Nevertheless there are still cultural and economic differences between West Europe and the ex-communist East European states and it has been naïve to think that opening up Europe's frontiers would result in immediate integration of people from other continents with different cultures, religion and traditions.

It has become apparent that instead of adapting to the Western culture many immigrants from other continents prefer to live according to their own traditions, laws and religion and, in fact, reject our way of life. Being alienated in a different environment has also regrettably led to several young people finding their way into crime or terrorist organizations or simply engaging in terrorist attacks alone after being attracted into radical groups. This applies particularly to people of the Muslim faith.

Their reluctance to abide by Western standards is understandable when one considers how our societies have lost all sense of morality and become degenerate allowing binge drinking and alcohol abuse, violence against women, pornography, paedophiles, and a general loss of family values. Nevertheless there is a growing tendency within the Muslim population to live according to sharia law, which is not only radically different to our State laws but overrides them. Muslims often resist mixing with people of other faiths and expect to run their own schools. Arranged marriages are still the norm for their children, women are obliged to wear the veil or the burqa, they want segregation of sexes in many aspects of daily life, call for food restrictions in schools and oppose allowing their children to enter into relationships with non Muslims. This has resulted in a number of tragic incidents in several European countries where some parents have been convicted of killing their own wives and children.

These cultural and religious differences make cohabitation and integration virtually impossible. Imagine, as someone remarked in the press, one hundred thousand young Europeans with their drinking, eating, sexual and leisure habits living in a strict Muslim country and the local population told to accept their behaviour. It simply would not be tolerated. One country which seems to abide by religious tolerance is Malaysia; a Muslim state, in which people of difference faiths and cultures live side by side in relative harmony. Shopping centres cater for Western tastes as well as abide by Islamic rules. There are bars with alcohol and those without. Some transport is segregated, others accessible to all. Women are free to choose whether they cover their heads or not. While visiting Kuala Lumpur, I was welcomed to visit one of the city's mosques by the local imams.

These differences are creating a vicious circle. Radical Islamic groups see the violence in Syria, the invasion of Iraq, Western military presence in Afghanistan and the plight of Palestinians as a deliberate war on Islam. The fact that there has been no Western military intervention in Syria does not seem to have altered their views. They extract their revenge by persecuting Christian communities in North Africa and the Middle East or engaging in terrorist attacks against the West and Western interests, which leads to more resentment against Muslim communities, which in turn ferments more anti-Western feeling throughout the Islamic world.

For many years France, with its substantial Muslim community, has faced urban violence in its suburban council run estates with a high rate of immigrants in Paris, Lyon and

Marseille. In these run down apartment blocks, where the satellite dishes on balconies all point to North Africa, the authorities seem unable to prevent drug gangs roaming about with Kalashnikovs assassinating each other in an orgy of gang warfare. The Paris attack against the cartoonists of Charlie Hebdo was the result of the failure to integrate and indoctrination by extremist elements among the Muslim population. After every violent death the politicians announce tough new controls combined with social measures, which never seem to materialize. Despite the cultural and religious differences, which make integration difficult, Western Europe remains the goal for the thousands of men, women and children escaping from the conflicts in Afghanistan, Iraq, Libya, Somalia, Sudan and Syria, or for economic reasons from Algeria, the Congo, Eritrea, Morocco, Nigeria, Tunisia and West Africa. It has been estimated that more than one hundred thousand illegal immigrants entered Italy last year.

The sectarian violence raging in North Africa and the Middle East is on the verge of reaching European cities as many of the migrants are of Muslim origin. When it would seem more natural for Muslims to seek refuge in the wealthy Arab states closer to home in the Middle East, why do they still prefer the long, perilous journey to Western Europe? Intellectuals argue that with a population of around five hundred million Europe could easily accommodate one hundred or two hundred thousand immigrants under a quota system. But given the rise of Islamic terrorism can Europe afford to accept any Muslim migrants? There are Muslim countries in Asia, easily accessible to asylum seekers from neighbouring countries where there are conflicts. For example an Asian country such as Kazakhstan could take in millions of Muslim refugees. It is more than ten times the size of the UK with less than twenty million people. Saudi Arabia is four times the size of France with thirty million people, while Turkmenistan, the same size as Spain, has a population of only five million. Migrants from Pakistan or Afghanistan reach Greece via Turkey where they could seek asylum.

The answer lies in the refusal of some of these nation states to take in immigrants, or if they do, to leave them in refugee camps rather than allow them to integrate into their societies, while liberal, Western countries are perceived as easy prey with no questions asked. The hundreds of thousands of refugees in these camps are not granted rights and are expected to return when circumstances permit, whereas those who reach Europe ask for resident papers and passports with the intention of staying. It is clearly not asylum they seek but a better life in Western Europe for which they are prepared to pay. And while our Governments seem incapable of stemming the tide, the trafficking gangs make fortunes.

There is a significant increase in the world's population and it has been estimated that there are more than two hundred million people waiting to emigrate from their countries of origin. Western Europe is the goal for millions of Africans and Asians, the USA is confronted by immigration from Central and South America while Australia faces the problem of dealing with so-called boat people from Indonesia. Malaysia and Thailand do not know how to deal with thousands of Myanmar and Bangladesh migrants reaching their coast. Africa's population, without urgently needed birth control initiatives, is expected to rise to two and a half billion by the middle of this century. It is becoming apparent that given the numbers involved, the rich Western nations will not be able to cope with this huge influx of desperate people for much longer. Granting double or triple nationality and handing out papers or passports is a recipe for disaster.

There is less money for social benefits or housing and with twenty million Europeans out of work, less opportunity for work. It is unacceptable to see photos of smiling illegal immigrants giving the victory sign when they reach Europe's southern coast. It is not a game in which those who succeed in evading border controls win the prize of staying and obtaining residents' permits. Laws regarding automatic nationality need changing to stop the abuse by pregnant women arriving in Western Europe illegally to have a baby in order to obtain nationality and social benefits for all the family. The policy of family reunification after a specific period is also being abused given the larger family units in Africa or Asia likely to place an unsupportable burden on our health, housing and social services. The Internet is being used to entice vulnerable women into false marriages with foreign men whose real aim is to obtain a resident permit. In California police discovered a huge business involving Chinese women arriving purely to give birth before returning home in order for their children to be automatically granted US passports. In our Western societies, which are based on the rule of law, no state should allow foreigners to enter its territory illegally without visas or financial resources. The only response, however drastic, is to refuse to accept any illegal immigrant and return them to their country of origin. A clear policy would have prevented thousands of homeless immigrants from camping in Calais in order to cross the channel to reach England. Their numbers have led to serious social problems causing resentment among the local population and especially to long distance truck drivers. Due to an increase in illegal immigrants trying to climb on to and hide in their trucks, they have turned their vehicles into fortresses. And should the immigrants succeed in reaching England to be caught by customs officers, the drivers are fined for bringing them into the country, which has led to a call for boycotting the port. The British Government has offered financial help to build walls and fences in Calais when it seems more sensible and cheaper as well as respecting the law, to send the immigrants without papers back to their country of origin before the situation becomes unmanageable and dangerous. Due to the lack of communication between English and French Governments, Calais has become a lawless jungle with traffickers in control. David Cameron, whose election victory, now gives him a free hand, has set out what seems to be a logical, albeit harsh, policy to crack down on illegal immigration within the UK even if it does not agree with Europe's methods to tackle the problem.

The recent events on the Italian border at Ventimiglia are another example of the chaos which prevails. Thousands of undocumented migrants believe they can simply ignore the law and force their way into France. For some reason the Italian authorities have been transporting thousands of illegal immigrants from Lampedusa to the Italian mainland, and in Ceuta and Melilla, Spain's enclaves in North Africa, instead of simply sending illegal immigrants across the border back to Morocco, they have been shipped to Spain. While granting permission to remain in Western Europe may be humanitarian, it simply sends a message back home that anyone reaching European territory will be allowed to stay. And most undocumented immigrants seem to carry mobile phones to convey the message.

The latest proposal from Brussels to fix quotas for asylum seekers confirms just how far Europe's leaders are from reality. So far nobody has explained how such a programme would be implemented. These people are not products to be packaged up and distributed. First there is the difficult task to determine whether a person is a genuine asylum seeker or economic migrant. Then there is the desire of most of the migrants to reach Northern European countries where they either have family or contacts or can find jobs. It is unlikely that anybody from Africa or Asia would wish to be sent to East Europe where they do not speak the language or would find jobs, housing or social benefits. If they did end up in say Romania, Hungary or Bulgaria the chances are that with no border controls, they would simply pack their bags and head west.

There is also the question of whether immigration is beneficial or a burden to the developed world. While most immigrants work, pay taxes and contribute to the local economy, the overriding aim is to send money back home. According to the Multilateral Investment Fund which promotes development between North and Latin America, more than sixty-five billion dollars was remitted by immigrant workers in the US to their families in Central and Latin America. It has been suggested that many poor countries encourage their youth to emigrate, legally or illegally and do not cooperate to repatriate citizens since they are considered as exports and provide badly needed revenue to develop their own economies. The influx of people from West Africa has given rise to a new fear; the spread of contagious diseases like Ebola.

And the European Union finds itself with its own immigration crisis within its member states. The aim of freedom of movement of people now encompasses the ex-communist, Eastern Bloc countries. But this movement is turning into one way traffic as thousands of workers, who earn less than 300 euros a month, head west to Germany, Great Britain, France, Spain and Italy looking for jobs with higher wages. It is hardly a surprise that the youth of Ukraine sees Western Europe as a dream.

But the crisis has changed the rules of the game. There is a limit to how many people from other member states can find jobs, homes and count on social benefits in the West. Free medical care in France has led to an increase in health tourism with thousands of foreign nationals seeking to benefit from the country's generosity from a health service deeply in debt. Britain and Germany are in conflict with Brussels. They want to change the current laws to restrict social benefits for non-nationals who arrive to seek work or medical care and deport those who end up on the streets begging. This would include both people from other European member states and from overseas. It goes against everything the European Union stands for, but the present situation calls for drastic action.

I have already made the point that allowing the ex-communist states to join the European Union together was a major political and economic mistake, akin to Germany's reunification, which led to West Germany saddled with seventeen million unemployed East Germans. Several of the old communist run countries, faced with massive corruption, have still not found equality, economic prosperity or democracy and there are some who retain a nostalgia for the protection that communism offered.

Western Europe is naturally concerned about the influx of workers from East European member states competing for jobs with nationals and immigrants, both legal and illegal, from outside Europe. As already mentioned, the nations of Eastern Europe should have been formed into a kind of second division with controls on the free movement of people to the West, allowing gradual entry as and when their economies reached required standards.

Switzerland is not part of the European Union and has always accepted the free movement of people from Western Europe. But a recent referendum voted to restrict immigration. This was clearly due to the growing fear, shared by eurosceptics, of seeing an influx of Eastern Europeans and non EU immigrants which could destabilize the country.

European Union laws allow foreign nationals from member states without resources or legal work to stay in another member state for a maximum of three months. So why have thousands of Roma families been allowed to remain when they have neither work nor resources? The result has been the setting up of illegal campsites and a life of crime, delinquency and begging. France's interior minister Manuel Valls was right to speak frankly about this issue, which is posing a serious threat to France as well as other European countries.

The case of a Kosovan family deported from France illustrates the problems Europe faces. Despite the publicity the case generated, the fact is that Kosovo is an independent country and is not in the European Union. There is no legal reason for France to take responsibility for its citizens. The family is believed to have now obtained Croatian passports in order to have free access to the EU. This demonstrates the chaos, which prevails. Whatever the Human Rights court decides in Strasbourg, Europe's governments need to determine whether it can be justified for the developing nations to export whole populations and expect other countries to house and feed them. Great Britain, Germany, France, Spain, Italy or Holland cannot look after thousands of impoverished people from other countries. Bulgaria and Romania would not allow Western European families without any resources to settle in their countries providing housing, social benefits or education for their children, nor would the majority of nation states.

We still live in separate nation states with governments and laws. Most countries in the world require visitors to possess passports, visas and sufficient resources and only allow foreigners to stay for a limited time. Restricting travel for some while encouraging or allowing illegal immigration for others is incompatible in a law-abiding society. The alternative is to face social unrest, chaos and anarchy.

Although Polish workers have tended to be the exception to the rule, the result of opening Europe's borders has been the transformation of many parts of European cities into ghettos or no go areas with more and more impoverished families without any means of support drifting into crime, prostitution, drugs and begging to survive, placing a strain on housing, health and police services.

The expansion of Europe has raised the issue of whether Europe can or should continue to accept any immigration at all from outside its own borders. Clearly there are no more economic reasons; there are more than enough Europeans to fill every available job legally.

It is accepted that Europe's populations are growing older and young blood is needed to sustain future economic development. But the call for more immigrants to respond to the shortage of workers does not seem to take into account the Internet age and advances in technology, which have led to a reduction in the need for manpower. Machines now carry out the most mundane tasks. In addition the effects of the crisis have led to an unacceptable erosion of the advances in social justice achieved during the twentieth century; a huge increase in unemployment, part time jobs at lower wages, laws which make it easier to lay off staff and a loss of negotiating power of the unions. One of the effects of the crisis is that while thousands of highly educated Europeans, especially from Spain and Portugal, are heading north to seek employment, uneducated and unqualified illegal immigrants from Africa and Asia take their place. They either add to the number of unemployed or are prepared to work for less. This creates economic, cultural and social problems.

With the added risk of terrorist attacks, illegal drugs, and the risk of transporting diseases, there is a strong case to re-establish border controls. European governments have failed to stem the flow of illegal immigrants from Africa or Asia trying to reach Europe via the Canary Islands, Spain, Lampedusa, Greece, Calais, or the two Spanish enclaves in north Africa, Melilla and Ceuta, which have become today's equivalent of Trojan horses. According to the Spanish newspaper, El Pais, Spain's most dangerous place is a suburb of Ceuta; it is a no go area for police with high unemployment, poverty, crime, drug dealing and has become a breeding ground for radical Islamists. And it is part of Europe! Spain has come in for criticism for using fences with extruding sharp knives in Ceuta and Melilla along the border with Morocco, which have injured several illegal immigrants from sub Saharan Africa attempting to climb them. And thousands have died in the Mediterranean trying to reach the shores of Europe.

Fences are usually designed to keep people in, not out. They have not worked on the Mexican border or in Greece and cannot work in North Africa or Bulgaria. The answer lies not in erecting more fences or walls but in dialogue with the countries from which illegal immigrants originate. If Spain expects Britain to relinquish sovereignty of Gibraltar, surely it would make sense for Spain to transfer their two North African colonies with substantial Muslim communities to Morocco.

It is hardly fair to blame Europe's Governments for the death of migrants risking their lives to reach Europe. Illegal immigration has become an industry. Thousands pay people traffickers for the dangerous journey to Europe. These Mafia gangs also attempt to introduce drugs into Europe as well as young girls, who end up in prostitution, plying their trade openly in deprived areas of Western cities, while the current political and military conflicts in North Africa and the Middle

East have led to an increase in demands for asylum. This situation has made it difficult to distinguish between genuine refugees, economic migrants or even potential terrorists taking the opportunity to infiltrate into Europe. Kosovo claimed and was granted independence but it has been reported that the country is so poor up to 50% of the population already want to leave, Granting legal status to any illegal economic migrant sends the wrong message to their fellow citizens. It only exacerbates the problem leading to an increase in the numbers of people prepared to risk their lives believing that they can all receive similar favourable treatment if they succeed in crossing borders.

The paradox is the Chinese community and the Chinatowns in cities around the world. They rarely integrate, live according to their own rules and customs, and generally, are not only tolerated, but accepted by governments and the people everywhere. Rarely do we see the Chinese at the job centre or benefits offices.

Nobody knows how many Chinese live outside China in the West. They keep to themselves, work long hours and their shops and restaurants are always popular and busy. Their workshops and stores operate as distribution centres for the vast Chinese manufacturing industry, giving it access to world markets without having to learn another language or local customs.

During a recent visit to Lima, Peru, I was looking for a particular gift to bring home. Unable to locate a toy shop in the city centre, I was directed to the city's Chinatown area. As well as the typical Asian markets and restaurants associated with the Chinese areas of our cities, I ended up in a five storey market run by Chinese, full of stalls selling an array of toys, all made in China. The fire which killed Chinese workers in Prato in Italy's Tuscany region, brought to light the unregulated situation of Asian businesses in Europe. There is without question a considerable amount of illegal Chinese immigration. Much of the merchandise manages to evade customs duty or VAT, perhaps through corruption, and astonishingly governments turn a blind eye to this illegal activity.

The cash businesses generate vast sums of untaxed money, which ends up in China or is recycled to Chinese to open more stores or workshops in the West. Governments and law enforcement agencies find it difficult to penetrate this opaque world given the language and cultural difficulties. Nevertheless a huge undercover operation in Spain in 2013 led to the arrest of both Chinese and Spanish nationals running a huge import and money laundering operation supplying the Chinese community. The growth in the penetration of Western markets by the Chinese is now being seen as a potential threat given the rise in economic power of the Asian giant.

Clearly there are going to be more people travelling and wishing to settle in another country. But Western Europe, the US, Canada and Australia should no longer be considered as the final destination for asylum seekers, refugees or economic migrants.

Despite ongoing conflicts, the world fortunately has less despotic dictators who threaten the lives of their people. Economic growth has allowed several African, Asian and South American countries to create wealth. There is therefore a need to review the whole question of asylum, immigration and demands for naturalization with the cooperation of the United Nations. This is not about racism or xenophobia but practical common sense to maintain social cohesion and national identity.

Surely it is not beyond the Security Council to compile a list of those states in which certain groups face persecution, discrimination, torture or death. Only people from countries on the list would be considered as genuine asylum seekers making it simpler for countries to determine their rights. In addition new rules could be established to make it mandatory for refugees to seek a neighbouring country with a similar culture on the same continent. It is not possible to stop people entering Europe or the US, but clear laws, which could be enforced without lengthy delays, could be introduced so undocumented foreigners could be deported immediately.

Almost every nation imposes strict rules requiring visas, passports, proof of financial resources and no criminal record for anyone wanting to take up residence. Any unauthorized extension to the period granted, results in arrest, prison or deportation. There is no reason why Western Europe should be any different.

With a coordinated European policy, it should be agreed with the governments of those countries from where the majority of illegal economic immigrants originate that they will not be allowed to remain and will be returned automatically to their country of origin; no benefits and no chance of naturalization.

This should apply also to travellers without jobs or sufficient financial resources, foreigners convicted of criminal offences, false marriages and women whose sole aim is to give birth purely to obtain resident status – nationality based on GPS – as one US senator called it, which can only lead to the abuse of our laws.

Governments have ignored the problems of integration in overpopulated Western Europe by handing out passports like charity. Our societies have reached the limit of tolerance with people from different ethnic, cultural and religious backgrounds attempting to live together. The concept of nationality, of being British, Spanish, German, French etc. is being lost, replaced by a nation of citizens called "residents".

A report by the Policy Exchange in the UK has forecast that by two thousand and fifty, one third of the UK population will be ethnic minorities, of which a substantial number will be Muslim. This has far reaching consequences for our society. Towns and cities could be controlled by people of foreign origin and adapt laws to suit their own communities. The Royal Family will serve no purpose since fewer and fewer people will feel any loyalty to it. The only positive aspect is that William and Catherine will not need to travel the world visiting the ex-colonies since so many of their people are now in the UK.

If people do not respect the laws and traditions of the country in which they live how can there ever be harmony? The answer is not to submit to the demands of ethnic minorities or religious groups at the expense of the majority. The violence which erupted across the Arab world following the Dutch film and French cartoon of Mohamed, albeit inspired by a minority of radical Islamists, demonstrated the difficulties which multiculturalism brings.

Governments cannot ignore the real threat which uncontrolled immigration poses to our societies. It can only lead to more ghettos within our cities. The situation is verging on anarchy as the recession leads to increased protectionism, racial and religious tension and anger over jobs and, more important, lack of security.

The violent backlash against illegal immigrants in Greece and rise of ultra right wing parties is a consequence of the failure by governments to recognize the wishes of the majority of the people. Yet there is a lack of political will to deal with the problem and impose strict and clear immigration policies and laws.

Western governments have often brought people of immigrant origin into their governments with the misguided view that it will improve relations with ethnic minority groups. This is in my view a mistake as loyalty can be divided and different backgrounds can lead to divergences of opinion. A Muslim, Sayeedi Warsi, appointed as a secretary of state, recently resigned from the British Government over David Cameron's support of Israel, yet she has remained silent over the rise of Islamic radicals and the killing of Christians in Iraq. A Congolese immigrant, Cecile Kyenge, was appointed Minister of Integration in the previous Italian government, where she was sympathetic to the demands of thousands of illegal immigrants arriving in Sicily or Lampedusa.

One consequence of illegal immigration is that Europe's prisons are overcrowded with illegal immigrants and foreign criminals since the courts do not seem to know how to deal with them. The prison population of Britain is around eighty-five thousand, France seventy-two thousand, Spain sixty-two thousand and Italy sixty-seven thousand. It has been estimated that between thirty and forty percent of prisoners are foreign and the number is rising each year.

It is well known that Mafia gangs, many from East Europe, Russia and West Africa, operate in the West engaging in robberies and fraud. They are also involved in transporting young girls to work as slaves in clubs in Western European cities while paedophile rings have proliferated in our societies.

Italy and Spain have witnessed an increase in immigrants from the Central American, Asian and African continent often accompanied by babies and children. But it has been established that many of the immigrants are not the parents and use the children as a means to avoid being deported. The USA has been confronted with thousands of children from Central and South America entering the country alone and illegally in the hope that their parents will be allowed to follow them. President Obama's plan to give around five million undocumented Hispanic immigrants resident status led to a confrontation with the republican dominated Congress and Senate.

The tragedy in Prato in the Italian Tuscany region in which Chinese workers died in a fire, in December 2013, was an accident waiting to happen according to a spokesman for the extreme right La Lega party. Officially there are supposed to be about seventeen and a half thousand Chinese residents but more than fifty thousand are believed to be living and working in Chinese run workshops in Prato, where the local authority has turned a blind eye to the unauthorized manufacturing and distribution facilities and the exploitation of illegal immigrants.

Further south, the Italian port of Castel Volturno, near Naples has become a notorious centre for Nigerian drug and prostitute gangs, which collaborate with the local Camorra Mafia. For reasons hard to comprehend, the government does not seem concerned about cracking down on the illegal traffic prevalent in many Italian cities, flooded with illegal foreign prostitutes plying their trade openly in the streets. It has been estimated that 50% of these prostitutes are foreign and 20% underage.

There is genuine concern in Western Europe that the adhesion to Schengen of all the Eastern European member states would simply open the flood gates to more criminal gangs and illegal immigrants from Asia and North Africa seeking to take advantage if our open borders. The only solution seems to be more draconian measures to stamp out these illegal practices. But why do governments seem to do so little to crack down on the exploitation of Asian workers, young girls or children?

Foreign prostitutes, mostly illegal, from East Europe, Africa or South America, operate with impunity in many European cities. They line streets, trade from parked vehicles or use small ads, with photos, to attract clients. So far some governments have introduced laws, which allow the selling of sex but not the paying for it. This seems incoherent as the two seem to go together.

Instead of laws to impose fines on clients, politicians should be working on eradicating the problem at source before it becomes a major humanitarian problem. With sufficient political will it is a problem which could be resolved overnight by removing the girls from the streets, outlawing advertisements and deporting all illegal prostitutes, pimps and drug dealers and arresting their Mafia protectors. Yet somehow little is done to end the illegal traffic, protect the young victims or crack down on the gangs, which can only operate with the connivance of local politicians, business people and even the judiciary and police.

Laws which make each country responsible for its citizens and allow all illegal immigrants as well as foreign criminals convicted of serious crimes, to be returned to their country of origin to serve their sentence, would relieve our prisons of undesirable elements, save a great deal of public money and might even be a deterrent.

Another phenomenon is that while governments announce measures to tighten up on the black economy and loss of VAT receipts, they do nothing to stop the increasing number of illegal immigrants, selling illegal products made in illegal workshops. Anyone heading for Europe's seaside resorts and cities will not fail to notice the presence of immigrants at traffic lights waiting to wash windscreens, selling tissues or just begging. Large numbers of immigrants from the African continent can be seen carrying large sacks. They contain a variety of goods ranging from sunglasses, hats, tee shirts, handbags, belts, jewellery, scarves and CDS, which are carefully laid out on the pavements or carried through crowded markets or along the beaches looking for buyers. They operate from morning until late at night.

Odd as it may seem, the police, local authorities, regular shopkeepers or market stall holders do not appear to object to their presence, and in coastal resorts sunbathers either politely take a peek at what is on offer or just shake their heads to express their disinterest. In rail and bus stations these traders can suddenly appear with umbrellas when it rains and hats and sunglasses when it shines attempting to force their wares on to travellers arriving or departing.

The goods are laid out on cloths, which have strings attached to the corners. From time to time the vendors will suddenly pull the strings, the goods will disappear into the cloth, deftly loaded on to their backs and they will disappear as fast as they arrived. This scenario takes places every time local police are on the prowl. But as soon as the police have gone the vendors and their goods reappear. Even when they confront illegal vendors carrying copies of designer watches, handbags and sunglasses, the police stroll past and do nothing.

It is fairly evident that much of, if not all, the merchandise is counterfeit and there is definitely no VAT paid. But where does it come from and how does it end up in the hands of immigrant traders, who may or may not have legal papers to reside or work in the European Union? They are like migrating birds, which head north each spring. Is the merchandise being made in clandestine factories in Europe or brought in by containers from Asia? At Christmas time each year hundreds of containers full of counterfeit goods, dangerous toys and pharmaceutical products are discovered and confiscated in European ports such as Rotterdam. The customs and tax authorities have a tough job tracing the origin of these goods and arresting those involved in the transport and distribution.

In some cities and resorts immigrant groups are abusing their position and often obstructing people going about their daily lives by selling goods outside cafes and supermarkets. The stories of Romanian families using their children to pickpocket tourists or beg throughout Western Europe are not fiction. Workers at the Paris Louvre museum were forced to go on strike in protest at Romanian children, who due to their age, were allowed free entry and were causing havoc with Asian tourists stealing wallets and bags. In London, police had to remove a group of Romanians who had set up a camp in Park Lane and in France a local mayor has come in for criticism for attempting to break up an illegal campsite leading to a demonstration by Romanians in the town centre; the law turned upside down. There is no moral or legal obligation for Western European countries to take in and look after thousands of impoverished people predominantly from Romania and Bulgaria. Their own countries should be forced to take them back and, with financial aid from the EU, provide schooling and improve their living standards.

Madrid has recently announced measures to deal with antisocial behaviour. This includes any person, legal or illegal, who congregates at traffic lights to wash windscreens, blocks the entrances to supermarkets and major stores, begs at cafes playing musical instruments, sells counterfeit goods or picks up prostitutes in the street. Is this a restriction of people's liberties or a necessity to clean up the city? So far the law has not been implemented.

We live in a hypocritical society. In the present economic crisis Europe's governments are introducing laws aimed at limiting people's rights to demonstrate, cracking down on VAT dodgers, unlicensed traders, tax evaders, benefits cheats etc. and are calling for everyone to declare their earnings and pay taxes. Yet consumers can be fined for buying counterfeit goods, clients can face fines for picking up prostitutes, while little is done to stop the illegal merchandise from being sold in the markets or stores, often by undocumented immigrants and illegal foreign prostitutes who are not apprehended.

Many illegal African immigrants or Bulgarian or Romanian workers who have lost their source of income in Western Europe, have resorted to collecting rubbish and metals to survive and send money home. Unfortunately the rise in price of certain metals especially cooper, has led to criminal gangs taking up cables along railway tracks or raiding builders' yards. Seeing these poor people rummaging through refuse bins in our streets shows how a global problem has become a local problem.

If people are illegal and selling counterfeit or unlicensed goods undeclared or engage in robbery, drug dealing, prostitution and fraud, they should simply be arrested and deported and the goods seized. There is no way that Western visitors would be allowed to remain without visas and sell goods illegally in any other country. It would simply not be tolerated and deportation would be immediate.

National identity cards, which are common in most European countries, should be introduced in the UK. It might be costly but would give the UK the perfect opportunity to clearly establish who has a legal right to be British or live in the UK. Potential legal immigrants seeking citizenship should have to pass a national identity test. This is mandatory in the US for every aspiring candidate before becoming a US citizen and obtaining a passport.

The whole question of being granted a passport needs addressing. For years Spain and Italy have been in the front line of the influx of boat people from North Africa. But the reaction of former Italian premier, Enrico Letta to grant Italian nationality to those who died seems a very poorly placed gesture. In the same way that stepping foot on European soil should not grant some divine right to resident status, nationality is not a charitable gift to hand out, nor the result of giving birth to a child regardless of the nationality of the mother, nor should it be considered as a reward for kicking a football or being able to run fast. Like soccer transfers, granting nationality has now become another marketing tool.

Nationality comes from blood, roots, history, family, culture, language and education. Nationality is what binds citizens together and forges our identity. That is why the United Nations exists and at major ceremonies and sporting events we fly the flag and pump out national anthems. It is why we have governments, presidents, monarchies, passports and above all a legal system. Loyalty to one's country is drummed into every citizen at birth and nationality should not be treated lightly.

But both nationality and residency are being abused. And this is what concerns the silent majority. Instead of a coordinated immigration policy, each EU member state, as well as the European Union, has been making its own rules while the Court of Human Rights is doing whatever it can to prevent illegal immigrants from being deported. The result is chaos. Governments do not seem to have considered the consequences of handing out passports, or allowing foreign residents to vote, while massive illegal immigration, which flouts the laws of the country, destroys the fabric of our societies.

By granting an illegal immigrant resident status, it gives them the right to live anywhere in the European Union with or without the agreement of other member states. Allowing foreigners to vote can result in communities with substantial immigrant communities winning council elections and changing the laws to suit their own cultural or religious interests. This has come to light in the UK where local elections are believed to have been rigged in favour of ethnic minorities and the number of Islamic schools has increased in many towns and cities.

Italy seems determined to offer nationality to asylum seekers, which will only send a message to hundreds of thousands of illegal immigrants to attempt to reach Western European shores believing they will be welcomed with open arms. It is inconceivable that any European Union nation should act unilaterally without consulting other member states first, especially in view of the growing influence of extremist and populist parties following the results of the Euro Election.

I was raised in a world where nationality was fundamental to a person's identity. I believe it is still the pillar of our societies. I have spent more than a quarter of a century in France. As a student I had the invaluable experience of a summer job in a small factory in the Dordogne region living side by side with the local population. I speak the language understand the culture and politics and I consider myself totally integrated. But I am still English. How can I suddenly become French when I never studied philosophy? I find it hard to adjust to the situation where a person of Algerian, Bangladeshi, Chinese, Cameroun, Eritrean, Nigerian, or Senegalese origin can become British, Spanish, French, German, Italian or Spanish. It would be equally strange to envisage a white Westerner becoming Cambodian, Congolese, Somali or Moroccan. Outside of Europe and the USA, few, if any, nations would grant nationality to foreigners who happen to enter or give birth on their territory. It makes a mockery of everything which nationality is supposed to represent. But the world is changing and perhaps I am out of touch.

Germany has recently taken a decision, which alters centuries of Teutonic thinking. It has always relied on the rule that blood determines nationality and not where one is born. But the new government has proposed allowing children born of foreign parents to automatically obtain dual nationality. Spain has recently proposed allowing Sephardi Jews, linked to families expelled from Spain by Isabel and Ferdinand in 1492, to be granted Spanish passports without giving up their current nationality. Israel has not reacted too kindly to Spain's decision but why stop at the expelled Jewish community. What about the Moors also expelled from Spain, or Italians and Irish who emigrated to the USA? If the European Union is to survive, decisions relating to the concept of nationality and residence status need discussing and agreeing at European level and not taken unilaterally.

Should there ever be a European passport, who will be eligible to obtain it? Will it be limited to Europeans only or anybody possessing dual or triple nationality? One of the major difficulties in Europe has been, and still is, the assimilation of immigrants. Granting double or triple nationality seems to reject the concept of full integration, which is vital for the future of every nation state.

In today's volatile world there is a strong case to abolish the concept of dual nationality. It is firstly rather unfair that a minority of people should have two countries of origin and move freely between them when it suits them. Everyone should be obliged to choose just one country. While nationality and integration might be considered less of a problem with children of Western origin, when it comes to children of immigrants from other continents with different cultures and religion it poses difficulties and has led to a loss of roots and loyalty. Should political or even military conflicts ever arise, whom would these young adults side with? Criminals with dual nationality are able to simply abscond to their second country of origin or worse, engage in terrorism. We should not forget that the terrorist attacks in the USA and Europe were carried out by young immigrants, who had the right of citizenship and thousands are now involved in the Syrian conflict or have joined radical Islamic groups in the Middle East.

Tightening up on issuing passports does not mean people cannot choose to live in another country if they are allowed to do so and obtain legal papers, become tax residents and abide by the laws of the country. But even this is being abused. Spain and Greece are offering resident status to anyone who purchases a property, making a mockery of European immigration laws. If the European Union is to have any meaning I repeat that no member state should be allowed to fix its immigration policies unilaterally.

Spanish king, Felipe VI, has to deal with seventeen presidents of the autonomous regions and preside over a nation with a growing number of ethnic minorities. The British Royal Family has to contend with a multicultural society with fewer and fewer loyal subjects. If Europe should become a federalist union with nation states accepting a loss of sovereignty, there will simply be no role or use for monarchies. Europe has tended to allow "a live and let live" policy which has clearly failed. The diverse, vibrant communities, vaunted by human rights activists, have turned out to be impoverished ethnic urban ghettos. Historian Stanley Payne wrote: "A multicultural society is a contradiction in terms. It is not a single society but several, making a unified society impossible." David Cameron and Angela Merkel admitted publicly, "multiculturalism has failed".

Either we live in law-abiding societies and abide by international laws, or the rule of the jungle in which anarchy and chaos will prevail. There cannot be different laws for different sets of people, whether they are the privileged elite or illegal immigrants without resources. If the future is for open borders and freedom of movement for all in a united Europe, then like monarchies – presidents, governments and nation states serve no more purpose.

It may seem harsh and drastic but strict immigration controls are the most humanitarian method not only to save lives of immigrants desperate to reach Europe or the US but to ensure our societies maintain a level of law and order and social cohesion. At present governments seem more prepared to look after illegal immigrants than take care of their own citizens, especially the increasing number of poor families and children without jobs, homes and who are below the level of poverty.

Fences, walls and tough immigration laws will never solve the underlying causes, which are gross inequality and a vast wealth gap between the rich Western economies and the poorer nations of the world. Today it is a question of numbers with the increasing populations of Africa and Asia outstripping the West. By mid century there is simply no way millions can expect to be welcomed in Europe. Christians and Syrians fleeing the conflict in the Middle East are also heading for Western Europe. America is facing an influx of thousands of unaccompanied children crossing the Mexican border from Central America in the hope they will be accepted and with the expectation that the parents can ultimately join them. How long can the Western countries cope with what is an invasion?

The time is appropriate to establish a new relationship with African, Asian and Central American governments to put an end to illegal immigration in exchange for investment in education, health, infrastructure and economic development. In retaliation for what it considers lack of cooperation by Algeria, Mauritania, Morocco and Senegal in stemming the tide of illegal immigrants from Sub Saharan Africa, Spain has cut back its financial aid. Could it contemplate the transfer of Melilla and Ceuta to Morocco, which are not vital to Spain's economic or strategic interests, and offer to repatriate the eighty thousand Spanish residents to the mainland? This is what happened to the French nationals in Algeria following the granting of independence by President de Gaulle. It would have the effect of solving the immediate problem of illegal immigrants believing they are on European soil.

The crisis in Melilla and Lampedusa led to a Euro-Africa conference in Brussels in April 2014, which came up with proposals to deal with the problem including repatriation coupled with financial aid. What the conference established was that the economies of several African states are now growing much faster than in Europe and the receipts from immigrants overseas provide more than international aid. Many African and South American countries are rich in minerals and natural resources. Asian economies are also growing fast with large populations transforming them into major manufacturing bases. This suggests there is no economic or moral reason for Western Europe to accept immigrant workers and certainly not illegal immigrants, whatever their reasons for wanting to live in Western Europe. Europe's colonies fought for, or were granted, independence. Their governments and people must learn to manage their affairs and not expect their old colonial masters to welcome them in and provide jobs, housing and benefits. There can only be order in the world if each nation takes responsibility for its own citizens.

Huge sums of money are being invested in Africa, Asia and South America, which have an urgent need for housing and infrastructure projects. If corruption can be eliminated and investment filters down to the people, their economies and the living standards will improve. Southern European countries are concerned about the loss of a highly educated youth to the stronger economies of northern Europe. But nobody seems to have considered the damage mass migration causes for the developing nations whose future will also be put in jeopardy by the loss of a large percentage of its young people. We should encourage and welcome students to Europe but on the understanding that they have to return to their country of origin at the end of their studies.

Reducing inequality and poverty around the world is the only way to resolve the hardship and desperation that leads people to want to seek a better life elsewhere. And this requires an end to conflicts, corruption, corporate greed and a doubling of international cooperation and investment with the ultimate goal of sharing economic wealth. Thirty-four year old German Melendez is a farmer from Salvador, one of Central America's poorest nations. As a teenager he entered the US illegally but was discovered and deported. Now a member of the Observatory, a citizen's environmental organisation, he is active in developing the country's agricultural industry. "The solution to poverty is not to flee to the United States as an illegal immigrant. To destroy the American dream we have to build the Salvador dream." His message should be conveyed to all the developing nations as a signal for them to begin to take responsibility for their lives and create their own wealth.

Religious Morality

The essence of all religions is one. Only their approaches are different.

Mahatma Gandhi

French writer, Andre Malraux, said, "The twenty-first century will either be spiritual or it won't be at all." His views related to the Muslim faith and we are all witnessing the consequences of the rise of radical Islam around the world. Throughout history religious wars have caused countless deaths while racism, linked to religion, is still a major social scourge. We should not forget that Catholics and Protestants fought each other in Europe for hundreds of years and during the colonial occupation caused countless victims wherever they tried to enforce their religion on the indigenous people.

In Spain in the 9th century the Moors brought with them a high level of culture to Europe and left a priceless legacy; philosophy, algebra, writing, art and architecture. The Alhambra in Granada and Mezquita in Cordoba stand as prime examples of their contribution. In Andalucia the Moors lived in harmony with Christians and Jews for three hundred years. Where are the Muslim cultural ambassadors today? Where are the artists, writers, architects and philosophers? Syrian writer and poet Ali Ahmed Said Esber, known as Adonis, who has spent many years living in Paris, has said that there can be no democracy without separation of religion from the state. He describes Islam today as "a religion without a culture".

In Europe, two world wars and loss of colonial power resulted in the migration of people of different cultures and faiths who have tended to live side by side, and if not cohabitating, at least tolerating each other; Hindus, Jews, Catholics, Protestants, Buddhists and Muslims have all lived together, with everyone free to pursue his or her faith without government intervention. 9/11 changed people's attitudes.

Bin Laden and Al Qaida declared war on the West. The US and European invasion of Iraq and long drawn out conflict in Afghanistan coupled with unfettered support for Israel was the excuse. Islam became synonymous with terrorism. But in many Muslim countries religious Islamic leaders chose to engage in sectarian massacres between the Shia and Sunni communities and an ideological battle to return to a stricter way of life adhering to the Sharia laws. Their objective has been to export their beliefs to the West, which they consider to be decadent and its people, infidel. Worse is the beheading of innocent civilians both in the Middle East and in Europe. But if the primary objective of the Islamic leaders is to ultimately transform Europe into a Caliphate then it should be made clear to all Muslims that they can never succeed.

One of the consequences of 9/11 has been the stringent control on travellers around the world obliged to waste time at airports and ports due to the introduction of draconian security measures. It has to be stated that all this inconvenience is due to the intolerance of a radical minority from one specific religious group.

Rising islamophobia in the Western countries should not be seen as a kind of 21st century crusade against Islam. It is primarily a backlash to what is considered to be a growing and unwanted influence of Islam in Western societies. Are Ramadan, the month long fast or daily prayers compatible with our western way of life? Allowing madrasa schools run by Salafist imams in the UK is surely a huge political error. In

France, which prides itself on its secular society, while town halls were advised to remove models of the nativity, there is an Islamic school in Lille, in Northern France, where prayers are obligatory, girls wear veils and the Qur'an is taught. The veil seen as a fashion accessory can be appealing but as a religious symbol it has no place. These policies at best segregate society, at worst form future terrorists. This is not the result of the multicultural divide but a planned and deliberate step in a long-term objective to create an Islamic state. The conquest of the West has begun and these schools should be banned together with the burqa, sexual segregation, genital mutilation, child marriages, polygamy and the sharia law which do not belong in our Christian based society.

Since 1905 France has relied on the absence of involvement of government in religious affairs and vice versa, but the demands of the Muslim community are threatening the country's secular laws. There are an estimated two thousand five hundred mosques in the country of which approximately ninety are run by salafists. Religion permeates through every aspect of Islamic life and its spread is creating mounting concern that several small towns could end up as Muslim enclaves. The French government seems frightened to act in case it is seem as stigmatizing the five million strong Muslim population. France's Jewish population is the largest in Europe and one of the consequences of rising anti-Semitism, violence and concern over the growing influence of Muslims in the country is that thousands are leaving each year to live in Israel concerned for the safety of their families. Incredibly, France's response to the beheading of one of its citizens by an Islamic extremist has been to add to the number of police checking unauthorised Uberpop drivers.

The Arab Spring was supposed to bring democracy to the Muslim states of North Africa and the Middle East. But this was unrealistic and naïve thinking on the part of Western governments. People of different cultures and traditions going back thousands of years, subservient to tribal rulers, dictators or harsh political and religious regimes, were unlikely to understand the system of voting to elect leaders or to embrace democratic values overnight.

Islamic groups have naturally taken advantage of the departure of leaders like Mubarak and Gaddafi to exert their influence. Women who thought the new political regimes would give them more freedom have realized they are unlikely to achieve their aims easily, while the youth, who embraced the Internet and mobile telephones, face a return to Islamic laws, violent resistance or are forced to emigrate.

While the West has been granting more religious freedom to Muslim groups, it did not prevent home grown Muslims from terrorist acts or murders in London, Madrid, Paris and Boston. One of the perpetrators of the Kenyan massacre is believed to have been a Somalian granted asylum and nationality in Norway. The Charlie Hebdo massacre in Paris was carried out by young men, who grew up in France. These bomb attacks have shown how some people find it hard to integrate into Western society and are vulnerable to join terrorist groups or act alone.

They also send a clear message that the West should not tolerate radical imams or fundamentalists like the Salafist movement, which preach hatred or violence or the murder of individuals simply because they may have said something about or drawn a caricature of the prophet. Clearly this one sided thinking makes it hard for the West to justify granting the construction of mosques, Islamic schools, the wearing of the burqa and the introduction of Islamic laws into Western society. Perhaps Winston Churchill had the answer. In 1899 in his book, The River War, he wrote, "The influence of the religion (Islam) paralyses the social development of those who follow it."

The Middle East remains the centre of religious conflict. Syria has been receiving world attention for the killing of its people. But it is a confusing situation and one where it is hard for the West to assess who is right or wrong. Assad and his regime will eventually be replaced. However for the moment he can count on the support of Shia Iran and the Hezbollah as well as Russia while the so-called rebels are made up of Sunni, Al Qaida members, Syrian opponents of Assad and other radical groups, each having its own intentions which do not always coincide.

The West is at a loss as to how to react. The only clear objective is to prevent Syria falling into the hands of Islamic groups, setting off a time bomb in the world's most volatile region, and prevent the radical Islamic group, ISIS establishing a Caliphate across the Middle East. Their persecution and killing of Christian communities, which have lived for centuries across the Middle East, cannot be tolerated in a civilized world. Israel's long-term security would be at risk and cannot be ignored. The country would face an uncertain future with an armed Hamas on one side, the Hezbollah in Lebanon, and a fanatical Islamic group in Syria and Iraq. Is permanent peace in the region an illusion?

The arrival of the new Pope has given the Christian world renewed hope at a time when Christians are being persecuted in many countries with Muslim majorities. Within the short time he has been in the Vatican, Pope Francis or Francisco I, has been initiating major internal reforms and, using the Vatican City's extensive diplomatic channels, begun to travel overseas following in the footsteps of Pope Jean Paul II. The new pope seems to be genuine in his calls to reform the church and bring the poor or oppressed nations of the world out of poverty but he cannot do it without the help of the world's rich nations. He plans to engage in dialogue with religious leaders of all faiths to try to end the conflicts, achieve peace and reduce the huge and unacceptable inequality in a diverse and complicated world. His visit to the Middle East, bringing together Shimon Peres and Mahmoud Abbas demonstrated his firm commitment to achieve peace in the region.

But where are the Arab States? Saudi Arabia and the rich Gulf States appear to be opening up their countries and modernizing their societies. But while the leaders study in

Western universities, embrace our Western culture and spend money in our hotels and stores, at home they maintain strict Islamic practices. With both their wealth and influence they seem to be well placed to take a more active role in achieving peace yet do not seem to be keen to become too involved in the region's conflicts and have even been linked to the financing of terrorist groups. Neither do they seem to be prepared to accommodate their fellow Muslims fleeing from Egypt, Iraq, Libya, Somalia, Sudan or Syria, who instead head for Western Europe.

There does not seem to be a simple solution and attempts to open talks with Islamic leaders, even the Taliban, do not seem to make headway. Those whom we consider terrorists are praised as freedom fighters in their own countries. But why has Islam turned the clock back to fundamentalism? The most radical Muslims claim the West has declared war on Islam and use it to radicalize their population. This is of course, far from the truth, but how can we change their opinions? France has tried to bring the two worlds together. The Institute du Monde Arab in Paris attempts to bridge the gap with its permanent and temporary exhibitions devoted to Arab culture and aimed at improving our knowledge and fostering understanding of the Muslim world.

Although it cannot be denied that the West expects the world to adhere to Western values and our way of life, every nation has a right to its own traditions, culture and laws. While we should respect Islam, surely Muslims too can learn to respect the Western culture with its Christian beliefs as well as their own different groups whether they are Shia or Sunni, moderate or radical. One thing is certain. We cannot combat an ideology with weapons. There is no alternative to dialogue and understanding if we are to live in a peaceful world.

Aid Morality

While poverty persists there can be no true freedom.

Nelson Mandela

Despite decades of aid and charity the situation in the world's poorest countries is still dramatic. The intervention of the International Monetary Fund and the World Bank, the United Nations, NGO organizations such as Amnesty international, Greenpeace, Human Rights Watch, Medecins sans Frontiers, Save the Children, Oxfam etc., as well as others, while doing as much as they can, do not seem to have made much headway in the fight against child deaths or disease, environmental damage, poverty, sexual violence etc. And the poorer the country the more its citizens will continue to seek a better life elsewhere. Haiti is a perfect example of the failure of the UN, the World Bank and FMI to alleviate the plight of its citizens and rebuild the country. Several years after the devastating earthquake, the country still lacks housing and infrastructure or any real form of government and has been left to fend for itself.

While the charity organizations endeavour to improve the lives of the people, for far too long Western governments have done little to prevent dictators and corrupt rulers from terrorizing their people or siphoning off millions of dollars from their countries. Selfish political and economic interests have prevailed. Western mining and financial interests continue to exploit the natural and mineral resources of many developing nations.

Latin America and Africa are rich in natural resources yet too many people remain uneducated and in poverty. Asia with its large population has become the manufacturing base of the world, but workers are exploited by the lack of social cover and low wages paid by major Western corporations. The Gulf States are notorious in the poor treatment of Asian migrants. Only well publicized events like the Bhopal chemical plant in India and Bangladesh factory tragedies wake up the conscience of the rich countries who have to change the unacceptable conditions, pay and risk of workers in some of the world's poorest nations.

There is no more Cold War and the G20 can and should do more. Less talk and more action is needed by the wealthy nations which have a duty to finance education, health, agriculture, energy, housing and infrastructure projects to enable the poorest countries to develop their economies and improve the living standards of the population. The large trading and mining corporations have a moral duty to improve the working conditions and pay of the indigenous population and redistribute their enormous profits.

This is not only a moral issue but an economic and social one which, if neglected, will inevitably add to the already massive number of immigrants, mostly illegal, who seek a better life elsewhere and result in more social and military conflicts from which the West will not be immune.

The fifty billion dollars a year, which Oxfam estimates is lost through tax evasion, is equivalent to the entire aid budget of the West. If governments acted to end the role of tax havens and crack down on tax evasion and avoidance it could recover this money. This is also where a Tobin tax could play such a useful role. It would raise revenue from those who can most afford it and provide much needed funding which could be allocated to the developing nations.

Enabling the so-called developing nations to improve their economies and provide housing, infrastructure, hospitals and schools is the only way to improve the living standards of the people and reduce the desire to emigrate. However at the same time the leaders and governments of the developing nations must take responsibility for their people and their future by ending the corruption, which has for too long obstructed social and economic growth.

Tragedies can often lead to action. Ebola galvanized Western governments and the UN, terrified of the potential consequences, into closer collaboration to control and eradicate the disease, which spread throughout West Africa. The earthquake in Nepal brought an immediate response from many countries sending not only food and supplies but qualified engineers and health workers to assess the damage and help alleviate the suffering. It was an example of what can and should be done. Of course intervention is more difficult when there is an absence of government, corruption or military conflicts leading to the persecution and forced migration of minority groups which have been taking place in the Middle East and Central Africa as well as in Bangladesh and Myanmar. In 2014 there were an estimated fifty million refugees fleeing from their countries.

Organizations such as One Campaign, Change and Avaaz are appealing to millions of people through the Internet to raise more awareness of the plight facing three quarters of the world's population. But it requires a commitment from our political leaders and, above all, as I keep repeating, a change of mentality in governments and the corporate and financial sectors.

Sporting Morality

If you are first you are first, if you are second you are nothing.
Bill Shankly

The Lance Armstrong affair exposed the corruption, which has become endemic in sport, now almost forgotten in the wake of the FIFA scandal. The reasons have to do with the way sport has been transformed into a major international business where too much money is involved.

Sportsmen and women, managers, agents, organizers, sports bodies and the media have been able to increase their earnings substantially thanks to the wall of money circulating via sponsors and TV, and often turn a blind eye to the dark side of sport.

It is difficult to believe that during almost a decade of drug taking, nobody knew that Lance Armstrong and many others were taking drugs to enhance their performance. Any follower of the sport would be more surprised if cyclists who ride a hundred kilometres every day or climb mountain passes in the heat of the sun followed by drenching rain and strong winds coupled with sudden changes in temperatures, can do so without performance enhancing drugs.

Doping, cheating, match fixing, tax evasion etc. have damaged the image of sport irremediably and it is not just limited to cycling. We have seen it in motor racing, tennis, boxing, horse racing, basketball and soccer. The investigation into the alleged corruption of directors of FIFA confirmed what many in and out of the game have known for many years but never made any attempt to expose it. FIFA has turned into a secret society laying down the rules of the game while being criticized for the lack of transparency relating to the millions of euros, which filter through its Zurich HQ each year. The coveted World Cup has come under suspicion with accusations of bribery being levelled at FIFA for allegedly engaging in secret negotiations with potential host nations. None has been more damaging than the scandal over the choice of Qatar for the 2022 World Cup with reports of million dollar payments being made to FIFA officials while thousands of poorly paid immigrant workers building the stadiums are treated like slaves. It typifies everything that is wrong with the beautiful game, transformed into an ugly business. Perhaps they should switch the dates so Russia hosts the games during the winter and Qatar in the summer. That would be interesting.

For Brazil, a nation passionate about soccer, to have protested against FIFA, says something about how the game has lost its way. The people turned against the government accusing it of neglecting public investment for the benefit of the country. Enormous sums were spent to build new stadiums, which have only benefitted the elite, while FIFA pocketed all the money from sponsors. FIFA's officials, holed up in their ivory tower in Zurich, counting the millions in their Swiss bank accounts, should understand that sport cannot just be about money and sponsors and pandering to corporate and elite interests while expecting the supporters to continue paying extortionate prices. To rub salt into the wound those who can most afford to pay to attend sporting events tend to get in free as celebrity VIP guests of sponsors and organizers.

An example of how soccer is now organized for the benefit of television is the way the international or European Soccer Championships have changed. Once the Champions League was for league champions, then the 2nd and 3rd placed clubs were invited to participate. Instead of a knock out competition over two legs, group matches were invented to ensure the TV money would flow over several months. Matches, which used to be played at a specific time on a specific day, are now spread over the weekend or over separate weeks and at times to suit Asian audiences. The winter months now have periods during which there are soccer matches every day and all shown live on TV. Good news for the increasing number of TV pundits, who fill any spare time available with their pointless comments.

The Europa league, formally the UEFA Cup, for eligible European soccer clubs, is no longer the correct description. It extends far beyond Europe's borders. Israeli and Turkish clubs can participate and I notice that Kazakh club, Astana, also takes part. According to my knowledge of geography Kazakhstan is on the Chinese border in central Asia, which hardly makes it eligible to play in a European competition. But then I am out of touch with the rules. However although it is logical and fair to give lesser known clubs from Central and Eastern Europe the opportunity to play against the big boys, I am under the impression that some of the leading clubs in Western Europe do not relish the idea of mid-winter games in harsh conditions against clubs such as Rubin Kazan, Shakhty Salihorsk, Ruch Chorzhow, Rudar Pljevlja Xazar Lankaran or Ludogorets Razgrad, whose names sound like villains in a James Bond movie. Most players would probably have difficulty in finding them on a map.

The rise of Internet betting has been one of the factors in the increase in match fixing with players and referees being bribed to throw matches in many European soccer championships and, according to recent reports, even the World Cup. The growing popularity of soccer throughout gambling mad Asia has led to the increase in match fixing by local Mafia gangs for whom gambling is a vital source of revenue and who are accused of attempting to influence results of matches across the world.

There is also a growing tendency for leading soccer clubs to benefit from some very advantageous decisions by referees, which in the current climate also raises suspicion of match fixing, even if they are unfounded. Nevertheless last minute penalties are awarded for non-existent fouls or diving, goals given from clear offside positions and players are sent off for no apparent reason. Is this fear of abuse by supporters on the part of referees and linesmen or something more sinister which is ruining the concept of fair play? And the prospect of video referees to spot the most blatant and costly errors, is still some way off.

Violence has not yet been eradicated. This was brought to light during last season's Italian Cup Final in Rome between Juventus and Napoli. A supporter from Naples was shot near the stadium by one of the Roma Ultras and then to avoid trouble inside the stadium once news spread, officials were seen negotiating with a member of Naples Ultras. It transpired that the gunman was a known criminal having spent several years in prison for killing a policeman, and the leader of the Neapolitan supporters was the son of a notorious boss of a Naples Mafia family. Tragically, after a long battle for survival, the victim died from his wounds in hospital. So much for sport. Many families are drifting away from watching games due to the risk and this incident forced the government to promise reforms and a crackdown on violent behaviour. With all the money flooding in from television and sponsors, there is a strong case for clubs to become fully responsible for policing and security at matches?

In Spain violence of another form erupted over the control of the Valencia soccer club. The ex-president, a leading real estate developer, was accused of attempting to kidnap his rival over a debt relating to an alleged multimillion unpaid share deal between the two men. The scandal linked dubious deals between the club, the Valencia city authorities, and accounts in offshore banks.

Events such as these have placed the world's most popular sport at a watershed, morally and economically. The risk to the game is so great there is a case for clamping down on the betting practices, which not only lead to fraud and match fixing but financial hardship for gambling addicts.

There are many European clubs on the verge of bankruptcy, only surviving thanks to the deep pockets of oligarch owners or the generosity of the taxman. The cost of tickets has escalated out of all proportion and genuine supporters have simply been priced out. It now costs almost two thousand pounds for a season ticket at Arsenal just to watch a handful of games. Even so the top Premier League clubs are attracting full houses. But this is not reflected in Europe, where, apart from the leading clubs in each country, there are more and more empty seats and terraces in the stadiums. Spare a thought for Stranraer currently languishing in Scotland's first division. Their average gate last season was five hundred and forty one supporters.

Players play musical chairs, changing clubs every year which enables their agents and club owners to make more money. If Tottenham had not sold Modric and Bale or Arsenal, Fabregas and Van Persie, they might have achieved success at the expense of their rivals. The influence of Qatar, with its bottomless pocket, owner of PSG and sponsor of Barcelona, is having a major effect on international soccer which may not be healthy since their money goes to the most successful clubs and is not distributed equally.

More and more players are brought from overseas, which affects the search for home grown talent. With the exception of PSG, French clubs rely heavily on imported African players, many of whom are not world class. Not everyone can be as talented as Samuel Eto'o or Didier Drogba.

Marketing gimmicks have become a big earner with clubs redesigning their strip every season – one for home, one for away games and one for Europe – in the hope of selling more expensive merchandise. It has become a fashion parade. Soon we shall see soccer stars on the catwalk presenting their new strip.

But the greatest problem remains the mounting debts which risk bringing down even the top clubs given the new rules introduced by UEFA, which will prevent them from spending more than they earn. This will impact on the level of transfer fees and salaries, which have reached unsustainable stratospheric proportions. Out of total debts of over three billion euros, Spanish clubs owe an estimated six hundred million to the tax man and it was a huge tax liability which triggered the demise of Scottish club Rangers. In 2012 it was estimated that the total debt of the English Premier League was approaching two billion four hundred thousand pounds. In Portugal the debt of the leading clubs, Benfica, Porto and Sporting Lisbon has left them virtually bankrupt. Italian club, Parma, is another victim. Relegated from Italy's Seria A with huge debts, its future is in doubt.

To attract David Beckham to Real Madrid, the Spanish tax authorities actually brought in the "Ley Beckham", the Beckham Law, which allowed him and many other foreign players to be exempt from certain Spanish taxes. But even this is not enough for some players. Leo Messi became embroiled in a court case involving tax evasion relating to unpaid tax on image rights, another tax gift for the sporting elite, which should be abolished. But football has such influence and there is so much money at stake, there is no way a court would ever contemplate prison for these privileged stars.

Despite millions on the poverty line in Spain, people actually cheered Messi when he arrived at court illustrating soccer stars' influence on society. They, like bankers, are the untouchables. Players like Bale and Ronaldo are believed to be paid in excess of ten million euros a year net. Lionel Messi, is believed to be on an annual salary of twenty million euros. If their clubs pay the taxes and charges, and this is by no means certain, it means the trio earn more than sixty million euros gross, which equates to three thousand workers on twenty thousand euros a year. Can one young man who kicks a ball around a field really be worth one thousand workers? This makes neither moral nor economic sense. Without the other players who form the team, Messi and Ronaldo cannot function and are worthless.

Too many soccer players, like many corporate CEOs, are highly paid for getting out of bed. Surely it would be fairer for the bulk of their earnings to depend on success, results and silverware. This is called incentive measures. And why doesn't UEFA adopt the system used for American Football? The USA is hardly a socially conscious nation yet when it comes to sport it sets an example for all to follow. Each year the teams which finish last have first choice of the top university sports graduates, while the previous year's champions wait until last. This ensures that no team dominates year in year out and creates a far more democratic and fair sport.

The influence of money has led to an increase in the number of court cases regarding opaque commissions to middle men, money laundering and tax evasion in the transfer market with so-called agents setting up deals with African and South American clubs to bring young players to Europe with the money never reaching the clubs directly. Not for the first time, France's Olympique de Marseille, has come under suspicion with regard to opaque commissions on recent player transfers and the club's alleged links to the city's underworld. A Spanish accountant investigating the financial situation of clubs in La Liga said that it was far more difficult to trace movements of money in soccer clubs than in most businesses. The transfer of Neymar to Barcelona is a perfect example of what he meant with ongoing investigations into precisely how much was paid and to whom.

Soccer has become such a social phenomenon that local politicians are afraid of the consequences should a town's club be declared bankrupt and disappear. They appease supporters for votes and have allowed the clubs to run up debts and turn a blind eye to the loss of tax revenue.

Real Madrid, one of the world's richest clubs, has submitted plans for a four hundred million euro commercial investment adjacent to the Madrid stadium. It is rumoured the Bernabeu could lose its revered name and become another Emirates Stadium. Yet ten years ago, saddled with debts, the club escaped insolvency thanks to some fancy financial engineering.

Club President Florentino Perez, who happens to be head of one of Spain's largest construction groups, is believed to have negotiated a deal with the planning authorities to change the zoning in order to build and sell four high-rise towers for use as offices and a hotel on the old club training ground on the northern perimeter of the city, which as well as saving the club, changed the city's skyline.

Sooner or later soccer will have to return to the real world too. When the supporters start to boycott stadiums or stop watching a bunch of overpaid, some not even talented, young men, mostly from foreign parts, kicking a ball – that is when they are not speeding, drinking or engaged to models, starlets or singers – prices will drop and so will the revenue. Then we may see a return to normality, club loyalty and in the UK, an English squad with a chance of actually winning some silverware.

Loyalty may be a thing of the past but Barcelona's Xavi Hernandez and Liverpool's Stephen Gerrard are two players who set an example through their talent on the pitch and humility off it. Having spent their entire careers with the same clubs and represented their countries, Hernandez, 35 and Gerrard, 34, were given standing ovations at the final whistle of their last home match of the season before moving on.

Television has become the lifeblood of soccer worth billions to the Premier League. But an English pub owner, Karen Murphy, put a spanner in the works by succeeding in her legal battle over pay-to-view, arguing that using a cheaper Greek TV decoder to play soccer matches in her pub was perfectly legal under European law. The European and British courts agreed. Despite losing the case, the major TV companies, which could face a dramatic loss of revenue from matches, have not surrendered and are prepared for a long drawn out battle.

Whenever there are vast sums of money involved and too much inequality it can only lead to corruption, disillusion and unrest. This is what is causing the increase in migration from the world's poor nations towards Western Europe. Soccer has been a major factor in reducing conflicts and forging relationships around the world but it has also instilled in many young people the impossible dream of coming to Western Europe and becoming rich. Soccer will also have to deal with the growing disparity in earnings between the leading West European clubs, whether they are public corporations or private enterprises, and those from the lower divisions or from East Europe and Africa.

Even the soccer showpiece of the World Cup has lost its aura. Up and until the 1970s the World Cup was where supporters all over the world had a rare opportunity to watch unknown teams and players from other continents. It was original and exciting. Spectators and television viewers were in awe at the talent of the Brazilian team with its stars including Pele, Garrincha and Carlos Alberta, to name but a few. Today most of the top players are with European clubs and seen every week on television around the world. Brazil versus Spain or Argentina versus Italy could be games between Real Madrid and Barcelona, or Milan and Juventus. The World Cup has been transformed into a money-spinning circus for FIFA and sponsors, stripping out the profits while leaving the host country burdened with huge debts.

An interesting anecdote is that while Monaco and Liechtenstein are independent states and tax havens, their soccer clubs are allowed to play in the French and Swiss leagues respectively. It obviously suits the French and Swiss governments as well as business interests. But why should teams from these tax havens be able to play in another country's championships? Has anybody considered what would happen to Barcelona if Catalonia ever seceded from Spain? Who would turn out to watch them play Terrassa or Manresa? Or would the obvious financial interests take precedent and the club would remain in the Spanish league?

Motor racing too has changed totally. Now known as F1, it has become so reliant on TV and sponsorship it is no longer an exciting and dangerous sport but a parade of computerized machines with wheels using circuits to advertise the sponsors' products or services. Bernie Ecclestone came under fire for accusing Sebastian Vettel and Nico Rosberg of being bad for business, lacking personality and not being seen enough in the German press. In a sport with international interests perhaps they need to spend more time in nightclubs with their trousers down, in the people magazines with models or other celebrity events in order to promote Formula One. This is the sporting world we live in. And the circuits are chosen increasingly for geopolitical reasons. There is such a gap between the wealthiest and poorest teams that apart from the first few laps, when the cars are bunched together, often no two cars can be seen on the same straight. There is so much strategy that pit stops, fuel consumption or choice of tyres determine who wins. Perhaps in the future, technology will lead to a sport in which there will be no need for drivers. Think of the savings.

This lack of competition is why MOTO GP has increased its popularity. This is what racing is about with no pit stops and shorter races where the riders and powerful machines in their colourful costumes can be seen bunched together at incredibly high speeds with the leadership constantly changing.

The IOC also needs reforming with regard to its methods of choosing the venue for the Olympic Games. Beijing was a political choice and after 2012 in London, it was perfectly obvious Rio de Janeiro would be chosen for the 2016 games. As one of the world's leading and most beautiful cities, from a nation that is a fast growing economic power in a continent that has never before staged the games, the contest was over before it began.

In Buenos Aires, Madrid's pride was shattered and its delegates humiliated by the IOC members. Was it worth it? What was the purpose of Madrid's third attempt when Spain had recently (in Olympic terms) hosted the games – Barcelona in 1992 – and it was highly doubtful that a European City would be chosen in 2020 after London in 2012. Madrid's officials must have known it was Asia's turn.

European IOC members, who supposedly pledged support for Madrid, reneged on any promises simply because choosing Madrid in 2020 would have ruined any chance of another European venue in 2024 -Paris has already thrown its hat into the ring. Political reasons and local interests prevail. Madrid is now a city of Olympic stadiums without the games.

What Pierre de Coubertin had in mind when he created the modern games was to fulfill his dream to bring athletes and sportsmen and women together from all over the world. Only what started as a ritual of goodwill and fair play has been gradually transformed into a global corporate and media circus requiring a massive financial investment.

So why do so many cities compete to organize a three week long, sporting event which requires years of preparation, causes upheaval and turmoil for the inhabitants, requires enormous and costly building and security measures, and once over is all but forgotten? The winter Olympics in Sochi was considered a success. Yet the legacy of the billions invested is a phantom city.

The answer lies in the way the IOC operates and the power it wields. But has its influence gone too far for the world to allow a handful of secretive individuals holed up in Switzerland determine where and who should organize a multimillion pound global business? Does anyone ask himself what is the role of the members apart from a talent to act like prima donnas and jet around the world in lavish style?

Their power is so far reaching it induces politicians to beg for their cities and then open their books to show they have sufficient resources to build and provide the required facilities. Their methods fuel accusations of corruption such as the Salt Lake City bribery allegations in 2002 and Tony Blair's last minute lobbying for London in Sydney.

But do they really need to assess the merits of the world's leading cities and subject elected political leaders to grovel before them when any reasonably intelligent person would acknowledge that all international cities possess the expertise and finance to develop and host a major sporting event?

Do the ends justify the means – the lobbying, the behind the scenes negotiations, secret meetings, and political involvement? The West loves to promote democracy around the world yet the decision making process of the IOC when it comes to determining the venue for the world's most important sporting event is far from transparent or democratic.

The choosing of the venue is the culmination of years of planning and research by the IOC members and at huge cost to the competing cities. It is more than likely that the decision is taken long before the delegations of world leaders, city officials and even royalty, setting aside any economic problems they face at home, travel halfway around the world to seek an audience with the IOC. They line up, like contestants in a beauty parade, to wait in suspense while the committee members lock themselves up to announce the winner. The IOC is judge and jury. At least in beauty competitions or Eurovision, the winner tends to be chosen by the audience.

Surely it is time to put an end to the IOC's monopoly and the charade of political and financial lobbying, and return to the ideal of using the Olympic Games to unite the people of the world. Many of the world's best athletes now originate from the developing nations. It is time they had the opportunity to hold the games instead of the usual merry-go-round of wealthy cities.

With Madrid's obvious readiness and capability established, with 80% of the infrastructure already built, why doesn't the IOC simply choose Madrid now for the 2024 games and avoid wasting more time and money for other cities during the next four years? This would herald a new era in choosing the venues for future games.

Rather than engage in the costly competition to organize the games which only benefits the globetrotting committee members, the IOC and G20 nations should work together as a team with the aim of giving more nations the chance to host the games and spending the IOC's cash more wisely. The sites for five or ten games over the next twenty to forty years should be determined in advance by mutual agreement. The venues should rotate between the continents in order for all the world's nations to have a chance to act as host. Finance would come from a consortium of wealthy G20 nations in order to spread the cost with private sponsors. This would enable poorer nations, currently excluded, to hold the games and reduce the risk of one city going bankrupt. If the decision to hold the games in an African or Asian country lacking the means was made a decade in advance, they would have time, with international cooperation and funding, to prepare for the games. It would provide badly needed investment in infrastructure, housing, transport and sports facilities that would be put to good use after the games were over, provide local jobs and assist in the economic development of the countries concerned.

Today, whether the games are held in Iceland or Mozambique actually makes little difference to the vast majority of spectators sitting in front of their televisions around the world. And ticket prices could be substantially reduced in the poorer nations as most of the revenue is generated from television coverage and sponsorship. In the aftermath of the FIFA corruption scandal, there is no reason why the World Cup venues should not be chosen this way too.

To uphold the Olympic spirit the right path is to make the games the catalyst for aiding the developing nations in a coordinated effort to achieve democracy and prosperity. And instead of remaining an elite, privileged club, the IOC should be transparent, come down to earth and look to how it can benefit the world rather than its own members. It is time for a real change of climate in the sporting world.

Justice Morality

If you tremble with indignation at every injustice then you are a comrade of mine.

Che Guevara

Justice has slowly but inexorably been turning away from the people it is supposed to represent. The cost of litigation prevents most of the population from being able to obtain redress from the courts. Justice systems are overworked and understaffed with courts unable to cope with an increasing number of cases either criminal or civil. Our legal systems are a charter for criminals and wrongdoers, as well as for the legal profession, while the victims are too often ignored and left uncared for.

I have been fortunate, or unlucky, depending on how you look at it, to see first hand how the law functions both in the UK and in France. Like many property owners I have had to deal with landlord and tenant disputes resulting in court hearings in the small claims court and the Royal Courts of Justice in London as well as tribunals in France. I have been represented by solicitors and counsel and sometimes handled the case personally, not always appreciated by the judges. It is invariably time consuming, stressful, requires an enormous amount of paper and files and, in the UK, given the need to appoint solicitors and barristers, is unnecessarily expensive. My experience is laid out in my lawyer's charter.

(See Appendix V)

Governments and Human Rights organizations have ignored the rise in crime, which has resulted from the growing diversity and ethnic mix in our societies, whether it is violence or fraud. They pass their time worrying about rights for gay communities, religious groups, ethnic communities and laws for abortion, euthanasia, drug addiction, prostitution, mendacity etc.; all perhaps worthy issues which need addressing, but concerning only a minority of the population. There are more than six hundred foreign criminals in UK prisons who can't be deported in case it affects their human rights.

Meanwhile the security of the vast majority of the population is ignored. The perpetrators of crimes are given more protection than their victims. Human Rights groups have campaigned successfully for the end of capital punishment and long prison sentences in many countries. But capital punishment still exists – for the victims of violent crimes who lose what is most precious, the right to live.

Decisions of the Court of Human Rights often seem contrary to any normal appreciation of what justice should be. They seem more interested in the rights of illegal immigrants, criminals and terrorists than the plight of poor children and families facing poverty or victims of violence at home. It is time the families of those murdered obtain justice for their loved ones. Criminals and delinquents amount to a tiny percentage of the population. Their human rights must be earned through respect for others and responsibility in society. Unfortunately this is rarely the case.

As financial crime increases with more people becoming victims of unfair charges, mis-selling, cyber crime or blatant fraud by major corporations or banks, there is little redress at present for the European consumer. To enable consumers to claim for fraud, losses or unfair practices we need the introduction of class actions similar to those allowed in the USA in order to create a more balanced legal environment and stop the largest corporations from using their financial muscle to escape legal action. Fraudsters and corrupt politicians, bankers and business people act out of personal greed. They should therefore be expected to pay for their crimes through losing any wealth accumulated by compensating their victims or returning illicit gains to the state.

Our liberal, democratic societies are in moral decline, faced with an increasing lack of respect for authority be it the police, teachers or even parents, by a disenchanted young generation, often from ethnic minority groups, who find themselves alienated and without jobs or any future. Of more concern is the virtual takeover of nations or parts of countries by criminal gangs as in Mexico, Colombia, Somalia and to some extent even Italy and some Eastern European states.

Despite the violence, America is divided as to whether the sale of guns should be restricted. The right to bear arms is written into the Constitution. But the people who drafted the laws could never have envisaged the development of automatic weapons, grenades, rockets and other deadly arms. There is absolutely nothing to prevent the government from outlawing the deadliest weapons on the streets used to massacre so many innocent people.

While Europeans are forbidden to carry arms this has not prevented a huge increase in gun crime by gangs, often linked to the drug trade. Parts of Marseille are notorious for gangland violence in which Kalashnikovs are used on a daily basis. The assumed perpetrator of the attack on the Jewish museum in Brussels travelled freely around Europe with a bag containing a Kalashnikov, an automatic pistol and ammunition. He was only arrested by chance in Marseille due to a routine police inspection during a drugs search. To demonstrate how the law is being turned upside down he was reported to have said that he did not want to be extradited. He should not have been given time to even consider it before being swiftly returned to Belgium to face justice.

Brazil used the World Cup competition as an excuse to clean up some of its favelas. The problem of whole communities under the rule of drug barons, virtually cut off from the state, became too much for the government to accept when the attention of the world was fixed on the country hosting the world's largest sporting event. Their solution was to send in the army. Heavily armed troops and tanks engaged in sudden coordinated attacks into the townships to root out the leaders and attempt to restore law and order. The USA and Europe too have reached a point where similar drastic measures might be the only solution to end the rise in crime and gang warfare linked to narcotics, which have created no go areas in the most deprived areas of many cities. Spain has seen a rise in crime from Latin American gangs, known as Latin Kings, whose members have somehow slipped through immigration controls and operate freely inside the country. The immediate deportation of foreign gang members to their country of origin would help eliminate this problem.

The southern coast of the country in and around Gibraltar and La Linea are notorious crime spots for the trade of illegal narcotics, cigarettes and contraband goods from North Africa and have become virtually no-go areas for the police. The Costa del Crime has earned its description by becoming home to hundreds of foreign criminals from the UK and more recently Eastern Europe. Many of these undesirable elements, who are known to the police authorities, should be deported before they have time to open the front door of their new luxury homes.

Italy's Mafia remains a mystery. It has always played a role in the political affairs of Sicily and the south of the country as well as being behind many businesses, especially in the construction and gaming sectors. Yet many of the arrested clan bosses were found hiding in the cellars of small farms in isolated villages. Despite the huge income from their criminal operations, the bosses were rarely seen driving luxury cars, wearing ostentatious jewellery or seen in fashionable resorts. Even in prison, Mafia bosses seem to be treated with respect. So why on earth don't they abandon the violence and crime, live normal lives and engage in legal activities.

Last year in Italy I picked up a leaflet explaining the dangers of purchasing contraband cigarettes; how it funded organized crime, the damage to the economy, loss of taxes, lack of guarantees, and punishment for those who bought the products. The sponsors were Philip Morris and British American Tobacco. Recently a Spanish judge ordered that confiscated branded goods be distributed to the poor rather than be destroyed according to the usual practice. It caused indignation in the boardrooms of several luxury goods companies worried about their image.

One of the failings in our justice systems, which has led to the general disaffection with politicians, is how the courts are failing to hand out strict punishment to dangerous criminals, pandering to human rights groups and becoming far too lenient in dealing with convicted criminals, especially those who are released early and commit more crimes. This is a problem affecting every European country with the public often appalled at the repeated robberies, rapes, child abuse, murders of innocent victims by people already condemned to serve long prison sentences but set free.

Incomprehensibly the Court of Human Rights ordered Spain to release ETA terrorists, many of whom committed diabolical crimes including the murder of innocent men, women and children in cold blood with bombs similar to those used in Northern Ireland by the IRA. Other prisoners freed include rapists and murderers of children and even those convicted of terrorist offences. These criminals are now free after serving less than thirty years behind bars.

The judges based their decisions on the reasoning that the life sentences handed down by Spanish courts was against their human rights despite committing crimes against humanity. Whether their interpretation of the law was right or wrong it is another example of how the courts seem to act in favour of the perpetrators of crimes rather than the victims.

Worse is the situation in which delinquents, drug dealers, car thieves, many of whom are foreigners, are not even sent to prison but released by the courts. This happens regularly in poorer areas of cities where there are substantial immigrant populations. This is often described as a means to keep social peace in the most sensitive areas and aimed at avoiding discrimination or ethnic violence, it has led to a minority of young thugs and gang leaders becoming heroes and created no go areas for the police, who are becoming increasingly disenchanted by judges. Officers risk their lives to arrest criminals only to stand by impotently as the courts release them back on to the streets. Prisons are overcrowded, despite early release programmes, which often send highly dangerous individuals back into society to commit more crimes, which invariably lead to more innocent victims. It is happening time and time again. Yet as crime increases, human rights groups continue to press for favorable treatment and lower sentences for convicted criminals while ignoring the rights of their victims.

Anyone who acts in self-defence in his or her own home or business or attempts to intervene, is treated more harshly than the burglar or attacker. Far more time and money is used to protect and look after a few thousand convicted criminals than the hundreds of thousands of their victims. The balance needs to be restored.

Those condemned should serve the full sentence handed down by the courts with little or no remission. Violence against the police forces has become commonplace. With terrorist attacks posing a threat to our societies, there is a case for bringing back the death penalty for the murderers of law enforcement officers, child rapists and murderers, professional killers and for terrorists. There is a universal call to end capital punishment but in a more precarious, complex and more violent world this needs to be counter balanced with severe lengthy prison sentences. If there is no capital punishment, life imprisonment should mean life for the most violent criminals, especially for terrorists convicted of bomb attacks. It is an outrage that the Omagh bombers, whose victims included innocent women and children, have never been brought to justice.

Whether governments like to admit it or not there is no doubt that the opening of borders has led to an increase in delinquency, fraud, money laundering, tax evasion, prostitution, drug dealing and begging. We have free movement of people in Europe but not when it comes to convicted criminals. Extradition between member states is rare and violent foreign criminals claim their human rights whenever a court seeks to send them back to their own country. There is no reason why foreign criminals and immigrants convicted of serious offences should not be deported either before or after serving their prison sentence to be dealt with by their respective governments and not be allowed back into the country for a minimum period, say five years, after serving their sentence. Why should any country have to look after foreign criminals for what could be half a lifetime?

Foreign girls from Asia, Africa and Eastern Europe, usually without papers, forced into prostitution should be sent home while their "protectors" should face prison and, if foreign nationals, be deported. They should also have their assets seized. There is no justification for whole parts of Western cities being used by prostitution gangs for the exploitation of young undocumented girls or women. Yet the only reaction of governments is to introduce laws to fine their clients.

IMPUNITY, definition: exemption from punishment or freedom from the injurious consequences of an action. No other word can so aptly describe how justice has been turned upside down to preserve and protect a privileged elite, which has lost all sense of morality and ethics. The law has not kept up with the globalization of crime. Despite the increase in white collar crime and fraud, prison rarely acts as a deterrent. Too many drug barons, organized crime bosses and non-violent but well-connected individuals benefit from impunity or lenient sentences. It would be a far greater deterrent if monetary gains and assets were seized to repay victims. Highly publicized cases such as Bernard Madoff have set an example but too often corrupt officials, tax evaders, drug traffickers, Mafia gangs and fraudsters are allowed to keep the proceeds of crime. Some crime bosses are often considered too powerful to arrest and with the knowledge of the police and magistrates, continue to live in luxury and pursue their criminal interests with impunity. This should not be tolerated in any civilized, law abiding society. Confiscating assets is becoming more commonplace for drug traffickers and it has to be a more effective method than a short prison sentence. Al Capone escaped justice until he was finally convicted for tax evasion. Where are the dedicated law enforcement officers like Eliot Ness today?

Convicted fraudsters and corrupt politicians who refuse to divulge the hiding place of their illicit and untaxed gains should remain locked up until the proceeds of crime or theft of public funds are recovered. The only alternative to prisons would be a requirement to repay the debt to society by undertaking civic duties or work and repay their victims out of earnings from any subsequent employment.

There should be an end to prescription in those countries where it exists. Why should a criminal who manages to hide from the law be allowed to escape justice because of time limits? All suspects should be liable to face criminal proceedings until a case is solved regardless of the time it takes. This already applies to crimes against humanity. Where it involves serious crimes, fraud or tax evasion, suspects should never be allowed immunity from justice or tax amnesties and they should be forced to repay what they owe to the state or, more important, to their victims. It is also time the courts refused to throw out cases on a technicality or procedural error which canny lawyers so often use to free their clients in what has become a game of wits.

Corruption and tax evasion has become a growing scourge in our societies. Elected representatives of the people and financial and corporate bosses have tended to benefit from political and judicial favours. They cling on to their elevated positions and do not understand the meaning of the word, resignation. It is standard procedure for members of the church, police, military, medical, legal and other professional bodies to close ranks and stand together to protect their own regardless of any wrongdoing.

The West has turned a blind eye to the massive political corruption, especially in Africa and Eastern Europe, which has stripped nations of their wealth, allowing dictators or oligarchs to buy luxury real estate or fill bank accounts in tax havens. But if justice is equal for all citizens, political figures and elected representatives and members of the professions convicted of corruption, bribery, negligence, crimes or taking public money should be banned from office for life or at least for a long period as well as be required to repay all the proceeds and face heavy fines and prison sentences.

The question of damages is an issue, ripe for reform. An innocent man, Glen Ford (no relation to the actor), who spent thirty years on death row before being released recently, received just two hundred and fifty thousand dollars, the maximum permitted. How many times do we hear about victims of car accidents or medical mistakes receiving paltry sums while celebrities in civil suits or libel cases receive millions of dollars? There is no sense or logic in the way damages are awarded. It is time for governments to fix fair and equitable sums, to give the courts guidance and end the present lottery system, which more often than not denies the real victims their rights while giving obscene amounts to those who do not deserve them.

It is wrong that celebrities claim huge sums in damages for having their privacy invaded when the only "damage" suffered is to obtain more publicity. The case in France of Julie Gayet being awarded fifteen thousand euros for a photograph with Francois Hollande published in a magazine should lead to thousands of people who have had a photo taken with the French president claiming their reward. It is necessary to control the abuses of the press but courts should give these kind of damages to charity not to the stars and celebrities who thrive on publicity. The same should apply to the celebrities who had their telephones hacked and received fortunes while the real victims of crimes or accidents, who remain permanently incapacitated, receive paltry amounts from the courts. This is immoral as well as unjust and the laws need changing.

Dealing with young offenders is always going to be difficult. Prison merely acts as a school for criminals especially among the more vulnerable ethnic minorities, while convicted terrorists often use prisons as a breeding ground for future terrorists. Countries with substantial Muslim communities have learnt to their cost that its prisons have been forming Islamic terrorists, who once released have been travelling to Syria to join the Jihad before returning to Europe, where they pose a serious threat to our security. By allowing foreign imams to preach in French prisons, the Government has exacerbated the problem.

While lack of integration, inequality and unemployment can be blamed on an increase in crime, there has to be more parental control and responsibility and especially education to ensure the young can obtain the necessary basic training in order to eventually find a job. This is easier said than done in the present crisis when many families are unemployed, but more effort is required by government and local councils to find an answer.

Detention centres with education and training facilities might be a short-term solution for violent young offenders but the answer must lie with governments providing adequate training and employment opportunities for the young or our nations will face an increase in urban disorder and a potential breakdown of society.

Judges' decisions have also lost all sense of reason. Violent delinquents and drug dealers are often released back on the streets with a warning, while citizens with no previous conviction are sent to jail for trivial offences. While it took years to obtain a deportation order for Abu Qatada, an Islamist who posed a serious threat to the security of the country, Trenton Oldfield a young Australian, who was jailed in 2012 for disrupting the boat race, was threatened with deportation.

In France, the *Institut pour la Justice*, is a non profit making organization with hundreds of thousands of members, whose aim is to lobby the government to protect victims of crime and punish offenders. The organization is opposed to the release of delinquents and criminals with a long history of violent crimes. There have been numerous cases where the release of dangerous criminals back into society without supervision, has resulted in the rape and murder of young girls. Several known paedophiles have also been released and committed further crimes.

Many young delinquents with police records evade prison due to suspended sentences and are allowed to go free. This has led to a loss of respect for authority by a generation of young people, who do not fear the law and astonishingly for a democratic society, deliberately target the police who find themselves facing armed gangs in certain areas of French cities.

The *Institut pour la Justice* is highly critical of the French justice minister, Christiane Taubira, for what it says is an intolerable situation in a civilized society. Some of her ideas to transform the French justice system have created tension in the French Parliament, where many MPs, including the Prime Minister, Manual Valls, openly expressed their opposition to her proposals. Nevertheless she managed to retain her position in the last reshuffle of the French Government.

One of the most controversial laws in France is the forty-eight hour ruling. If a squatter enters someone else's property and is undetected for more than two days by the owner, the police cannot evict them. They need a court order which can take months leaving the owners helpless as well as face opposition from lawyers representing squatters' rights organisations. A recent high profile case brought to light the anomaly and injustice of this law, which was actually introduced during the Sarkozy presidency. An elderly widow moved into her brother's home leaving her cottage empty. When her brother died and the property was put on the market by his family she naturally expected to return to her home but in the meantime it had been occupied by squatters and she has been involved in a lengthy court procedure to recover it.

Leniency seems to be a recurring theme. In Britain a judge allowed an alleged Mafia boss to remain in the country rather than be extradited to Italy. Foreign criminals seem to be given the right to choose whether they want to be extradited when it should be automatic. Italy showed how weak its justice system is by condemning Silvio Berlusconi, with all his convictions, to the severe regime of visiting an old people's home to assist residents, where he arrived in his chauffeur driven car with bodyguards accompanied by journalists and TV cameras. A judgment in Spain recently condemned a notorious female Bosnian pickpocket gang with nothing more than a warning to keep away from metro stations, leaving them on the streets, while Romanian gangs who have been using the Louvre Museum in Paris as their hunting ground, stripping tourists of their money and papers, were merely told to stay away from the museum. Perhaps convicted jewel thieves should be barred from approaching jewellers! Where on earth is the logic and justice in these cases, which do nothing to stop the same people, often children, who steal for their parents, pursuing their criminal activities?

For some inexplicable reason the Romanian community has been allowed to set up illegal camp sites and squats on the edge of many towns and cities in France, Spain and Italy from where they have been engaging in unsociable and criminal activities. Mafia trafficking gangs seem to operate with impunity exploiting illegal immigrants or young foreign girls forced into prostitution. Why are the ringleaders not arrested and deported together with undocumented foreigners? The government seems to ignore the problem while the police and local councils seem impotent. The situation in some cities has become so drastic the only recourse is for the local population to take action.

Should drugs be depenalised? The wall of money generated from the production and sale of drugs has overtaken many poorer countries' GDP with a consequent increase in the underground economy, organized crime, violence and delinquency. Considering that prohibition in the US was the principle cause of the rise of organized crime across America, there is a strong argument to liberalize soft drugs and even hard drugs under strict supervision.

In Mexico's fight against the violent drug gangs, which have virtually taken over parts of the country, President Enrique Pena Nieto has become frustrated with the USA. "They pump money into Mexico and Colombia to help fight the war on drugs yet it is American consumers who finance the drug barons." Nevertheless he can't blame the US for the murder of over forty students or the corruption by officials and drug cartels, which culminated in so many demonstrations by a population whose tolerance has reached breaking point with the government and police.

Removing the criminal element would undoubtedly relieve police forces and investigators from chasing users and dealers, reduce drug related crime and the prison population while governments would have more money to invest in education, prevention and medical help. Opponents of liberalization of drugs argue it would lead to an increase in consumption. The only way to find out is to give it a test for a year or two. A great deal of attention will now be focused on Colorado, where the State authorities have given the go ahead to cultivate marijuana for certain purposes.

Any plan aimed at putting an end to the transport and dealing of drugs, which are destroying whole communities and reduce the circulation of drug money, would be a step in the right direction. The situation in Central America and Mexico, where Mafia gangs have engaged in a war to the death and intimidate as well as massacre thousands of innocent people, should surely convince the most ardent objector that anything to reduce the violence is worth trying.

The bosses of organized criminal gangs or drug cartels seem to be revered as being too powerful to arrest and often spend their lives living in luxury. Most are well known to police forces so why are they untouchable? Is it due to political connivance and mutual agreements between crime bosses and politicians? Certainly in Italy this seems to be the case where iconic judges Giovanni Falcone and Paolo Borsellino were murdered in 1992 in Palermo, Sicily, but it took years to arrest and imprison the presumed Mafia assassins. A decade earlier in 1981 in France, magistrate, Judge Pierre Michel, was gunned down in Marseille while investigating the drug operations of what was known as the French Connection in the city, and one of the conspiracy theories surrounding the death of President John Kennedy involved US organized crime families.

Cities like Chicago, Marseille and Naples have a reputation of corruption where links between politicians and Mafia families have always existed. The Triads in China and the Yakusa in Japan are an integral part of Asian society, where bribery and corruption are accepted as a way of life. There is so much money circulating, the temptation to take a share also affects law enforcement officers. Police investigators are looking into the disappearance of over fifty kilos of cocaine from the Paris police headquarters at 36 Quai des Orfevres, which so far have not been recovered. The theft from the mythical address which houses one of Europe's most efficient police forces, shocked the country and the removal of its senior police officer for obstructing the course of justice has severely dented its image.

It is equally clear that the drug money cannot circulate without the cooperation of and connivance of banks and politicians. The removal of monetary controls and the global economy have been a boon to criminals as well as tax evaders. To combat the transfer of the proceeds of crime there needs to be far more control over large amounts of money being handled through the banking system, especially by banks in tax havens, without whose cooperation organized crime and tax evaders would not be able to accumulate or launder illicit gains. Would Ukraine be in such a dire economic state if billions belonging to the state had not been allowed to disappear into the world's banking system?

On a positive note since laws now exist whereby courts have the power to seize assets of convicted criminals, it is time bankers started to be arrested and condemned as accomplices for illicit transfers and money laundering. Meanwhile as proof of the colossal earnings derived from prostitution rackets and illicit drugs and the failure to combat them, the EU has come up with the idea of including the proceeds in every member state's PIB.

Who chose to print the five hundred and two hundred euro notes and why? In the age of credit cards or bank transfers for virtually all large purchases, they are rarely used for daily transactions and are the perfect tools for the illicit transfer of large amounts of cash. Despite new laws requiring banks to disclose all transfers using high denomination notes, there is a strong case for removing them from circulation. So far only Spanish ex-leader of the socialist party, Alfredo Perez Rubalcaba, raised the issue. There is simply no justification to keep them in circulation.

The European Central Bank with its plans to impose stringent bank regulations could initiate the beginning of a new era in this respect and implement Rubalcaba's proposals. But ultimately it needs elected governments to agree on ways to bring transparency and stability to the financial sector.

In a rapidly changing world, laws have to adjust to changing circumstances with far more international cooperation. Justice has to be for the people. More important, justice needs to be seen to be done. Without a fair legal and justice system our democracies face irremediable decline.

Conclusion

Freedom has to be a continuing process in order not to degenerate into a banal formula. The fields in which plots are cultivated also sprout weeds. Excessive power prolonged for too long degenerates into a caste system. With the caste comes interests, elevated status, the fear of losing them, scheming to maintain them. The castes keep to themselves and support each other.

Jose Marti

A crossroads without signs requires making a choice. But fortunately our societies have sufficient signs to guide us even if they are often ignored. The road to recovery will be long and winding and fraught with instability with a new world order taking shape. The difference between left and right wing parties has become blurred to the point of extinction requiring a new form and style of politics and politicians. Politicians should take heed of the desires of the majority of the population seeking employment, more security, justice, social cohesion, an end to violent crime, delinquency, mass illegal immigration and corruption. We must end government of the elite, by the elite, for the elite. A new "Renascimento" where culture, liberty of expression and freedom will herald a new world order to replace the excesses of political power, capitalism and consumerism.

Communications, air travel and the Internet have made the world smaller. The global village has arrived and, as JFK pointed out, we all inhabit this small planet. This requires compromise, tolerance and an acceptance of different cultures, religions and way of life. We cannot impose our democratic, liberal ways on nations or people who have lived for centuries under dictators or tribal chiefs or whose religions require stricter rules of behaviour. But conversely other regimes or religious groups cannot expect to enforce their views, laws and way of life on people of different faiths either in their own or other nations of the world. Fanatical religious groups prepared to kill and die for their cause are doomed to fail.

In an interconnected world a new form of global capitalism is needed which balances the need for risk taking entrepreneurs and innovators with stricter, regulated financial markets and environmental issues. International trade has to be regulated to avoid unfair competition and comply with environmental and health requirements. Universal health cover and education for every man, woman and child must be the goal of every government and remain under state control.

Banks must return to their role as servants of the economy not its masters; to act as providers of credit to industry and individuals and guardians of people's savings, not speculators. The re-introduction of the Glass-Steagall Act should be high on the political agenda.

While quoted corporations and stock markets have a role to play, the importance to every economy of small companies, which account for more than seventy-five percent of our PIBs as well as creators of new jobs should not be underestimated and should be receiving far more attention.

Remuneration packages in the financial sector and corporate boardrooms need to be adjusted downwards and based on long-term growth with an end to the short-term bonus culture. We need a redistribution of wealth to create a fairer and more equitable society in the rich nations while helping the developing nations develop their economies in order to reduce poverty. Governments must implement necessary infrastructure and energy conservation programmes. Climate change cannot be ignored any longer.

In a global economy, tax regimes must adapt. A review of the current tax regimes is needed to bring an end to tax evasion, the use of tax havens and avoidance schemes and restore the balance between rich and poor. The Tobin Tax is a logical step towards this goal. At the same time laws should be introduced to make it illegal for any person to hide behind opaque trusts, companies or foundations, using lawyers or third parties. The real holders and beneficiaries of bank accounts, directorships or real estate need to be known.

Justice must be seen to be done, and criminals pay in full their debt to society. We live in a world where wealth is seen as the ultimate goal. Financial crimes and corruption should therefore be punished by the repayment of the proceeds of crime coupled with heavy financial penalties as a deterrent. In any democratic society everyone must be equal before the law and the elite should not benefit from impunity, which is causing so much resentment and disillusionment. The rule and respect of law are the pillars of our society. Without justice and equality they cannot function and so long as greed prevails and wrongdoers are granted impunity our democracies hang on a thread.

In short the middle and poorer classes can no longer subsidize the rich. We need to instill a sense of fairness and morality throughout the political, financial and business sectors to make the world a more prosperous and safer place for all its citizens. Economic wealth cannot be concentrated in the hands of the elite while ninety-nine percent of the population struggle to survive. Experts never cease to warn that endless economic growth is leading to the destruction of the planet. We have to find other goals than the mere obsession to accumulate wealth and the often, destructive power it exerts. Happiness and satisfaction can be found by spending more time with one's partner or family than blindly spending money in the pursuit of an illusionary, luxurious lifestyle.

A final simple message for political leaders if they wish to accede to or remain in power is to listen to the wishes and aspirations of the majority of the people.

At the World Peace Congress in Lausanne on 4 September 1869, Victor Hugo gave a speech expressing his vision of a better world. It was addressed to the Citizens of the United States of Europe and almost 150 years later it still sends a powerful message.

Allow me to give you this name, because the Federal European Republic is founded in law in the expectation of becoming a reality. You exist, therefore it exists. You show by your presence that you are united. You are the beginning of a great future.

You confer on me the title of honorary president of your congress and I am deeply touched.

Your congress is more than a group of minds. It is a kind of editorial committee of the future legal doctrine. An elite only exists on the condition it represents the masses, you are this elite. From this moment you notify to whoever it may concern that war is bad, that killing, even glorious, boastful or royal is odious, that human blood is precious, that life is sacred. A solemn formal command.

But that a final war is necessary, alas, I cannot deny it. But what is this war about? A war of conquest. What is there to conquer? Freedom.

The first requisite for every man, his first right, his first duty, is freedom. Civilisation tends invincibly towards unity of language, unity of measure, currency unity and the fusion of nations into humanity, which is the supreme unity.

This harmony has a synonym: simplification; in the same way that wealth and life have a synonym: circulation.

The first servitude is frontiers; who says frontiers says ties, cut the ties, eliminate the frontiers, remove the customs official, remove the soldier, in other words be free, peace follows.

A real peace. Peace established once and for all. Inviolable peace. A normal state of work, trade, supply and demand, production and consumption, a huge common effort, attracting industry and circulation of ideas, the movement of people.

Who has an interest in frontiers? Kings. Divide and rule. A frontier implies guards, guards imply soldiers. Do not pass, word of all the privileges, of all that is forbidden, of all the criticisms, of all the tyrannies. All human calamity stems from frontiers and soldiers.

The King, being the exception, in order to defend himself, needs the soldier, who in turn needs to kill to live. Kings need armies, armies need war. Otherwise their purpose evaporates. Strangely man accepts to kill his fellow man without knowing why. The art of the tyrant is to transform the people into an army. One half oppresses the other.

Wars have all kinds of pretexts, but only one cause, the army. Eliminate the army, you eliminate war. But how do we abolish the army? By getting rid of despotic regimes.

How everything is linked. Abolish the parasites in all their forms, civil lists, paid idle functionaries, salaried clergy, kept judges, sinecure aristocrats, free concessions to public buildings, permanent armed forces, sweep them out and you endow Europe with ten billion a year. By one stroke of a pen the problem of poverty is simplified.

But the thrones do not want this simple approach. Thus the forest of bayonettes.

Kings agree on one single point. Prolong wars. We think they quarrel, not at all, they assist each other. I repeat that the soldier has to have a reason to exist, maintaining an army is to maintain the despots, excellent, ferocious logic. The Kings exhaust their sick, the people, by the shedding of blood, there is a strong brotherhood of the glaive from which results the serfdom of men.

To sum up, I mentioned somewhere about the reintegration of the soldier in the citizen. The day when this metamorphose takes place, the day when the people will no longer see themselves as men of war, this enemy brother, the people will be united as one, loving each other and civilization will be called harmony and will have the means to establish on one side wealth and on the other illumination, this strength, work and this spirit of peace.

Victor Hugo Lausanne, 4 September 1869

Apart from substituting presidents and governments in the place of "Kings" and automatic weapons replacing "bayonettes" and "glaives" little has changed since Hugo's speech. His vision has partly come true with the establishment of the European Union but the elite has never been more privileged and soldiers and wars, more destructive than ever, are still with us.

I would like to end on a note of optimism and nothing conveys this more appropriately than the final scene in Charlie Chaplin's movie, Modern Times. Out of work and destitute, the two characters sitting forlornly by the roadside, smile at each other, rise to their feet and begin walking down the empty road towards a better world with hope in their hearts.

Appendix I: Capitalist Pyramid cartoon 1911

Appendix II: European parliaments

Country	Parliament	Senate
Austria	183	62
Belgium	150	71
Bulgaria	240	
Croatia	151	
Cyprus	59	
Czech Republic	200	
Denmark	179	
Eire	166	60
Estonia	101	
Finland	200	
France	577	343
Germany	662	69
Greece	300	
Hungary		386
Italy	630	315
Latvia	100	
Lithuania	141	
Luxembourg	60	
Malta	69	
Netherlands	150	75
Poland	460	100
Portugal	230	
Romania	332	137
Slovakia	150	
Slovenia	90	40
Spain	350	259
Sweden	349	
United Kingdom	646	800
European Parliament	751	
USA	435	100
Japan	512	252

Appendix III: Arms Suppliers

NATO countries with highest military spending (in billions of dollars):

USA:	600
UK:	57
France:	52
Germany:	44
Italy:	25
Canada:	16
Spain:	11.5
Turkey:	10
Netherlands:	10

Source: International institute of strategic studies.

World's leading arms exporters in billions of US dollars

United States	10.0
Russia	6.0
China	2.5
France	2.0
Germany	1.2
United Kingdom	1.0
Spain	1.0
Israel	0.8
Italy	0.7
Ukraine	0.6

Source: Stockholm International Peace Research Institute 2014

Appendix IV:

The Lawyers Charter

The rules:

Laws are drafted by the legal profession

Laws are designed to leave as many grey areas as possible to prevent the lay person from understanding them and courts from interpreting them, to enable the legal profession to justify high fees for their "legal expertise".

The law is a game run for the benefit of a closed shop of professionals, not for the paying customer, sorry, client.

The dual role of solicitors and specialist barristers leads to duplication, delay, often misunderstanding and higher fees.

While everyone has the right to handle their own case, judges do not appreciate dealing with laypeople and are not always sympathetic.

The Experts:

Solicitors always tell their clients that they need counsel's advice.

Solicitors and barristers invariably say that the case is a complex issue.